Bernard Clayton's

COMPLETE BOOK

OF

SMALL BREADS

MORE THAN 100 RECIPES FOR ROLLS, BUNS, BISCUITS,
FLATBREADS, MUFFINS, AND OTHER SMALL BREADS
FROM AROUND THE WORLD

BERNARD CLAYTON, JR.

Illustrations by Stephanie Osser

SIMON & SCHUSTER

SIMON & SCHUSTER
Rockefeller Center
1230 Avenue of the Americas
New York, NY 10020

Copyright © 1998 by Bernard Clayton, Jr.
Illustrations copyright © 1998 by Stephanie Osser
All rights reserved,
including the right of reproduction
in whole or in part in any form.

SIMON & SCHUSTER and colophon are registered trademarks
of Simon & Schuster Inc.

Designed by Karolina Harris

Manufactured in the United States of America

10   9   8   7   6   5   4   3   2   1

Library of Congress Cataloging-in-Publication Data
Clayton, Bernard.
    Bernard Clayton's complete book of small breads : more than
100 recipes for rolls, buns, biscuits, flatbreads, muffins, and other
small breads from around the world / Bernard Clayton, Jr.
        p.   cm.
    Includes bibliographical references and index.
    1. Breads.   2. Cookery, International.   I. Title.
TX769.C5327   1998
641.8′15 — dc21   97-46552
                                                      CIP

ISBN 0-684-82692-5

Permissions will appear on page 280.

With Thanks

To write an all-inclusive accounting of those who have contributed to this book, I would need to go back three-plus decades to when I was first beguiled into the kitchen — never to depart — by Julia Child and her first book, *Mastering the Art of French Cooking.* It has been a love affair ever since. And from that moment forward, I have been mindful of my debt not only to Julia but also to cooks, chefs, cookbook authors, food writers, teachers, friends, readers, and students in a number of countries around the world, north and south of the equator, for what I have written about foods.

My special thanks, however, to those who gave me permission to use and adapt recipes from their books for inclusion in this volume. I have written about them in text pieces of this book as well as placing them in a special panel of permissions.

B. C., Jr.

DEDICATED TO MY TESTING/TASTING
PANEL OF NEIGHBORS
WHOM I ASKED TO THINK SMALL,
AND THEY DID MERITORIOUSLY.
THEY LOVED THEIR ASSIGNMENT,
AND STAND AT THE READY FOR THE NEXT.

Contents

Introduction

SMALL is a bagel. Small is a croissant, a *brioche à tête*, a scone. Small is a Parker House roll, an English muffin. Small is a beaten biscuit, a hot cross bun, a doughnut.

While the more than one hundred breads in this book are small in size — any one of them can fit easily on the palm of the hand — they are the pick among breads.

Some are spiced or sweetened, enriched, flavored or filled. Some are unleavened and pancake flat, or lightened by soda or baking powder or both instead of yeast or starters or beaten egg whites. Most are baked in the oven and some are cooked on a griddle. Some are deep-fried. Bagels are poached before baking.

The range of these breads from around the world encompasses French bagels, English hedgehog rolls, Czech *kolaches*, Syrian *sum-sums*, Chinese steamed buns and Swiss *Gipfelteigs*, Hawaiian plantation biscuits, Indiana corn muffins, and Puget Sound cinnamon buns, with delicious stops along the way.

The book will appeal to those home bakers with small families or those with limited kitchen facilities. The yield of most of the recipes is small, reduced to about half the quantity found in others. A dozen muffins, for instance, rather than two or three dozen. There are exceptions, of course, when the bread must be made in larger quantities for a barbecue or buffet for a number of hungry guests.

The book is written, too, for the experienced home baker who appreciates a comprehensive gathering together of longtime favorite small breads in one volume.

The appeal of baking breads in the home has never been as great as it is today. And with good reason. Ingredients and equipment in catalogues and kitchenware shops abound. Not that I had to walk through deep snow to shop when I wrote my first breads book a quarter of a century ago, but I did drive more than one hundred miles to buy bread, whole-wheat, and rye flours. Today, those flours are five minutes away in several stores in my nearby shopping center.

In a recent King Arthur Flour catalogue for the home baker, I could order not only every kind of U.S. and Canadian hard, soft, and in-between wheat flours, but also flours from France, Ireland, and Italy, not to mention a flour that I thought bordered on overkill—a blend of eight grains: wheat, triticale, rye, millet, oat, buckwheat, barley, and soy.

Equipment? A quarter of a century ago, I fashioned my own baguette pans with metal shears and a hammer from black stovepipe I bought in a country store. Now there are catalogues unnumbered and store shelves stacked high with baking pans of every composition and size, *bannetons* with or without cloth linings, razor-sharp *lames* to cut designs on dough, *couches* to hold dough, baking stones, and on and on.

In my books and baking classes, I urge the home baker to see baking as a relaxed art. The rules are not strict. There is no step in the bread-making process that cannot, in some way, be delayed or moved ahead just a bit to make it more convenient to fit into a busy schedule. This does not hold for making pastries, which is an art calling for precise measurement and timing. But in bread making, if the dough you are shaping gets stubborn, pulls back, and refuses to be shaped, walk away from it for a few minutes. It will relax and so will you.

Baking is an inexact art, and a forgiving one. A few grains more or less of sugar or salt, a few degrees more or less in oven temperature, will make little difference in the results. After all, the kitchen is not a high-tech laboratory in which every element is controlled.

The exception is the baking itself. The only time I pay strict heed to a schedule is when the dough is in the oven. Normally, I never leave the kitchen during the bake. If I must, I carry a small clock-timer to remind me when to return.

When kneading yeast-raised dough by hand, bread making is not necessarily a gentle art. Don't baby it. Break the kneading rhythm by occasionally throwing the ball of dough down hard against the work surface. Smack it down. The developing gluten loves it. A properly kneaded piece of dough can be stretched between the hands without tearing.

On the other hand, quick breads, those leavened chemically with baking powder and baking soda, take tender care. No kneading. Mix just to blend the ingredients.

All recipes in the book stand alone without reference to another recipe except for bread made with sourdough starters. For these, there is a chapter devoted to a selection of starters and how to make them.

The recipes in this book have been collected in travels across this country and many parts of the world, both east and west. Many breads have been adapted from recipes in my *Complete Book of Breads* as well as *The Breads of France* and *Cooking Across America*. Some are favorites of readers who have sent them to me. I am indebted also to several cookbook authors whose small breads recipes have contributed much to the tone (and flavor) of this book. All of the recipes, new and old, and from wherever they came, have been tested and tasted in my kitchen. Each is timed step-by-step so that you will know exactly how much time to devote to preparation and baking.

This book has been a delight to write. It has meant new sources, new recipes, new techniques, new thoughts, new ideas, new places to visit, and, yes, an excuse to buy yet another baking pan.

Enjoy!

Buns

Among all of the small breads, the bun is one of the most versatile. It is the bun that holds the hamburger and hot dog at the family picnic. With a cross of icing, it becomes a hot cross bun for Easter. It is the soft and puffy steamed bun served at an Asian meal.

The bun is good eaten anywhere and at any time of the year.

19

PAN DE SAL
(Crumb-Coated Breads)

[ONE DOZEN BUNS]

In the Philippines, *pan de sal* is the traditional bread for breakfast — crusty on the outside, soft on the inside, and a touch sweet and a bit salty. Yeast-raised, the dough is given several rest periods to double in volume and gain in piquancy and good taste through long fermentation. After it is shaped, it is rolled in fine bread crumbs to give it a lightly speckled coat when baked.

It is more than a breakfast bread, of course. It is served as dinner rolls, and street vendors with small ovens make and bake them with a variety of fillings.

The recipe came from Reggie Aspiras, a colleague from Manila, who is a chef, food writer, restaurateur, and teacher. In order for me to taste as well as visualize *pan de sal* and other Filipino breads, Aspiras baked a dozen different breads, which were delivered to me half a world away the next day — or did I get them before they were baked, thanks to the international date line? Just kidding.

INGREDIENTS

3 cups bread flour, approximately
1 package dry yeast
2 teaspoons salt
1/2 cup sugar
1 cup warm water (90°–100°)
2 tablespoons butter or margarine, room temperature
1 cup fine bread crumbs, to coat

BAKING PAN

One baking pan. Need not be greased, for the bread crumbs will keep the dough from sticking.

BY HAND OR
MIXER
15 mins.

Measure 1½ cups of bread flour into a bowl or mixing bowl and add yeast, salt, and sugar. Stir to blend. Pour in the water and stir with a large wooden spoon or mixer flat beater blade. It will be a smooth batter. Add shortening. Beat until it has been incorporated. If using a mixer, attach the dough hook. Add the balance of the flour, ½ cup at a time, to make a rough mass that will clean the sides of the bowl.

KNEADING 8 mins.	If by hand, place the dough on the floured work surface and knead with a strong push-turn-fold motion until the dough is elastic. A test is to stretch the dough several times without it tearing. The dough under the hook will form a ball around the hook that will clean the bowl. Knead for 8 minutes.
BY PROCESSOR 5 mins.	Attach the steel blade for this small amount of dough. Measure 2 cups of flour into the work bowl and add the yeast, salt, and sugar. Pulse to blend. With the processor running, pour the water through the feed tube, followed by the 2 tablespoons of butter. Add the balance of the flour, ¼ cup at a time, with the machine running. Don't overpower the dough with too much flour. Remove the cover and pinch the dough. It should be soft, elastic, and slightly sticky.
KNEADING 45 secs.	With the machine on, knead for 45 seconds.
FIRST RISING 2 hours	Place the dough in a bowl that has been greased, cover with plastic wrap, and leave at room temperature to double in volume and increase in bouquet, about 2 hours.
SECOND RISING 30 mins.	Punch down the dough, replace the cover, and allow to proof for 30 minutes.
SHAPING 10 mins.	Punch down the dough, roll into a foot-long piece, and cut into a dozen pieces. Each piece should weigh about 1½ ounces. Roll each piece into a ball between the palms. If the dough resists, let it relax and come back to it later. Spread the bread crumbs in a plate. Roll each bun in the crumbs to coat.
REST 30 mins.	Place the pieces on the baking sheet, cover, and put aside to rest and rise for 30 minutes.
PREHEAT	While the buns are resting, preheat the oven to 400°.

BAKING
400°
25 mins.

Uncover the buns and lightly coat them again with a sprinkle of bread crumbs.

Place in the middle shelf of the oven and bake for about 25 minutes until a golden brown. The bottoms should be hard when tapped with a finger.

FINAL STEP

A rack covered with these to cool is so attractive that it seems a shame to break up the cluster to serve.

OLD MILWAUKEE RYE BUNS

[SIXTEEN BUNS]

When I began baking, Old Milwaukee rye was the first bread out of my oven that was an unqualified success, and has since become a classic in many kitchens. It is among a half dozen of my favorite breads.

It begins with a sponge (or sour) rising and falling in a bowl under a taut plastic wrap that will bubble to its maximum goodness in about 3 days, give or take a few hours. After a day or so, a whiff of the fermented sponge will make manifest the historic relationship of the baker with the brewer.

Rye dough, even though it is made with equal amounts of white and rye flour, is a heavy dough and bakes into a heavier-than-white bun. Big appetites love them. Slices of the bun, toasted or not, are at home at a buffet for company or for snacks after work or after school.

Note: This is a heavy dough. If you're using a food processor, I suggest doing just half the recipe.

INGREDIENTS

Sponge:
2 cups medium rye flour
1 package dry yeast
1 tablespoon caraway seeds
1½ cups warm water (100°)

Dough:
All of the sponge
1 cup warm water (105°–115°)
¼ cup molasses
1 tablespoon caraway seeds
1 egg, room temperature
1 tablespoon salt
2 cups rye flour
4 cups bread or all-purpose flour, approximately
3 tablespoons vegetable shortening
1 egg, beaten with 1 tablespoon milk, to brush

BAKING
SHEETS

Two baking sheets, greased, Teflon, or sprinkled with cornmeal.

PREPARATION
1–3 days

Set the sponge in a large bowl by measuring in the flour, yeast, seeds, and water. Blend well with 25 strokes of a wooden spoon. Cover the bowl snugly with plastic wrap so the sponge loses none of its moisture, which will condense on the plastic and fall back into the mixture. The dark brown pastelike batter will rise and fall as it develops flavor and a delicious aroma. Stir once each day.

The sponge, which will resemble a wet mash that's too thick to pour and too thin to knead, may be used anytime after 6 hours, although the longer the better—up to 3 days, when it will have ceased fermentation. If it fails to bubble up after falling back anytime during the 3-day period, don't think it's dead. It's not. It's resting but gaining flavor all the time.

BY HAND OR
MIXER
20 mins.

On bake day, uncover the bowl and add water, molasses, caraway, egg, salt, rye flour, and about 2 cups of the white flour. Beat till smooth—about 100 strokes—or 3 minutes with the mixer flat blade. Add shortening.

Stir in the balance of the white flour, ½ cup at a time, first with the spoon and then by hand or with the mixer dough hook. The dough should clean the sides of the bowl, but it will be somewhat sticky, thanks to the perverse nature of rye flour.

KNEADING
8 mins.

Turn the dough out on a floured work surface and knead by hand (with the help of a dough blade) or under the mixer dough hook.

Knead with strong push-turn-fold rhythm until the dough is smooth. Add sprinkles of flour if necessary to control stickiness.

BY PROCESSOR
5 mins.

Attach stubby plastic dough blade.

Pour the sponge into the processor work bowl and add warm water, molasses, caraway seed, egg, and salt. Pulse to blend into a light batterlike dough. Add all of the rye flour. Pulse. Add shortening. With the machine on, measure in the bread flour — ½ cup at a time. Add the last portion of the flour with care — no more than necessary to create a ball of dough that will ride the blade around the work bowl, cleaning it as it whirls.

KNEADING
45 secs.

Leave the machine running, and knead for 45 seconds. The dough will be somewhat sticky when it comes from the work bowl, but a few sprinkles of white flour will make it easy to shape into a ball.

FIRST RISING
1 hour

Place the dough in a greased bowl and place plastic wrap over the top of the bowl. Leave at room temperature until the dough has doubled in bulk, about 1 hour.

PUNCH DOWN
10 mins.

Punch down and let rise an additional 10 minutes.

SHAPING
15 mins.

Divide the dough into 16 pieces. Shape each into a ball. These will weigh about 4 ounces. Press each into a patty that is about 4" across and ¾" thick.

SECOND
RISING
40 mins.

Cover the buns with waxed paper. Leave until the buns have doubled in bulk, about 40 minutes.

PREHEAT

Preheat oven to 375° 20 minutes before the bake period.

BAKING
375°
40 mins.

Brush the tops with the egg-milk wash for a shiny crust (or water for an unglazed one). Bake the buns for about 40 minutes, or until they test done — tapping the bottom crust yields a hard, hollow sound. The buns will be a dark brown.

FINAL STEP   Remove from the oven and allow to cool on metal racks. These rolls will keep for at least a week or more in a plastic bag, and freeze for several months at 0°.

Suggestion: If not all are eaten the first go-around, thinly slice those remaining, and save for a buffet. Then toast and serve with a spread or nibble out of hand for the joy of it.

PECAN STICKY BUNS

[A DOZEN OR MORE BUNS]

The great thing about making sticky buns with dough already rich with butter and eggs is the fact that you can let yourself go and make them as gooey and good as you wish. Blanket them with pecans (or other nuts) in a sea of soft caramel, fill the interior with good things — raisins or currants and perhaps more nuts, a sprinkling of date pieces, and dust with cinnamon.

A real sticky bun is a celebration! Go for it!

The buns may be baked immediately after the first rising, or, instead, put in the refrigerator, where they will rise slowly to be baked later at a more convenient time.

The glaze that is to be poured over the bottom of the baking pan and encrusted with nuts can be done before the dough is made or during the interval when the dough is set aside to rise.

INGREDIENTS   Glaze:
½ cup firmly packed brown sugar
½ cup corn syrup
4 tablespoons butter or margarine
1½ cups or more pecan halves or pieces to blanket the bottom of the pan

(continued on next page)

Dough:
4 cups all-purpose flour, approximately
2 packages dry yeast
2 teaspoons salt
¼ cup nonfat dry milk
1 cup warm water
4 tablespoons butter or margarine (reserve 1 tablespoon to brush later)
2 eggs

To Layer (choice or all):
1 tablespoon cinnamon
½ cup (4 ounces) date crystals or chopped dates
1 cup pecan bits
¾ cup currants or raisins

BAKING PAN	One or more baking pans depending on the number and thickness of pieces to be cut from the dough. Greased or Teflon. Usually an 8"-x-10" pan for a dozen buns, or a 9"-x-13" pan for 16.
GLAZE 10 mins.	Heat the brown sugar, corn syrup, and 3 tablespoons butter in a small saucepan until the sugar melts, stirring often. Pour into the baking pan(s), and arrange pecans, top side down, evenly over the bottom.
BY HAND OR MIXER 15 mins.	In a large bowl or mixer bowl, combine 1 cup of flour, the yeast, salt, and nonfat dry milk. Pour in the water and stir to make a batter. Add the butter and eggs. Beat by hand or with the flat beater blade for 2 minutes. Stir in additional flour, ½ cup at a time. If using a mixer, attach the dough hook. Continue mixing; add flour until the dough becomes a mass that can be lifted from the bowl and placed on the floured work surface.
KNEADING 8 mins.	By hand, knead with a strong push-turn-fold motion. Add sprinkles of flour if necessary. The dough will become soft and elastic, after about 8 minutes. In the mixer, add sprinkles of flour if needed to keep dough from sticking to the sides of the bowl. Knead for 8 minutes.

BY PROCESSOR 5 mins.	Measure 1 cup of flour and the other dry ingredients into the work bowl. Cover and pulse to blend. Pour the water through the feed tube. Turn on the processor and drop butter through the feed tube, followed by the eggs. Add remaining flour, 1/4 cup at a time, until a mass develops that cleans the sides of the bowl and rides the blade. Stop the machine. Pinch the dough. It could be slightly tacky but not sticky wet. If it is, add sprinkles of flour.
KNEADING 45 secs.	Knead for 45 seconds with the machine running.
FIRST RISING 1 hour	Place the dough in a greased bowl, cover with plastic wrap, and put aside until doubled in volume, about 1 hour.
SHAPING 20 mins.	Punch down the dough and place on the floured work surface. With a rolling pin and the hands, shape a large rectangle, about 1/4″ thick. If the dough resists and pulls back, walk away from it for a few minutes to let it relax. Melt the tablespoon of butter or margarine and brush the sheet of dough. Sprinkle with cinnamon, date bits, nut pieces, currants — or whatever else you wish to include. Beginning with the long side, roll up the dough like a jelly roll; pinch the seam to seal. With a sharp knife, cut the length of dough into 12 to 18 pieces, depending on how thick you want the buns. The more buns, the thinner they will be. Place the pieces, cut side down, on the bottom of the pan(s). The pieces should just touch. Don't crowd. They must have room to rise.
SECOND RISING 30 mins.	For immediate baking: Cover the pan and put aside to rise for about 30 minutes before putting in the oven. For baking later: Cover pan tightly with plastic wrap or slip it into a plastic bag for 2 hours at room temperature or overnight in the refrigerator (The buns will rise in the cold over a period of time.)
PREHEAT	Preheat the oven to 375° 20 minutes before baking.

BAKING
375°
25 mins.
35–40 mins.

If to be baked immediately, uncover pan and place in the 375° oven. Bake for 25 minutes, until golden brown on top.

If refrigerated, uncover the pan and leave at room temperature for 20 minutes. Bake for 35 to 40 minutes, or until golden brown.

Remove from the oven and let cool in the pan(s) for 5 minutes so the glaze will set, then invert onto a serving tray or platter. Allow whatever glaze is left sticking to the bottom to dribble down onto the buns or scrape it off with a spatula.

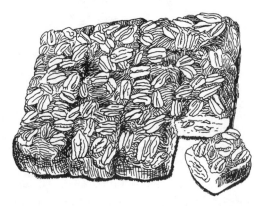

FINAL STEP   Eat! Celebrate!

Note: To freeze after the dough has been cut and the pieces placed in the pan: Wrap airtight with plastic wrap. Freeze up to 4 weeks. To bake, remove from the freezer; unwrap. Thaw at room temperature 1 to 2 hours. Let rise in warm place until doubled in volume, about 1½ hours. Bake as directed above.

HAMBURGER BUNS

[NINE BUNS OR EIGHTEEN ROLLS]

I combined two of my favorite hamburger bun recipes for this particular one. A batter of flour, yeast, and other ingredients is allowed to ferment and bubble for an hour to develop flavor. Egg gives the dough a golden richness.

Made small, they are fine for brunch or buffet; shaped large, they are great for large hamburgers at a picnic that caters to large appetites. The recipe can be doubled or quadrupled as need be.

INGREDIENTS	*3 cups bread or all-purpose flour, approximately*
	1 package dry yeast
	1 cup milk, room temperature
	2 tablespoons butter, room temperature
	2 tablespoons sugar
	1 teaspoon salt
	1 egg, room temperature
	1 egg, beaten with milk or cream, to brush
	1 tablespoon celery or poppy seeds, to sprinkle (other seeds may be substituted)

BAKING PAN

One baking pan, greased or Teflon.

BY HAND
OR MIXER
15 mins.

In a large mixing or mixer bowl, measure 2 cups of flour and sprinkle in the yeast. Stir in the milk and add small chunks of butter, the sugar, and salt. Lightly beat the egg in a small bowl and add to the batter. Beat with spoon or mixer flat beater until the egg is absorbed.

FERMENT
1 hour

Cover the bowl with plastic wrap and leave to ferment and become puffy, about 1 hour.

DOUGH
5 mins.

Stir down the spongy batter. Add the balance of the flour — ¼ cup at a time — to form a heavy, dense mass that can be lifted to the work surface, or left in the bowl under the dough hook. If wet, add flour.

KNEADING
10 mins.

Knead the dough with a forceful 1-2-3 rhythm of push-turn-fold until the dough is soft and elastic, about 10 minutes. If under the dough hook, the dough should pull away from the sides of the bowl and form a ball around the revolving hook, about 10 minutes. If it sticks to the sides, add liberal sprinkles of flour.

BY PROCESSOR
8 mins.

Attach the steel blade.

The sequence of adding ingredients varies from above.

Measure 2 cups of flour into the processor work bowl. Add the yeast, sugar, and salt. Pulse to blend. Pour the milk through the feed tube and add the butter. Stop the machine. Break the egg into a small bowl, stir to blend, and pour into the work bowl. Pulse 4 or 5 times to mix all of the ingredients together.

FERMENT
1 hour

Put the cover of the work bowl in place or use plastic wrap. Leave the batter to ferment and rise, about 1 hour.

Pulse to stir down the batter. With the machine on, add flour — ¼ cup at a time — until a heavy mass has formed that will pull away from the sides of the bowl and spin with the blade. Add flour if the dough continues wet and sticky.

KNEADING
45 secs.

With the processor on, knead for 45 seconds. The dough may be slightly sticky when taken from the bowl; if so, dust with flour. Form a ball to drop into a greased bowl to rise.

FIRST RISING
45 mins.

Place the dough in a greased bowl, cover with plastic wrap, and put aside to rise until doubled in volume, about 45 minutes.

SHAPING
15 mins.

The dough, which will weigh about 2 pounds, can be shaped into 18 small rolls (2″) or 9 large (4″) buns.

Push down the dough and lift to the work surface. Roll the dough into a cylinder, measure with a yardstick, and cut off pieces of equal length.

Cupping the hand, press down hard on one piece of dough, rolling it in a circle until a tight ball is formed. Set aside to rest, and proceed with the balance.

Starting with the first piece, knock flat with the side of the fist or press with the palms into an oval of dough about ½″ thick. Place the disk of dough on the bake sheet, and continue with the other pieces. If the dough resists, you may need to flatten the buns several times with your fist or fingers to get them to accept their role as 4″ buns.

SECOND
RISING
40 mins.

Cover the bake sheet with waxed or parchment paper, and set aside to rise until puffy and doubled in volume, about 40 minutes.

PREHEAT	Preheat the oven to 425°.
BAKING 425° 20 mins.	Brush the buns with the egg-milk wash, and liberally sprinkle with seeds of choice. Place on the middle shelf of the hot oven and bake until crusts are golden, about 20 minutes. Turn a bun over. If the bottom is nicely browned, buns are indeed done.
FINAL STEP	Remove from the oven and cool on a metal rack. Allow them to cool before serving. Split and toasted they are delicious. If any remain, they may be frozen and kept for 6 months at 0°.

KOLACHES
(Czech Sweet Buns)

[THIRTY-TWO BUNS]

There is a farmhouse on a country road on the high plains of Kansas where I have had the best-tasting Czech sweet buns — kolaches — of my life. They were baked by two women, mother and daughter, Amelia Branda and Ida May Goodman, who have a remarkable baking operation in their small kitchen, making the delicious fruit-, nut-, and cream-filled buns that are to a Czech what croissants are to a Parisian or bagels to a New Yorker.

Each week, they bake about 750 kolaches in an ordinary kitchen range. All of the mixing and kneading is done by hand. No mixer. No blender. There is a standing order for all of their production at Shaw's Grocery in nearby Wilson.

The two women use a variety of fillings for their kolaches — apricot, cherry, prune, poppy seed, raisin, cottage cheese, apple, and pineapple. Recipes for making the fillings follow. You may wish to make these beforehand. Store-bought jams, jellies, and pie filling may also be used.

As to choice of shortening: I like butter combined with vegetable shortening. Most Czech cooks prefer lard.

INGREDIENTS

³/4 cup (6 ounces) shortening, room temperature
¹/2 cup sugar
1 teaspoon salt
3 egg yolks
1 cup milk
5 cups all-purpose flour, approximately
2 packages dry yeast
Fillings (see recipes below)
1 tablespoon melted butter, to brush
Confectioners' sugar, to sprinkle (optional)

BAKING SHEET

One baking sheet, greased.

BY HAND
OR MIXER
10 mins.

In a mixing or mixer bowl, cream by hand or with the mixer flat beater the shortening, sugar, salt, and egg yolks. Mix the milk with the shortening and egg yolk mixture. Measure in 2 cups of flour. Add the yeast. Stir to blend well.

When the batter is smooth, add flour, ¹/2 cup at a time, and each time stir vigorously. When the dough has formed a mass that can be lifted out of the bowl and placed on the floured work surface, the dough is ready to knead. Or, if using a mixer, attach the dough hook. Add sprinkles of flour if the dough continues to be sticky during the kneading period.

KNEADING
10 mins.

Knead the dough with an aggressive push-turn-fold motion or under the dough hook for 8 minutes, or until the dough is smooth and elastic. At this point, it should not stick to the work surface or the sides of the mixer bowl. Add sprinkles of flour if the dough continues to be sticky during the kneading period.

BY PROCESSOR
10 mins.

Insert the metal blade.

The order of adding ingredients varies from above.

Pulse to cream the shortening, sugar, salt, and egg yolks in the work bowl. Add the milk and yeast. Pulse to mix thoroughly. Measure 2 cups of flour and add to the mixture. Pulse. When the batter is smooth, add flour, first ¹/2 cups at a time and then finish with ¹/4 cups or even tablespoons so you don't find suddenly that you have added too much and the dough is too dense. After each addition, pulse several times to form a mass.

KNEADING
1 min.

When the dough cleans the sides of the bowl and rides on the blade, let the processor knead the dough for 1 minute. Remove the cover and pinch the dough. If wet, and too sticky to lift out of the bowl, add sprinkles of flour.

FIRST RISING
1 hour

Place the dough in a greased bowl, cover tightly with a length of plastic wrap, and put aside at room temperature to double in bulk, about 1 hour.

FIRST
SHAPING
20 mins.

Punch down the dough and place it on the work surface. Divide the dough into 4 equal pieces. Roll each piece into a long cylinder about 1½" in diameter. With a knife, cut each cylinder into 8 equal pieces.

Roll each small piece into a tight ball and place on a greased baking sheet. Space 2" apart. Cover with a length of waxed paper and set aside to rise.

SECOND
RISING
20 mins.

Allow the balls of dough to rest and rise for about 20 minutes.

SECOND
SHAPING
15 mins.

Press each ball into a circle about 2½" across, and form a small rim around the edges. This is more than just a depression made with the thumb — this calls for pressure and pulling by opposing index fingers to flatten the dough, leaving the rim intact. If the dough is not pressed down sufficiently, it will rise and push out the filling.

Place a tablespoon of filling of choice in the center of each.

To make a square packet: Pat out a 3" square. Place a full teaspoon of filling in the center. Bring the 4 corners together on the top, pressing them together to stick. Brush with melted butter.

THIRD RISING
30 mins.

Cover the *kolaches* loosely with waxed paper and let rise again until the dough is "light" (puffy), about 30 minutes.

PREHEAT

Preheat oven to 375° while the buns rise.

BAKING
375°
25–30 mins.

Place the *kolaches* in the preheated oven and bake for 25 to 30 minutes, or until the dough is a golden brown.

Don't overbake.

FINAL STEP

Remove from the oven and, if you wish, sprinkle with confectioners' sugar. Place on racks to cool. These freeze well.

FILLINGS

Prune or Apricot (will fill 36 *kolaches*):
1 pound pitted prunes or dried apricots, cooked in water to cover
1 cup cooking liquid, from above
½ cup sugar
1 tablespoon lemon juice
1 teaspoon grated lemon rind
½ teaspoon cinnamon

Cover fruit with cooking liquid; stir in sugar, and bring to a boil. Reduce heat and cook slowly, stirring constantly until smooth and thick. Remove from heat and add lemon juice, grated rind, and cinnamon.

Poppy Seed (will fill 36 *kolaches*):
½ pound ground poppy seed
1 cup water

> *1 cup milk*
> *1 tablespoon butter*
> *1 teaspoon vanilla*
> *½ teaspoon cinnamon*
> *½ cup raisins*
> *1 cup sugar*
> *½ cup crushed graham crackers*

Boil poppy seed in 1 cup water until thickened, add milk and boil over low heat for about 5 minutes. Add butter, vanilla, cinnamon, raisins, and sugar. Continue cooking for about 5 minutes. Take from heat, add graham crackers.

Both of these will keep indefinitely refrigerated.

HOT CROSS BUNS

[SIXTEEN TO EIGHTEEN BUNS]

A hot cross bun speckled nut-brown, rich with cloves, nutmeg, currants, and candied fruit, is served traditionally on Good Friday but is delicious any day of the year. A cross of confectioners' icing is the distinctive mark of this bread that is in every child's book of nursery rhymes. Despite its Christian overtones, the bun is supposed to have originated in pagan England. Even today, a hot cross bun baked and served on Good Friday is believed to have special curative powers.

The dough may be prepared on Maundy Thursday if you wish to serve it hot from the oven on Good Friday. Bake enough for Easter breakfast, too.

INGREDIENTS
> *¼ cup sugar*
> *2½ tablespoons melted butter (reserve ½ teaspoon to brush)*
> *2 eggs, separated*
> *¾ cup milk, warmed*
> *2½ cups all-purpose flour, approximately*

(continued on next page)

1 package dry yeast
1 teaspoon salt
½ teaspoon nutmeg
¼ teaspoon powdered cloves
½ cup currants (or raisins)
¼ cup chopped candied fruit

Glaze:
1 egg yolk mixed with 2 tablespoons water

Icing:
1 cup confectioners' sugar mixed with 1 tablespoon milk and
1 teaspoon lemon juice, to make a paste

BAKING SHEET   One baking sheet, greased or Teflon.

BY HAND   In a large bowl, mix the sugar, melted butter, egg yolks, and warm
OR MIXER   milk. Stir to blend and set aside for a moment.
30 mins.   Into a mixing or mixer bowl, measure 2 cups flour, yeast, salt,
             nutmeg, and powdered cloves. Blend. Pour the liquid mixture
             into the flour and mix well with 50 strong strokes with a wooden
             spoon or 2 minutes with a flat beater blade in the mixer. Add the
             currants and chopped candied fruit. Blend.
                  Beat egg whites until frothy but not quite stiff and work into
             the batter.

KNEADING   Incorporate remaining ½ cup of flour with the dough hook until
6–8 mins.   it is a rough mass. Knead for 8 minutes. Don't make it a stiff
             dough but leave it soft and elastic.

BY PROCESSOR Attach short plastic dough blade.
5 mins.   Prepare the sugar/butter/egg/milk mixture, as above.
                  Measure 2 cups of flour, yeast, salt, nutmeg, and cloves into
             the processor work bowl. Pulse to blend. With the processor run-
             ning, pour the liquid through the feed tube to make a batter.
             Uncover the bowl and scrape down the sides with a spatula. Drop
             in the currants and candied fruit. With the processor on, add
             beaten egg whites and additional flour to form a rough, shaggy
             dough that cleans the sides of the bowl and rides on the blade.

KNEADING 1 min.	Process to knead for 1 minute. Stop the machine, uncover, and pinch the dough to determine if it is wet and needs more flour. If not, turn out of the bowl and dust lightly with flour (to prevent sticking).
FIRST RISING 1½ hours	Place the dough in a greased bowl, cover with plastic wrap, and let stand at room temperature while it rises to double in bulk, about 1½ hours.
REFRIGERATION Overnight	If the dough is to be held and baked the following morning, punch down, cover, and store in the refrigerator overnight. On the following day, remove bowl from the refrigerator and allow to stand for about 1 hour at room temperature.
SHAPING 12 mins.	Roll the dough into a cylinder and divide into equal parts in successive steps: — 2-4-8-16 — and shape into balls. Place the balls about 1 inch apart on the baking sheet. Flatten each slightly with the palm of the hand.
SECOND RISING 1 hour	Brush each with melted butter, cover with waxed or parchment paper, and put aside to rise until double in volume, about 1 hour.
PREHEAT	Preheat oven to 375° 20 minutes before baking.
BAKING 375° 20 mins.	Remove the paper covering the balls. With a razor or scissors, cut a cross on the top of each bun. Also, a cross can be pressed but not cut into the buns with the blunt edge of a knife. Brush with egg yolk and water. Place in the oven until nicely browned, about 20 minutes.
FINAL STEP	Remove buns from the oven. Place on wire racks. When cool, fill the indentations on each bun with confectioners' icing.

BATH BUNS

[SIXTEEN BUNS]

Delicately browned and sparkling with a sugar glaze, these sweet buns were popular with visitors to the city of Bath, famous for its therapeutic "spa" waters. The bun is flavored with mace, the ground outer coating of the nutmeg.

Bath, west of London on the river Avon, has the only mineral springs in Great Britain, and Roman colonists were inspired to build a spa there — hence the name.

INGREDIENTS
3 to 4 cups bread or all-purpose flour, approximately
1 package dry yeast
¼ cup sugar
1 teaspoon salt
½ teaspoon mace
¼ cup nonfat dry milk
½ cup hot tap water (120°–130°)
2 eggs, beaten
2 tablespoons butter, room temperature
1 cup raisins or currants, plumped

Glaze:
1 egg yolk beaten with 2 teaspoons cream or milk
1 tablespoon lemon juice
3 tablespoons sugar

BAKING SHEET   One baking sheet, greased or Teflon.

BY HAND
OR MIXER
10 mins.

In a mixing or mixer bowl, measure 2 cups of flour and stir in the yeast, sugar, salt, mace, milk, and water. Add eggs and beat by hand or in the electric mixer with flat beater at slow speed for 30 seconds. Add butter and beat at medium speed for 3 minutes, or for an equal length of time with a wooden spoon.

Stir in the balance of flour, ½ cup at a time, first with the spoon and then by hand — or under the dough hook in the mixer. The dough will be a rough, shaggy mass that will clean the sides of the bowl. However, if the dough continues moist and sticky, add sprinkles of flour.

KNEADING
8 mins.

If by hand, turn the dough onto a lightly floured work surface and knead with the rhythmic 1-2-3 motion of push-turn-fold. The dough will become smooth and elastic and bubbles will form under the surface of the dough. In the electric mixer, dough will form a ball around the moving dough hook. The sides of the bowl will be wiped clean.

BY PROCESSOR
8 mins.

Attach the short plastic dough blade.

The sequence for adding ingredients differs from above.

Measure 2 cups of flour into the work bowl, add yeast, sugar, salt, mace, and nonfat dry milk. Pulse to blend. Remove cover and drop in the butter in pieces. Pulse until the butter becomes tiny rice-size bits. With the machine running, pour the hot water slowly through the feed tube. Pour in the beaten eggs to form a thick batter.

KNEADING
1 min.

With the machine running, add the remaining flour, ¼ cup at a time, until the dough forms a ball. If the dough is wet and sticks to the sides of the bowl, add flour by the tablespoon. If dough is dry, add water by the teaspoon. Once the ball of dough has formed, process for 1 minute to knead.

FIRST RISING
1½ hours

Place the dough on a floured work surface and knead into a ball. It will be soft, smooth, and slightly sticky (until dusted with flour).

Drop the dough into a greased bowl, turn to film all sides, and cover the bowl with plastic wrap. Put aside at room temperature to allow the dough to double in volume, about 1½ hours.

While the dough is rising, soak the raisins or currants in water for 1 hour, drain, and pat dry.

SHAPING
15 mins.

Begin by punching down the dough and kneading in the raisins or currants. Shape the dough under the hands into a long roll. Measure off and cut into 16 equal-size pieces — each about the size of a large egg, weighing about 2 ounces. Roll the pieces into balls, and then flatten to ½″. Place them on a baking sheet about 1½″ apart.

Mix the beaten egg yolk/cream with the lemon juice and brush the buns. Sprinkle liberally with sugar.

SECOND
RISING
45 mins.

Place the baking sheet in a warm place, cover carefully with a length of waxed or parchment paper. The buns will double in bulk in about 45 minutes.

PREHEAT

Preheat the oven to 350° about 20 minutes before the bake period.

BAKING
350°
20–24 mins.

Bake in the moderate oven until the buns test done, about 20 minutes. Rap on the bottom crust. A hard, hollow sound means the bun is baked.

FINAL STEP

Remove from the oven. Place on a metal rack to cool before serving. These keep well for several days wrapped in plastic or foil, or for several months frozen at 0°.

CHINESE STEAMED BUNS

[ONE DOZEN PLUMP BUNS]

This recipe for the soft and puffy Chinese steamed buns came from China by way of Hawaii, where for years street vendors sold them from baskets hanging at the ends of long, sturdy poles balanced on their shoulders.

Steamed buns, which have no crust, are soft and light, fluffy yet firm. They make a delicious alternative to rice.

Especially good when served with duck and pork, the buns can be easily transformed into *boa*, "bread with a heart," with a number of different fillings. Almost any cooked meat or seafood mixture can be used to fill the versatile bun. A favorite is *char siu* — barbecued pork brushed while cooking with a sweet reddish sauce. It can be bought in Chinese markets in large American cities.

A recipe for making *char siu* follows.

While a bamboo steamer set over boiling water is ideal, metal steam-

ers work as well. Line the bottom of the steamer with a layer of dampened cheesecloth or muslin so the buns do not stick and yet will allow
the steam to circulate freely. The alternative is to place each bun on a
2″ square of waxed or parchment paper.

INGREDIENTS

2 cups bread or all-purpose flour, approximately
1 package yeast
2 tablespoons sugar (more if you want them sweeter)
½ teaspoon salt
2 tablespoons nonfat dry milk
¾ cup hot water (120°–130°)
1 tablespoon vegetable shortening
¼ teaspoon baking powder

SPECIAL
EQUIPMENT

See text above.

BY HAND
OR MIXER
10 mins.

Measure 1 cup of flour into a mixing or mixer bowl and add the
yeast, sugar, salt, and nonfat dry milk. Stir to blend, and fashion a
well in the flour. Pour the hot water into the well and drop in the
shortening. Let stand for a moment to soften the shortening. With
a wooden spoon or mixer flat beater, stir vigorously for 2 minutes.
Sprinkle in the baking powder.

Add remaining flour, ¼ cup at a time, mixed into the body of
the dough until it forms a rough but elastic mass that can be lifted
from the bowl. If in the mixer, attach the dough hook.

Note: Don't overload this dough with flour. It must be soft and elastic
so that later the small pieces can be stretched over the filling with ease.

KNEADING
5 to 6 mins.

If by hand, lift the dough to a floured work surface and knead
with the strong 1-2-3 rhythm of push-turn-fold. Add sprinkles of
flour if the dough is sticky — but keep it on the moist side rather
than making it a hard ball.

If under the dough hook, the dough will clean the sides of the
bowl and form a ball around the hook. If it sticks to the sides, add
small portions of flour — but be niggardly.

Knead for 5 to 6 minutes.

BY PROCESSOR
3 mins.

Attach the steel blade.

Measure 1 cup of flour into the work bowl and add the yeast, sugar, salt, and nonfat dry milk. Pulse to blend. With the processor running, pour the hot water through the feed tube, and add the shortening. Stop the machine and sprinkle in the baking powder. Add remaining flour, 1/4 cup at a time, with the processor on. The amount of flour is sufficient when the dough cleans the sides of the bowl and rides on the blade.

KNEADING
45 secs.

Process with the machine running for 45 seconds.

The dough will be somewhat sticky when taken from the machine, but a dusting of flour will make it possible to work.

FIRST RISING
30 mins.

Place the dough in a greased bowl, cover tightly with plastic wrap, and put aside at room temperature to rise.

SHAPING

Punch down the dough, and roll it into an 18″ length about 1½″ thick. Cut into 1½″ pieces. Form each into a ball by rolling under a cupped palm of the hand.

If the buns are to be filled, form the dough into balls as above. Let them rest a moment and then flatten each into a 4″ circle. Place a scant teaspoonful of filling in the center of each circle; gather the dough over the filling, make small pleats, and pinch the seam tightly closed.

REST
5 mins.

Place each ball with the seam down on the dampened cloth or circle of waxed or parchment paper on the steamer rack. Let the balls rest for 5 minutes.

While the buns are resting, bring the water to a boil.

STEAMING
15–20 mins.

Set the steamer in place. If the steamer cover is metal (rather than bamboo), fold a small towel and place under the cover (and above the buns) so the cloth will absorb the steam and not let drops of moisture rain on the buns as they are being cooked. Cover and steam.

FINAL STEP

Lift the rack out of the steamer. Let the buns cool for a moment and, if desired, serve from the bamboo steamer.

To reheat the buns, cover with foil and place in a 350° oven for 15 minutes.

Thin slices of day-old unfilled buns make excellent toasts.

When the buns have lost their freshness, slice ¼"-thick pieces, dip in an egg-milk mixture, and fry or deep fry. Sprinkle with confectioners' sugar and serve.

CHAR SIU

While any cooked meat or seafood mixture can be used to fill a steamed bun, this one is the author's favorite.

INGREDIENTS

½ *teaspoon sesame oil*
½ *pound* char siu *or roast pork or ham, finely diced*
3 *tablespoons chopped green onions*
2 *tablespoons sugar*
1 *tablespoon soy sauce*
¼ *teaspoon salt*
1 *teaspoon grated fresh ginger*
2 *teaspoons all-purpose flour*
2 *teaspoons cornstarch*
¼ *cup water*

PREPARATION

Heat the oil and stir-fry the diced meat for 30 seconds in a saucepan. Add the onions, sugar, soy sauce, salt, and ginger.

Mix the flour and cornstarch with water. Stir into the *char siu* mixture. Cook over medium heat for about 3 minutes, until the mixture thickens. Put aside to cool.

If you wish the filling smooth, as I do, process for 3 seconds.

Char siu can be refrigerated for a week or frozen for several months.

AUSYTES
(Lithuanian Bacon Buns)

[TWO DOZEN SMALL BUNS]

This small, three-bite bun filled with a nugget of sautéed bacon and onion is served as a special treat in a Lithuanian home during the holiday season. It would be accompanied by the greeting *Linksmu Kaledu* — Merry Christmas!

INGREDIENTS

½ pound bacon, finely chopped
1 small onion, finely chopped
¾ cup milk
2 ounces (½ stick) butter, room temperature
1 egg, lightly stirred
2½ cups all-purpose flour, approximately
1 package dry yeast
1 teaspoon salt
2 tablespoons sugar
1 egg beaten with 1 teaspoon milk, to brush

BAKING SHEET

One baking sheet, greased or Teflon.

PREPARATION
1 hour,
approximately

Beforehand: Place the chopped bacon and onion in a heavy skillet; barely cover the mixture with water. Place the skillet over medium heat and boil off the water. When the water is gone, in about 1 hour, the mixture will have cooked into a rich brown filling, but it must be stirred during the last 15 minutes or it may stick to the skillet and burn. It will crackle and pop to announce that it is done. Remove from the heat. Drain the grease through a sieve and allow it to drip while it cools.

When cool, chop again with a knife or in a food processor to be certain the mixture is finely chopped. Set aside.

BY HAND
OR MIXER
15 mins.

In a small saucepan, heat the milk and butter until the butter is melted. Don't bring to scald, however. Remove the milk from the burner, and when it has cooled to lukewarm, stir in the egg. Set aside.

Measure 1½ cups of flour, the yeast, salt, and sugar into a mixing or mixer bowl. Stir to blend, and slowly pour in the liquid mixture. It will make a heavy batter.

Add remaining flour, ¼ cup at a time, to form a rough mass that can be lifted from the bowl, or left under the dough hook. Add sprinkles of flour if the dough is sticky. The dough under the hook should clean the sides of the bowl and form a ball around the hook as it revolves. If it sticks to the sides, add sprinkles of flour.

KNEADING
10 mins.

Turn the dough from the mixing bowl onto a floured work surface, and knead aggressively with a strong motion of push-turn-fold. The dough will become smooth and elastic. Knead by hand or in the mixer for 10 minutes.

BY PROCESSOR
6 mins.

Prepare the bacon-onion mixture, as above. Heat the milk and butter in a saucepan. Allow to cool and add the egg.

Attach the plastic dough blade.

Measure 2 cups of flour and the other dry ingredients into the processor work bowl. Pulse to blend. With the processor running, pour three-quarters of the liquid mixture slowly through the feed tube, keeping some of the milk in reserve until it is absorbed by the flour. Add the balance of the flour and pour in the rest of the milk mixture.

Stop the machine, remove the cover, and pinch the dough to test its consistency. A slight stickiness is acceptable, but if wet, more flour should be added.

KNEAD
45 secs.

When the dough cleans the sides of the bowl and rides the blade, process for 45 seconds to knead.

FIRST RISING
45 mins.

Place the dough in a greased bowl, cover tightly with plastic wrap, and put aside to double in volume, about 45 minutes.

SECOND
RISING
30 mins.

Punch down dough with extended fingers, cover the bowl again, and let rise to double in size, about 30 minutes.

SHAPING
20 mins.

Remove the dough from the bowl, knead for a few moments to press out the bubbles, and roll until it is about ½″ thick. Cut out circles with a 2″ biscuit or cookie cutter or pinch off pieces that weigh about 1½ ounces.

Lay the dough circles aside as you cut them.

With your fingers, press and stretch each piece into a 4″ circle about ¼″ or less thick. The dough may pull back. If it does, let it relax. Be patient.

Put about a teaspoon of cooled bacon mixture in the center of the circle of dough. Draw sides of circle up and over the bacon. Tightly pinch the seam together, and place roll (seam under) on the baking sheet. Continue with the others.

THIRD RISING   Cover the rolls with waxed paper or parchment paper and allow
1 hour   to double in size, about 1 hour.

PREHEAT   Preheat the oven to 375° about 20 minutes before baking.

BAKING   Brush the rolls with the egg-milk wash. Place in the oven on the
375°   middle or bottom shelf. The glossy brown rolls will bake in about
20 mins.   20 minutes.

FINAL STEP   The buns are best served warm from the oven. They can be
                frozen, however, and reheated for 20 minutes in a 350° oven.
                            Linksmu Kaledu!

PAN DULCE
(Mexican Sweet Bread)

[SIXTEEN BUNS]

Pan dulce, an egg-and-butter-rich Mexican yeast-raised sweet bread, is fashioned into three different shapes: shells *(conchas)*, horns *(cuernos)*, and ears of corn *(elotes)*. Streusel, a crumbly topping, is pressed onto small rounds of dough for the shells, while the streusel is rolled up into the horns and corn ears.

The buns may be made with plain egg streusel and some may be topped and filled with chocolate streusel. I usually do several of each.

INGREDIENTS

Dough:
4 cups all-purpose flour, approximately
1 cup milk, room temperature
1 package dry yeast
1 teaspoon salt
⅓ cup sugar
2 eggs, room temperature
6 tablespoons butter or margarine
1 egg yolk beaten with 1 teaspoon milk, to brush

Streusel:
½ cup sugar
⅔ cup all-purpose flour
3½ tablespoons butter or margarine
2 egg yolks, lightly beaten
2 tablespoons cocoa or ground semisweet chocolate, if desired

EQUIPMENT

Two baking sheets, greased or Teflon; a razor blade.

BY HAND
OR MIXER
12 mins.

In a mixing or mixer bowl, measure 2 cups of flour and add the milk, yeast, salt, and sugar. Stir to blend well. Add the eggs and shortening. Blend with a wooden spoon for 100 strokes, or for 1 minute with a mixer flat beater.

Add remaining flour, ¼ cup at a time, until the dough has formed a soft ball.

KNEADING
10 mins.

If by hand, turn onto a floured work surface to knead. Knead with a strong push-turn-fold rhythmic motion, adding sprinkles of flour if the dough sticks to the hand or the work surface. In the mixer, add sprinkles of flour as needed, until the ball of dough cleans the sides of the bowl and rotates with the dough hook. Knead by hand or with the mixer for about 8 to 10 minutes, until the dough is smooth, soft, and elastic.

BY PROCESSOR
10 mins.

Attach the steel blade.

Measure 2 cups of flour into the work bowl and add the milk and dry ingredients. Pulse to blend. With the machine running, pour in the eggs and drop the shortening through the feed tube. Add remaining flour, ¼ cup at a time, through the feed tube until the batter becomes a mass that cleans the bowl and rides with the blade.

KNEADING
50 secs.

With the machine running, process the dough for 50 seconds.

FIRST RISING
1 hour

Turn the dough into a greased bowl, cover tightly with plastic wrap, and put aside at room temperature to double in volume, about 1 hour.

STREUSEL
10 mins.

Prepare the egg streusel, both plain and chocolate, if you wish.

Plain: In a small bowl, mix sugar and flour. Cut in the shortening with a wire pastry blender or by rubbing the mixture between your fingers until the crumbs are tiny. With a fork, stir in egg yolks until well blended and the mixture is crumbly.

Chocolate: This is the same mixture as above but with the chocolate stirred in.

SHAPING
20 mins.

Punch down the dough and turn onto a floured work surface. Divide into 16 equal pieces and shape each into a smooth ball.

It is your choice as to the number of each of these three *pan dulce* buns you may wish to shape.

For the *concha*, flatten a ball under the palm of your hand into a 3″ round. Top with streusel, pat smooth with a spoon, and roll and press it into the dough with a rolling pin. With a razor blade or a very sharp knife, cut a pattern (tic-tac-toe, for example) through the streusel into the dough. Place on the prepared baking sheet. Place buns about 2″ apart.

For the *cuerno*, flatten a ball and shape into a triangle, about 8″ from top to bottom. The base should be about 4″ wide. Spread streusel over the dough. With the fingers, roll bottom to top, slightly stretching the dough as it is rolled. Halfway to the top, fold in the sides, about ¼″, to hold in the streusel and make neat margins. Shape into a half-moon crescent and place on the prepared baking sheet.

For the *elote*, roll the ball of dough into an oval, 6″ by 4″, spread the streusel, and roll from one end to the other, stretching the ends as you roll. With a razor blade, make 5 or 6 cuts across the top of the corn shape through to the filling. Place on the baking sheet.

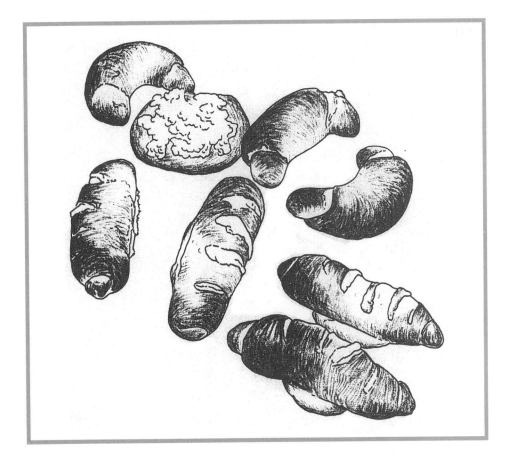

SECOND RISING 45 mins.	Cover the buns with waxed or parchment paper and put aside until almost double in bulk, about 45 minutes.
PREHEAT	Preheat the oven to 375° about 20 minutes before baking.
BAKING 375° 20 mins.	Brush the filled buns with the egg-milk mixture. Bake in the 375° oven for 18 to 20 minutes, or until the tops are lightly browned.
FINAL STEP	Place on a metal rack to cool. Delicious when warm out of the oven or when reheated.

CHELSEA BUNS

[NINE BUNS]

Characteristically square in shape, spicy and rich with raisins and nuts, and crusty with sugar, these buns got their name from the Chelsea Bun House in London, where they were a specialty in the seventeenth and early eighteenth centuries. King George III and Queen Charlotte were frequent guests of the proprietor, Captain Bun, who wore a dressing gown and a fez whether serving commoner or king.

While they closely resemble Danish pastry, they are more breadlike in texture. Serve with butter and jam.

Some bakers fill their Chelsea buns with mixed fruit rather than raisins and nuts, and glaze with honey.

INGREDIENTS

Sponge:
1 cup bread or all-purpose flour
1 package dry yeast
1 tablespoon sugar
¼ cup nonfat dry milk powder
¾ cup of warm water (80°–100°)
1 egg, lightly beaten, room temperature

Dough:
All of the sponge
½ teaspoon salt
¼ cup sugar
2 cups bread or all-purpose flour, approximately
¼ pound (1 stick) butter, room temperature
1 tablespoon butter, melted to brush
⅓ cup sugar
1 tablespoon cinnamon
1 cup raisins (golden or dark)

Topping:
⅓ cup sugar, to sprinkle liberally over baked buns
    or
1 cup confectioners' sugar, 1 tablespoon milk, and ⅛ teaspoon
    vanilla stirred together to ice

BAKING PAN	One 9″-x-13″ baking pan, greased.

PREPARATION
30–45 mins.

BY HAND
OR MIXER
10 mins.

Sponge: In a large mixing or mixer bowl, measure the flour and add the yeast, sugar, milk, and water. Stir to make a batter. Add the egg and beat until absorbed into the batter.

Cover the bowl with plastic wrap and put aside to ferment for 30 to 45 minutes.

Dough: Uncover the bowl and stir in the salt, sugar, and 1 cup of flour. Beat with strong strokes 45 times with a wooden spoon, or 3 minutes at medium speed in an electric mixer. Drop pieces of the soft butter into the mixture and thoroughly blend. Add remaining flour, 1/4 cup at a time, until the dough has become a shaggy mass that can be lifted from the bowl — or left in the mixer bowl under the dough hook.

KNEADING
10 mins.

If the dough is sticky under the hands or in the mixer bowl, add small portions of flour. Knead the dough with the rhythmic motion of push-turn-fold. It is to be a soft dough, so don't overload it with flour. It will be velvety smooth and a pleasure to work under the hands. Knead by hand or under the dough hook for 10 minutes.

BY PROCESSOR

8 mins.

Note: Because the batter is thin, mix the sponge in a separate bowl, cover, and set aside to ferment.

Attach the steel blade.

The mixing sequence differs from above: Measure 1 cup of flour into the work bowl and add the salt and sugar. Stir down the sponge and scrape it into the work bowl on top of the flour. Pulse to blend. Uncover and drop pieces of the soft butter into the mixture. With the machine running, add flour, 1/2 cup at a time, to form a rough mass that will ride the blade and clean the sides of the bowl. If the dough is dry and stiff, add water by the teaspoon, with machine running; if it is wet, add flour by the tablespoon.

KNEAD
60 secs.

Process the dough for 60 seconds to knead. Dough should be slightly sticky and very elastic when kneading is completed. Pull and stretch dough between your hands to test consistency; if necessary, return dough to work bowl to process a few seconds more.

FIRST RISING
45 mins.

Shape the dough into a ball, put it in a greased bowl, cover with plastic wrap, and put aside at room temperature to rise for 45 minutes.

SHAPING
18 mins.

Roll out the dough into a 10″-x-18″ piece. Place the dough lengthwise in front of you. Brush with melted butter, leaving a narrow ½″ strip at the upper edge.

Sprinkle sugar over the surface and dust with cinnamon. Scatter the raisins over the dough and roll up from the buttered long edge, stretching the dough slightly while rolling so that the sugar and raisins are gripped tightly. Seal the roll by pinching the edge firmly .

Brush the roll with melted butter, then cut into 9 slices 1½″ thick. After each slice, wipe the sticky blade clean. Lay the pieces about ½″ apart in the prepared pan with the cut side uppermost.

SECOND
RISING
40 mins.

Cover with waxed or parchment paper and put aside to rise for 40 minutes or until the rolls have doubled in volume.

PREHEAT

Preheat the oven to 400° 20 minutes before baking.

BAKING
400°
18–20 mins.

Place the pan in the oven and bake for 18 to 20 minutes. As the buns rise and bake, they will spread together and become square.

FINAL STEP

Either sprinkle sugar liberally over the tops when the buns come from the oven, or drizzle with the icing after the buns have cooled somewhat.

Separate the buns when they have cooled.

Biscuits

W HILE biscuits are popular for the speed and ease with which they can be made, a greater popularity rests on the fact they are delicious on almost all occasions—breakfast, lunch, and dinner, buffets, tailgate parties, wilderness trips, snacks after band and football practice.

Webster's description: "A quick bread, made light with baking powder, soda or yeast, and baked in small pieces." *Webster's* might have added that it requires a light hand in kneading to give the biscuit its treasured flaky results.

While this chapter is introduced by the southern biscuit and suggestions on how to make them, the rules apply generally to all of the biscuit recipes that follow.

In my bachelor days in New York City, my roommate for a time was a soon-to-be-groom, as was I. He was raised a South Carolinian with all the requisite birthrights of a southern gentleman. I was deeply impressed that he had a promise from the bride-to-be that she would make him baking powder biscuits for breakfast every day of their lives, as his mother had for his father. At last report, she had! On the other hand, while my Indiana bride did occasionally bake biscuits, she wanted it understood up front that it was not one of her wedding vows.

SOUTHERN BISCUITS

[ONE DOZEN BISCUITS]

Several years ago, a group of fine Georgia cooks were determined to create the best southern biscuit from among scores of recipes collected by their grandmothers as well as those found in old cookbooks.

The recipe chosen was by Shirley Corriher's grandmother, who left this notation as one of the ingredients: "Don't forget to add a touch of grace." It was her way of saying that biscuit making should be a joy.

Here, according to these and other southern cooks, are some important dos and don'ts in the art of making a true southern biscuit. At the same time, many of the rules apply to other biscuits as well.

- The less flour used, the better. Southern flours, usually labeled "made with soft winter wheat," have less gluten strength than most other flours and therefore make lighter biscuits. In the South, most home bakers use White Lily Flour. Don't hesitate to use other all-purpose flours, however. The difference in baking quality is very small.
- The chief leavening agent in biscuits is baking powder. Self-rising flour, widely used and popular in the South, has baking powder added. Use shortening rather than butter for a lighter biscuit. Lard gives biscuits a pronounced flavor and it is lighter than butter.
- The moister the dough, the lighter the biscuit. The dough should be as wet as possible and yet hold a shape. This is especially true of drop biscuits.
- Use a pastry blender or 2 knives to cut the shortening into the flour. Mixing by hand tends to soften the shortening, making a sticky, difficult-to-handle dough.

• Blending the fat completely with the flour, or using a liquid shortening, produces a mealy biscuit rather than a flaky, tender one. The most tender biscuits are those that are handled and kneaded just enough to mix the dry ingredients with the fat and the liquid — perhaps 5 to 10 quick kneads in all. More than that, and the flour's gluten tightens up and a tougher biscuit results.

• The amount of flour used in shaping varies with the method of shaping. A rolled dough calls for more flour than one dropped from a spoon.

• Dough that is ½″ thick is ideal for a tender, crumbly, light biscuit.

• Press the biscuit cutter straight down to get straight-sided, evenly shaped biscuits. Don't twist the cutter or it will smear the cut edges together.

• Bake close together for soft-sided biscuits; for crusty sides, 1″ apart.

• The hotter the oven, the better. Between 450° and 500° will make a golden biscuit that is moist on the inside.

• For a brown finish, brush the tops of the biscuits with milk or butter.

INGREDIENTS	*2 cups all-purpose flour*
	1 teaspoon salt
	1 tablespoon baking powder
	⅓ cup vegetable shortening or lard
	¾ cup milk for rolled biscuits, 1 cup for drop biscuits

BAKING SHEET   One baking sheet; biscuit cutter of desired size, large or small.

PREHEAT   Preheat the oven to 500°. This is a *hot* oven.

BY HAND
OR MIXER
5 mins.

Sift the flour, salt, and baking powder together into a bowl. Cut in the shortening with a pastry blender or 2 knives — or briefly with the mixer flat beater.

Pour in all of the milk at once. Stir with a fork or beater blade until just mixed. Add more milk if the dough is dry. The dough should be wet but able to retain its shape.

BY PROCESSOR
4 mins.

Use the steel blade.

Measure flour, salt, and baking powder into processor work bowl. Pulse to aerate. Add shortening, pulsing briefly to cut shortening into flour until it resembles coarse meal. Add the milk and combine by quickly turning processor on and off only 2 or 3 times, just enough to mix. Lengthy processing after adding the milk will toughen the biscuits.

SHAPING
CUT BISCUITS
8 mins.

Gather the dough into a ball; place on floured surface, sprinkle lightly with flour if necessary to prevent sticking. Work with the hands for a moment or so to pull all the dough pieces together. Dust again with flour if necessary.

Pat and roll with a rolling pin to ½″ thickness, cut into rounds, and place them on a lightly greased baking sheet. Knead scraps gently together and cut again.

BAKING
500°
10–12 mins.

Bake on the middle shelf of the hot oven for 10–12 minutes, or until golden brown.

FINAL STEP

Remove the biscuits from the oven and serve right away.
Pass the butter, and praise all grandmothers.

GREEK FETA BISCUITS

[TWENTY-FOUR SMALL OR TWELVE LARGE BISCUITS]

Biscotakia me feta is a delicious Greek biscuit with a mild cheesy flavor that is made with feta cheese from sheep's, goat's, or cow's milk.

While it is sold in most supermarkets, some feta cheese is ready-packaged in plastic and is a poor substitute for the real thing. Instead, look for the authentic feta in Middle Eastern food shops where the white, semisoft, and crumbly cheese usually is stored in brine. Always wash off the brine in clear running water before using. It can be stored for several weeks in the refrigerator immersed in a jar of nonfat milk mixed with a teaspoon of salt.

INGREDIENTS
2 cups all-purpose flour
½ teaspoon salt
3 teaspoons baking powder
1 tablespoon sugar
6 tablespoons butter
¾ cup milk
¾ cup feta cheese, rinsed and crumbled
1 egg yolk beaten with 1 tablespoon water, to brush

BAKING
SHEET

One baking sheet, ungreased.

BY HAND
OR MIXER
5 mins.

Sift the flour, salt, baking powder, and sugar into a large bowl. Quickly cut butter into the mixture with a pastry blender until mixture resembles coarse oatmeal. Pour in the milk, add cheese, and stir about 30 seconds to make a soft dough.

BY PROCESSOR
4 mins.

Attach the steel blade.

Pour all of the dry ingredients into the processor work bowl; pulse to blend. Drop the butter and cheese in the bowl. Pulse rapidly while pouring the milk through the feed tube.

When the ingredients have come together in a ball, stop the machine and turn the dough onto a floured work surface. Don't overprocess; process on the short side.

KNEADING
3 mins.

Knead the dough quickly for another 30 seconds on a lightly floured work surface. Press dough flat and fold in half. Repeat pressing down and folding 6 or 8 times. Roll out with a rolling pin to about ½".

PREHEAT

Preheat oven to 425°.

CUT ROUNDS
10 mins.

Cut dough into rounds of preferred size. For trim, browned-all-over biscuits, leave space around each on the pan. For biscuits that are high, soft, and golden in color, place them in the pan touching.

Place on an ungreased baking sheet and brush with egg yolk–water mixture.

BAKE
425°
12–15 mins.

Bake in 425° oven until lightly browned. This will be about 12 minutes for the small biscuits and 15 for the large.

FINAL STEP

Serve hot or, if for hors d'oeuvres, cool and split open for ham slice or spreads.

To freeze, seal in plastic bag. To reheat, place biscuits in a brown paper bag and heat in a 300° oven for 10 minutes or until warmed through.

BUTTERMILK CHEESE DROP BISCUITS

[ONE DOZEN BISCUITS]

Forget the diet. This is the morning to serve drop biscuits. The recipe came from tasting and testing favorite biscuits over the years and then selecting the things I liked best about each.

Not having been constrained by a metal biscuit cutter, a drop biscuit has a rough shagginess about it. Some biscuits will be bigger than others and all will have rugged hills and deep valleys. They will be crusty with bits of melted cheese peeking through the sides.

Don't use packaged grated cheese, which is nothing more than powder and can't establish its identity in the mixture. I favor a grated sharp Cheddar — a Kraft brick or a cheese from the Cabot creamery in Cabot, Vermont.

INGREDIENTS

1½ cups all-purpose flour, approximately
1 tablespoon baking powder
1 teaspoon salt
⅓ cup lard, chilled in the refrigerator
1 cup cold buttermilk
⅔ cup grated cheese, Cheddar preferred

BAKING
SHEET

One baking sheet, greased, Teflon, or lined with parchment paper (melted cheese bits will stick).

PREHEAT

Preheat the oven to 450°.

BY HAND
OR MIXER
5 mins.

In a mixing or mixer bowl, stir together the flour, baking powder, and salt. Drop pieces of chilled lard into the flour. If by hand, cut the lard into the flour with a pastry cutter or 2 knives slicing together across the shortening. Don't use fingers. They will smear the lard into the flour rather than leave the tiny crumbs intact. If in the mixer, use the flat beater blade to break the lard into the flour. Don't overmix.

Pour the buttermilk into the bowl and stir together with a wooden spoon or spatula to draw in all of the ingredients. Stir the cheese into the dough.

A tablespoon of dough should clump like cottage cheese. If the mix is dry, add 1 or 2 teaspoons of buttermilk. If too wet, add a teaspoon or two of flour.

BY PROCESSOR
4 mins.

Insert steel blade.

Measure the dry ingredients in the work bowl. Pulse to blend. Drop the lard into the bowl; pulse once or twice until the mixture resembles coarse grain. Pour the buttermilk through the feed tube. Add cheese. Pulse to mix, but only briefly. Test and correct for body as above.

SHAPING   Drop dough from a tablespoon — pushed off with a spatula — onto
5 mins.   the prepared baking sheet. For a crispy biscuit overall, leave room
                 between so they don't touch.

BAKING   Place baking sheet in the middle shelf of the hot oven. Bake for
450°   about 20 minutes until nicely browned and hard when tapped
18–20 mins.   with a fingernail.

FINAL STEP   For a real down-home touch, serve hot from the baking sheet.
                     While best right from the oven, drop biscuits may be reheated
                 at 250° for 10 minutes.

SODA BISCUITS

[TWO DOZEN TWO-INCH BISCUITS]

A soda biscuit has been described as "two crisp crusts with very little in
between." It is an uncomplicated biscuit for holding good things like
butter, jams, jellies, and honey. Or a small slice of southern ham.

Unlike the baking powder biscuit, its plump cousin that rises grandly
in the oven, this slender biscuit relies solely on buttermilk and soda
working together for its levitation, such as it is.

The soda biscuit is so easy to put together by hand, I find it isn't
worth the time it takes to clean up a machine to do otherwise.

INGREDIENTS   *1½ cups all-purpose flour, approximately*
                 ½ teaspoon baking soda
                 ½ teaspoon salt
                 ⅓ cup vegetable shortening
                 1 cup buttermilk
                 1 tablespoon melted butter or margarine, to brush

BAKING SHEET   One baking sheet, greased, Teflon, or lined with parchment
                 paper.

PREHEAT   Preheat the oven to 450°.

BY HAND   In a medium bowl, place the flour, soda, and salt and blend
12 mins.   together. Drop the shortening into the flour and cut into small
               pieces with a pastry cutter or 2 knives slicing against each other.
               Don't use fingers, for they tend to smear the shortening into
               the flour rather than leaving the tiny granules distinct and sepa-
               rate.

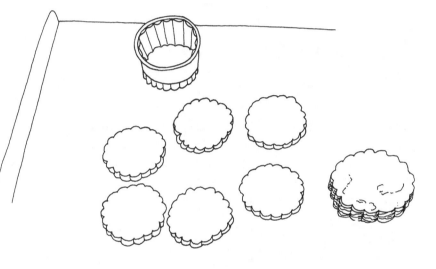

               Make a well in the center of the flour and pour in half the
               buttermilk. With a fork, draw the flour into the buttermilk and stir
               together. Carefully add just enough buttermilk to make a rough
               mass that can be lifted from the bowl and placed on a lightly
               floured work surface. Add sprinkles of flour if the dough is too wet
               or sticky to work with the hands.

KNEADING   Lightly knead only 4 or 5 times — only enough to draw the dough
1 min.   together. Don't overwork, or gluten will form and the dough will
               toughen.

SHAPING   Pat or roll out to ¼″ thickness and cut with a medium-small
5 mins.   biscuit cutter and place on the prepared baking sheet. Brush with
               melted butter or margarine.

BAKING 450° 12–15 mins.	Bake on the center shelf for about 12 to 15 minutes or until biscuits have a good suntan on their faces.
FINAL STEP	Brush again with the melted butter when they are taken from the oven. Serve hot or warm from the oven but, mind you, they are just as good when eaten later. Next day, even.

PLANTATION BISCUITS

[EIGHT WEDGE-SHAPED BISCUITS]

From the kitchen of the manager's house on one of the sugar plantations on the Big Island of Hawaii came this recipe made with milk soured with vinegar. The dough is patted and rolled into a circular piece, then cut into 8 wedges rather than into the usual biscuit shape. It is especially good spread with guava jelly.

INGREDIENTS	*3/4 cup milk* *1 tablespoon vinegar* *2 cups all-purpose flour* *2 teaspoons baking powder* *1/2 teaspoon sugar* *1/2 teaspoon baking soda* *1/2 teaspoon salt* *4 tablespoons butter*
BAKING SHEET	One baking sheet, greased or Teflon.
SOURED MILK	Half an hour before making the dough, mix the milk with the vinegar and set aside.
PREHEAT	Preheat the oven to 425° and place rack in top third.

BY HAND OR MIXER 5 mins.	Sift together the flour, baking powder, sugar, baking soda, and salt. With pastry blender or fork or flat beater blade, cut butter into the flour until the mixture has a fine-crumb consistency. Stir the soured milk and pour into the flour mixture. Stir only until the dough is lightly blended.
TO SHAPE 4 mins.	Turn the dough onto the floured work surface and pat into an 8″ circle. Cut into 8 wedges and place on the prepared baking sheet.
BAKING 15–18 mins.	Place in the hot oven and bake for 15 to 18 minutes.
FINAL STEP	Spread with jam and think of Hawaii.

SOURDOUGH BISCUITS

[TWELVE TWO-INCH BISCUITS]

For those who have a starter or can beg, steal, or borrow a cup from a friend, or those who wish to make their own, this delicately soured biscuit is worth whichever route you choose to take.

If you wish to make your own starter, I have included a chapter from my *New Complete Book of Breads* on the basics and five starter recipes. Turn to pages 262 to 266.

INGREDIENTS	*1 cup starter* *¾ cup lukewarm milk* *2 cups all-purpose flour, approximately* *¾ teaspoon salt* *3 teaspoons baking powder* *¼ cup vegetable shortening*
BAKING SHEET	One baking sheet — need not be greased.

BY HAND
OR MIXER
15 mins.

Stir together the starter and warm milk in a mixing or mixer bowl. In a second bowl, sift or stir together the flour with the salt and baking powder. Drop chunks of the shortening into the flour and cut into coarse bits with a pastry blender or 2 knives. If in the mixer, use the flat beater blade. Don't overbeat or the shortening will blend or smear into the flour.

Pour half of the milk into the flour and stir together. Add additional milk to make a shaggy mass that can be lifted from the bowl and placed on the work surface. Too much milk makes the dough too sticky to handle; not enough milk makes the biscuits dry. Don't overmix.

BY PROCESSOR
5 mins.

Attach the steel blade.

Stir together the starter and warm milk in a mixing bowl.

Measure all of the dry ingredients into the work bowl. Pulse to blend. Remove the cover and scatter pieces of the shortening over the flour. Replace the cover; pulse 5 or 6 times to cut the shortening into the flour. Pulsing the processor on and off, slowly pour the milk through the feed tube. The dough is not to be kneaded — only mixed. Turn the dough onto the lightly floured work surface.

SHAPING
12 mins.

Pat or roll the dough into a sheet ½″ thick. Cut with a biscuit cutter, dipping each time into flour so it won't stick or smear the dough as it cuts. Push straight down on the cutter. Don't twist or it will bind the dough. For crusty-sided biscuits, place about 1″ apart. For soft-sided biscuits, cluster with sides just touching.

Cover biscuits and set aside while oven heats.

PREHEAT

Preheat oven to 400°.

BAKING
400°
15–20 mins.

Bake on the middle shelf of the hot oven for 15 to 20 minutes until lightly browned.

FINAL STEP

Serve hot with lots of butter.

CORN STICKS

[FOURTEEN TO SIXTEEN STICKS]

There is an appealing roughness about this corn bread made into corn sticks. Each grain is distinct and separate. Delicious.

The cast-iron "ear of corn" pan — seen often in antique stores or hung on kitchen walls as decorative pieces — is a superb instrument for baking corn bread that is crusty on the bottom and golden brown on top. The thick cast iron holds the heat and prevents the crust from burning before the interior is cooked. It may take two 7-ear pans to bake this recipe. They are relatively inexpensive, and most kitchenware shops carry them.

INGREDIENTS

½ cup all-purpose flour
2 teaspoons baking powder
1 teaspoon sugar
½ teaspoon salt
1½ cups cornmeal, yellow or white
1 egg, room temperature
¾ cup milk, room temperature
3 tablespoons butter, melted

BAKING
MOLDS

One or 2 corn stick pans, oiled.

PREHEAT

Preheat the oven to 450° while preparing the batter. At the same time, place the prepared cast-iron pan(s) in the oven to be heated before they are filled.

PREPARATION
8 mins.

Sift and stir together the flour, baking powder, sugar, and salt in a bowl. Mix in cornmeal and blend thoroughly. In another bowl, beat egg until it is light in color, and stir in milk and melted butter. Using as few strokes as possible, stir the egg mixture into the cornmeal. The batter will be lumpy.

FORMING
4 mins.

With care, take the hot cast-iron pan from the oven. Spoon or pour the batter into the molds three-quarters full.

BAKING
450°
20–25 mins.

Bake until crisp, about 20 to 25 minutes.

FINAL STEP

Remove the sticks from the mold. Admire. Serve hot with lots of butter.

BEATEN BISCUITS

[ABOUT THREE DOZEN BISCUITS]

The beaten biscuit came from the South, where the sound of a wooden beater crashing against a ball of dough could be heard in the early morning coming from many nineteenth-century kitchens as slaves or members of the family began the ritual of making the small, crisp, short, and delicious biscuits for breakfast.

It is not an easy chore, but the results are outstanding. Flailing with a rolling pin, a flatiron, or the side of a cleaver, the beating goes on for 30 minutes, if just for family, 45 minutes for guests. My first beater was an ax handle.

A beaten-biscuit party can be a crashing success. Let the guests take turns beating on the dough for 45 minutes, then they will have a half hour to recharge their energies before *their* biscuits come out of the oven.

A recent development in the biscuit's long history has been the food processor. In some mysterious way, the force of the whirling steel blade has almost the same effect on the dough as a wooden beater. And in dramatically less time.

The traditional biscuit is 1½" to 2" in diameter and about ½" thick. It is fashioned with a special cutter that presses 6 holes through the top of the biscuit as it cuts. These holes can also be made with the tines of a fork. It is customary to form the biscuit by squeezing the dough between the thumb and forefinger to make a ball the size of an egg. Pinched off, it is patted or rolled flat and pricked with the fork.

A southern cook would most likely use self-rising flour and delete baking powder and salt from the list of ingredients.

INGREDIENTS
3½ cups sifted all-purpose flour
1 teaspoon salt
1 tablespoon sugar
1 teaspoon baking powder
4 ounces (½ cup) vegetable shortening or lard
1¼ cups milk, approximately

BAKING
SHEET
One baking sheet, ungreased or Teflon.

PREPARATION
Note: There is an antique hand-cranked beaten-biscuit machine extant, but it is unlikely one is readily at hand, so two ways are suggested: beating with a rolling pin or in a food processor.

BY HAND
OR MIXER
15 mins.

Sift flour into a large bowl and add salt, sugar, and baking powder. Stir to mix. Cut shortening into small pieces and drop into the dry ingredients. With the fingers or a pastry cutter or mixer flat blade, work shortening into the flour until it resembles grains of rice.

Slowly pour 1 cup of milk into the bowl and work it into the mixture. Slowly add balance of milk if it is needed to hold the dough together. Remember, it is to be a fairly stiff dough — be sparing of the liquid. Work the dough with the hands or with the beater blade for 2 or 3 minutes until you are certain it will cling together and not fragment with the first blow of the blunt instrument.

BEATING
30–45 mins.

Select a place on a countertop or table that is the height for prolonged beating. Don't beat frantically. Use measured blows. When the dough has been beaten crosswise in one direction, shift the dough or your position so that you are beating across the previous pattern. When the dough is flattened, fold and continue beating. The dough will become silky and elastic. Bubbles will form and pop when the dough has been beaten enough.

BY PROCESSOR
4 mins.

With the steel blade in place, add flour, salt, sugar, and baking powder to the work bowl. Pulse to aerate the mixture. Add the shortening and pulse 2 or 3 times. With the machine running, pour the milk through the feed tube in a steady stream. When the milk has been absorbed, remove the cover and pinch the dough to determine the consistency. It should be soft but not sticky. If it is wet, add a small portion of flour. If dry, add a teaspoon or two of water.

KNEADING
2 mins.

Process until the mixture forms a ball, then process/knead for 2 minutes.

Remove the dough from the work bowl and flatten with 50 whacks of a rolling pin. Turn the dough crosswise and give it another 50 blows. Not only does this let the dough know that it is a *beaten* biscuit but also prepares it for the next step.

PREHEAT

Preheat the oven to 400° shortly before the biscuits are to be cut.

SHAPING 10 mins.	Roll the dough into a ½″-thick sheet. Use a 1½″ or 2″ biscuit cutter to make about 36 rounds. Pierce each round with the tines of a fork. Place on a baking sheet.
BAKING 400° 25–30 mins.	Bake in the moderately hot oven until the biscuits begin to tan or brown, but only lightly, after 25 to 30 minutes.
FINAL STEP	Remove from the oven. Serve warm. These will keep for several days in a tightly closed paper bag. Wrap in foil to reheat. They freeze nicely for up to 6 months.

ANGEL BISCUITS

[EIGHTEEN BISCUITS]

   With wings folded, angel biscuits are as soft and fluffy and light as one might suppose an angel to be.

   The levitation for these angels, however, comes from yeast, baking powder, *and* baking soda. (For those on a low-sodium diet, substitute 2 teaspoons low-sodium baking powder and 2 teaspoons cream of tartar for baking soda.)

   The dough is rolled flat, cut, brushed with melted butter, and folded in half. The layers open in the oven like angels' wings, or so it can be imagined. I have also sprinkled grated Cheddar cheese over the biscuits before they are folded.

This convenient dough can be refrigerated up to 4 or 5 days, and baked as needed.

INGREDIENTS	
	1 package dry yeast

INGREDIENTS

1 package dry yeast
1 tablespoon warm water
2½ cups all-purpose flour, approximately
2 teaspoons baking powder
½ teaspoon baking soda
2 tablespoons sugar
½ teaspoon salt
¾ cup (6 ounces) vegetable shortening
1 cup buttermilk
2 tablespoons butter, melted, to brush

BAKING SHEET One baking sheet, greased or Teflon.

BY HAND OR MIXER 12 mins.

In a small bowl, dissolve the yeast in 1 tablespoon of water, and set aside.

In a large bowl or mixer bowl, stir together the flour, baking powder, baking soda, sugar, and salt. The mixer flat beater is good for this.

Drop chunks of shortening into the flour. Work in the shortening either with 2 knives or a pastry blender. The flour will resemble grains of rice or smaller. If in the mixer, the flat beater blade will cut the shortening into tiny pieces.

Stir the yeast into the buttermilk. Stir the buttermilk into the flour; mix it thoroughly but do not knead. If in a mixer, slowly pour in the liquid to form a moist dough. It may be sticky to handle, so dust with flour. It will become stiff and workable when it has been chilled in the refrigerator.

BY PROCESSOR 6 mins.

Attach the plastic blade.

Mix the yeast with the tablespoon of water. Measure all of the other dry ingredients into the processor work bowl. Pulse to blend.

Uncover the bowl and scatter pieces of the shortening over the flour. Replace the cover; pulse 6 or 7 times to cut shortening into the flour. Pulsing the processor on and off rather than allowing it to run, slowly pour the yeast and buttermilk through the feed tube. It is not to be kneaded, only mixed.

REFRIGERATE
Overnight

Place the dough in a greased bowl, cover with plastic wrap, and leave overnight in the refrigerator. (It can be used immediately but an overnight rest enhances its fluffiness.)

SHAPING
12 mins.

Roll out the dough into a rectangle. Fold in thirds, and roll again. Dough should be about ½" or less thick. Cut circles with a 2" cookie cutter. Brush each with melted butter (sprinkle with cheese, if desired). Fold in half. Press down hard along the crease. Place on the baking sheet.

REST
20 mins.

Cover the biscuits with waxed paper and set aside to rest for 20 minutes.

PREHEAT

While the dough is resting, preheat the oven to 400°.

BAKING
400°
15–17 mins.

Place the sheet of biscuits on the middle shelf of the hot oven. Bake for 15 to 17 minutes until the wings have unfolded and the tops are nicely browned.

FINAL STEP

Serve with lots of butter and other good things.
   My wife loves them with honey, which goes nicely with angels.

BENNE SEED BISCUITS

[ABOUT TWO DOZEN BISCUITS]

Known to southern cooks as the benne seed, the sesame seed lends an uncommonly good flavor to this biscuit that is rolled wafer-thin and baked for less than 10 minutes.

INGREDIENTS

¹/₂ cup toasted benne, or sesame, seeds
2 cups all-purpose flour, approximately
1 teaspoon baking powder
¹/₂ teaspoon salt
¹/₂ cup butter or margarine, room temperature
¹/₂ cup milk

BAKING SHEET

One baking sheet, greased or Teflon.

TOAST
350°
10 mins.

Beforehand: Spread the seeds on a cookie sheet and toast in a 350° oven for 10 minutes. Toasting (or roasting) greatly enhances the seeds' flavor.

PREHEAT

If the oven has cooled after toasting the benne seeds, heat again to 350° before starting the dough.

BY HAND
OR MIXER
10 mins.

Measure flour, baking powder, and salt into a mixing or mixer bowl. If by hand, rub in the butter or margarine with fingers or cut with a pastry cutter or drop small pieces into mixer bowl under the flat beater. Add the milk. Blend thoroughly with 30 or 40 strokes — or 1 minute in the mixer. If the dough is sticky and moist, add small portions of flour. Add the benne seeds and work them into the dough.

BY PROCESSOR
3 mins.

Attach the steel blade. This is a quick operation, so pulse processor only enough to mix the ingredients.

Place all the ingredients, in the order above, including the benne seeds, in the work bowl. Pulse 5 or 6 times — just enough to mix thoroughly. Feel the dough. If it is too sticky to be rolled, add flour.

SHAPING
5 mins.

Lightly flour the work surface and turn out the dough. Roll wafer-thin (¹/₈″ or thickness of two benne seeds placed side by side) and cut circles with a 2″ cutter. Arrange the circles on the baking sheet.

BAKING
350°
8–10 mins.

Bake for 8 to 10 minutes.

FINAL STEP   Remove biscuits from the oven. Place them on a metal rack and sprinkle lightly with salt. Serve while still warm.

BAKESTONE HERB CAKES

[EIGHTEEN TWO-INCH BISCUITS]

These biscuits, speckled with green flecks of oregano, a member of the mint family, are splendid companions for soup and salad. The biscuits hold promise beyond a delicious bite. Oregano has long been praised as an aphrodisiac and widely used as a medicinal herb, especially to improve the appetite. Based on an English recipe, these are quickly made and baked on the griddle — a boon in hot weather.

The recipe comes from *The Kitchen Garden Cookbook*, by Sylvia Thompson, a talented writer and a friend for many years. Our friendship began aboard the French passenger barge *Palinurus* on the Bourgogne Canal near Dijon, where both of us were writing about good things to eat.

INGREDIENTS   *⅓ cup fresh oregano leaves, tightly packed*
1⅔ cups all-purpose flour
1 tablespoon baking powder
¼ teaspoon salt
4 tablespoons butter, cold
½ cup plus 2 tablespoons half-and-half or milk

PREHEAT   Heat cast-iron griddle or heavy skillet over medium heat.
15 mins.

BY HAND   Chop the oregano leaves by hand or in the food processor before
OR   adding flour, baking powder, and salt. Blend with the fingers or
PROCESSOR   pulse 6 times if using the processor. Cut the butter into small dice
15 mins.   and drop into the flour. Rub into the flour or cut with a wire pastry blender or pulse in the processor until the butter is the size of small peas.

KNEAD
1 min.

Turn the mixture into a bowl. Stir in the half-and-half with a fork with as few strokes as possible. Knead briefly to pull the dough together into a ball.

BAKING
12 mins.

Pat or roll out dough to ½″ thick. Cut into 2″ rounds and fit close together on the unbuttered griddle or skillet. Turn when the bottoms are browned, 5 to 6 minutes, exchanging biscuits on the center and sides. In another 4 or 5 minutes, they'll be browned on the bottom. To be certain they are baked, split one open.

FINAL STEP

Serve hot in a basket — to be split and buttered.

PETITES GALETTES SALÉES
(Little Salted Biscuits)

[ABOUT FIFTY BISCUITS]

I discovered this recipe for bite-size biscuits on a trip to Grenoble, on the Isère River in southeastern France. They are ideal for entertaining, served alone or with spreads. While there is salt among the ingredients, additional coarse salt or poppy or sesame seeds can be sprinkled on for added flavor and appearance.

Depending on how they are to be served, the dough is cut into 1″ or 2″ squares. The choice is large or small.

INGREDIENTS

½ cup (1 stick) butter, room temperature
½ cup hot water (120°–140°)
2¼ cups all-purpose flour, approximately
¼ cup nonfat dry milk
4 teaspoons sugar
2 teaspoons salt
1 egg and 1 tablespoon milk or water, stirred together
Kosher or sea salt, poppy or sesame seeds, to sprinkle (optional)

BAKING SHEET	One baking sheet, which does not have to be greased because of the high butterfat content of the *galettes*.
BY HAND OR MIXER 15 mins.	Cut butter into several pieces and drop into mixing or mixer bowl. Pour in the hot water, which will further soften the butter. Let stand for 5 minutes. By hand or with the flat beater, stir in 3/4 cup of flour, dry milk, sugar, and salt. This will be a soft batter. Add the rest of the flour, 1/4 cup at a time, to form a ball of soft dough.
KNEADING 3 mins.	There is no leavening in this dough, so it is not necessary to develop gluten as for a yeast-raised product. The kneading or working the dough is simply to blend ingredients and make a smooth dough. If by hand, turn dough onto work surface dusted with flour and work until the dough is smooth. If in a mixer, attach dough hook. It may need additional sprinkles of flour to give body to the dough. Work (or knead) the dough for about 3 minutes.
BY PROCESSOR 4 mins.	Attach the steel blade. Prepare the butter and hot water as above. Place 1½ cups of flour and the other dry ingredients in the work bowl; pulse to blend. With the processor running, pour the liquid through the feed tube into the bowl. Stop the machine. Add remaining flour, 1/4 cup at a time, through the feed tube or by taking off the cover. Stop the processor, and feel the dough. If it is soft and smooth, process for 5 seconds. It may be slightly sticky, but it will become manageable with a dusting of flour.
REST 20 mins.	Place dough in a bowl, cover with plastic wrap, and put aside to relax at room temperature for 20 minutes.
PREHEAT	Preheat oven to 400°.
SHAPING 10 mins.	Turn dough onto floured work surface and roll into a rectangle — no more than 1/8″ thick. Don't rush. Pulling gently with the hands will help form the rectangle. I keep a yardstick handy to measure the area, mark off 2″ squares, and guide the pastry wheel or knife — or do it freehand.

A pastry wheel or jagger — especially the latter, which is a wheel with a scalloped edge like pinking shears — makes a handsome *galette* and does not tear or pull the dough as a knife would do.

Prick each with the sharp tines of a fork. Lightly brush each *galette* with the egg-milk mixture and sprinkle on salt or seeds, if desired.

Lift *galettes* carefully and place on the baking sheet. If sheet won't hold them all, cover balance with paper and leave on the work surface.

BAKING
400°
12–15 mins.

Place in preheated oven but stand by because these bake rapidly. Look at them after 8 minutes. They should be light brown with somewhat darker edges and brown on the bottom when done. Don't be afraid to shuffle them around to achieve uniform baking. If some are fatter than others and feel soft when pressed on top, return to the oven. But watch them!

FINAL STEP

Place biscuits on metal rack to cool.

Delicious warm. They will stay fresh for days in a closed container and they freeze well.

MOTHER'S BISCUITS

[TWO DOZEN BISCUITS]

The recipe for this delicious biscuit I found in a delightful book, *Cross Creek Cookery*, by Marjorie Kinnan Rawlings, author of *The Yearling*. The mother is hers. My mother's recipe was never committed to paper. But after a consultation with my sister, I am satisfied this biscuit is as good as my mother's.

INGREDIENTS

2 cups all-purpose flour
4 teaspoons baking powder
½ teaspoon salt
2 tablespoons butter
1 cup milk (scant), room temperature

BAKING SHEET	One baking sheet, greased and cornmeal-dusted, Teflon, or lined with parchment paper.
PREHEAT	Preheat oven to 425° before starting biscuit preparation.
BY HAND OR MIXER 10 mins.	Mix flour, baking powder, and salt together in a mixing or mixer bowl. Work in the butter with a wire pastry blender or mixer flat blade until it resembles coarse grain. Add only enough milk to hold the dough together. The exact amount varies with the flour.

BY PROCESSOR 4 mins.	Insert the steel blade.
	   This will be a quick mixing operation, on-off pulses only. Don't let the machine run.
	   Measure the dry ingredients into the work bowl. Pulse to blend. Drop in the butter, pulse 3 or 4 times until it resembles coarse grain.
	   Pour in half the milk through the feed tube. Pulse 3 or 4 times. Add more milk, but only enough to hold the dough together. Pulse 2 or 3 times. Remove the cover and feel the dough. It should be slightly sticky. Dust with flour to make it easy to handle.

SHAPING 6 mins.	While it is considered heresy to handle biscuit dough needlessly, Mrs. Rawlings's mother believed that to make a flaky, layered biscuit, one should roll out the dough, fold it over itself in 4 layers, roll out again to a thickness of ½″, and cut with a 2″ cookie cutter. Place biscuits on the baking sheet.
BAKING 425° 12–14 mins.	Bake in the oven until a golden brown and raised to about 1½″ to 2″, about 12 to 14 minutes
FINAL STEP	Remove biscuits from the oven. Serve hot.

BISCUITS AU MAÏS
(Corn Biscuits)

[FOUR DOZEN BISCUITS]

Biscuits au maïs get their rich look from eggs, yellow cornmeal, and butter. This is a dessert bread—a light golden disk, a bit on the sweet side, perhaps, but a fine complement to a dish of strawberries or a half grapefruit.

While it is unleavened, it achieves a pleasant plumpness in the oven, thanks to the eggs.

INGREDIENTS	*½ cup (1 stick) butter, room temperature*
	½ cup sugar
	1 cup yellow cornmeal
	2 eggs, room temperature
	1 teaspoon salt
	1¼ cups all-purpose flour, approximately

BAKING SHEET   One large baking sheet, greased or Teflon.

PREHEAT   Preheat oven to 375° before preparation begins.

BY HAND
OR MIXER
15 mins.   In a large bowl, stir the butter into a soft mass with a wooden spoon or with the mixer's flat beater. Slowly add sugar, and cream together—about 75 strokes or 2 minutes with the mixer. Add cornmeal, eggs, and salt. Beat until smooth. Add 1¼ cups of flour. The mixture will be soft and moist but can be rolled flat with a rolling pin to a thickness of about ¼″.

If too wet to work, add sprinkles of flour, blend in with hands, and flatten with rolling pin.

BY PROCESSOR
5 mins.   Use the steel blade for this small quantity.

Drop the butter and sugar into the work bowl. Turn on the processor and add the cornmeal, eggs, and salt through the feed tube. Add flour, ¼ cup at a time, to make a mixture that will form a soft ball and ride with the blade. If the dough is wet or slack, add sprinkles of flour. Turn from the bowl onto the work surface and roll flat.

The dough is not kneaded.

SHAPING
5 mins.

Use a 1½″ cookie cutter to cut about 48 pieces. Reassemble the scraps, roll again, and cut. Place together on baking sheet but do not let them touch.

BAKING
375°
22 mins.

Place the baking sheet on the center rack of the 375° oven. Near the end of the bake period, turn the baking sheet around. If those on the outer edge are browning too fast, either remove them if they are done (brown on the bottom) or move to the center while pushing the lighter biscuits to the outside. Bake about 22 minutes.

FINAL STEP

Remove from the oven and cool on metal rack. Delicious served warm or equally good frozen and warmed for serving later.

SAGE BISCUITS

[ONE DOZEN BISCUITS OR FOUR COVERS FOR POT PIES]

Served aboard the big passenger steamboat *The Mississippi Queen*, this biscuit—with green flecks of sage and the distinct but light fragrance of fresh-roasted cumin—is the creation of its chef, Keith Bryant.

While it is served aboard mostly at breakfast, the chef cuts the same dough into large round pieces to fit atop individual servings of chicken pot pie. The sage, cumin, and chicken blend together beautifully.

To bring cumin to the peak of its flavor, roast the seeds in a small skillet over medium heat for 4 or 5 minutes until the seeds turn a dark brown and the air is filled with the smell of cumin. Crush the seeds with a mortar and pestle or in a small coffee/spice grinder. With roasting, the cumin flavor is greatly enhanced not only for this recipe but for all dishes that call for the spice.

INGREDIENTS

2 cups all-purpose flour, approximately
4 teaspoons baking powder
1 teaspoon salt
6 fresh sage leaves, finely chopped, or 2 teaspoons dried
½ teaspoon ground cumin or cumin seeds to roast and grind
6 tablespoons vegetable shortening
¾ cup milk
1 teaspoon water, if necessary
Melted butter to brush tops

BAKING SHEET   One baking sheet, not greased.

PREHEAT   Preheat the oven to 450°.

BY HAND
12 mins.

In a mixing bowl, combine the flour, baking powder, salt, sage, and cumin. With a wire pastry blender or 2 knives, cut and work the shortening into the flour until it is crumbly. Stir in the milk to moisten the dough to make a ball. Add sprinkles of flour if the dough is wet or a spoonful of water if dry.

SHAPING
5 mins.

Pat or roll the dough into a ½″ sheet. Cut with a biscuit cutter, dipping each time into flour so it won't stick. Place on the baking sheet. If to cover pot pies, scribe the large circles around an inverted saucer. Brush with melted butter.

BAKING
450°
12 mins.

Bake on the middle shelf of the hot oven for 12 minutes or until brown.

FINAL STEP   Serve hot with butter. Use the larger pieces to cover pot pies.

DOG BISCUITS

[ABOUT TWO HUNDRED BISCUITS]

Dogs have long been a part of the Clayton ménage, so I have had a lively interest in what they eat — partly because I am fascinated by the manufacturers' promises of an ever-better life for a dog. I also discovered early on that I could make cheaper and better-tasting dried dog food than I could buy at the store. My dogs like it and so do I.

When I began the search for the ultimate dog biscuit I sampled leftovers from my neighbors' dog's dinner. They thought I was slightly daft then and they still do, many years later, even though their dogs rank me tops among gourmet cooks.

But the proof of the biscuit is the volume of thank-you cards and letters I have received, beginning in 1975, especially at Christmastime, from dogs all across the country who have received presents of these biscuits from the dog next door.

The ingredients for all commercial products are much the same — wheat flour, cornmeal, wheat-germ meal, meat meal, poultry by-products, condensed fish solubles, and on and on through a dozen more ingredients. "Glandular meat" is not my idea of haute cuisine.

My creation, I decided, must be palatable to beast and man alike, for who knows how many dog biscuits have been eaten by two-year-olds.

Here is the recipe:

3½ cups all-purpose flour, approximately
2 cups whole-wheat flour
1 cup rye flour
1 cup cornmeal
2 cups cracked wheat (bulgur)
½ cup nonfat dry milk
1 tablespoon salt (or less)
1 package dry yeast
1 pint chicken stock or other liquid, approximately
1 egg and 1 tablespoon milk, to brush

No sugar. No shortening. The cracked wheat would give an interesting speckled texture to the dough.

In a large bowl combine the dry ingredients (except yeast). In the refrigerator I found chicken stock made a week before with chicken necks, wings, backs, and giblets. In the meantime I dissolved the yeast in ¼ cup of warm water, which together with the chicken stock I poured into the dry ingredients. I kneaded this for about 3 minutes into a stiff dough.

I rolled the dough into ¼″ sheets, which I cut with cookie cutters into stars, circles, trees, bears, cats, and rabbits, any one of which should pleasure your dog. I brushed them with the egg-milk mixture.

Since there was no need to let them rise beforehand, I put them directly into a 300° oven for 45 minutes, turned off the heat, and left them overnight. In the morning they were bone-hard, guaranteed to clean a dog's teeth in hours.

This is a wonderfully versatile food. It can be nutritionally tailored any way you and the dog want. If he is on a salt-free diet, omit the sodium. If his diet requires vitamins, include them. I could have used butter, margarine, or cooking oil, as well as the more economical lard, suet, or bacon drippings. If eggs had been cheap, I might have included a half dozen or so for a rich golden batch.

A veterinarian could suggest other ingredients that only a dog's doctor can prescribe, but personally I will stick with the original recipe since neither my dogs nor I can get enough of them.

And the price—roughly 50 cents a pound—is less than half the cost of biscuits bought in one of those expensively designed bags and boxes that seem to promise life everlasting for a pet.

La Brioche

BRIOCHE dough is rich with butter and eggs. It is versatile. It can be baked into the tall, elegant *mousseline* or into the hugely popular *brioche à tête*, the small brioche with a topknot, or into a child's favorite, *petit pain au chocolat*. It can be wrapped around a sausage or enclose a fish.

If I were given to superlatives, I would praise the brioche as a bread almost without peer.

Following are five recipes for using the three different brioche doughs, one of which is made in a food processor. The quantity of dough in each recipe is modest—usually sufficient for four or six pounds of dough. All can be doubled, but be forewarned that twice as much dough may be twice as much as you want to handle. At least for the first time around.

The soft and sticky dough must be chilled before it is given a shape.

Don't attempt brioche unless there is room in the refrigerator for chilling. After it is shaped, it will soon come to room temperature and begin to rise.

BRIOCHE DOUGH

[TWO AND A HALF POUNDS]

This recipe is for the traditional French brioche. It offers an opportunity to make the dough the old-fashioned way — by hand, crashing it down into the bowl or on the work table. It can also be prepared in a mixer or in a food processor (page 86).

Bear in mind that the dough is soft and elastic — not firm — until it has been refrigerated. It will stick to your hands as you work it, but slowly it will begin to pull away from the sides of the bowl and your hands. It will become glossy. With the final addition of flour, the dough can be kneaded.

Because brioche dough must be well chilled in the refrigerator, plan to make the dough in the late afternoon or evening to bake the following morning.

Regular milk may be substituted for the water and nonfat dry milk below.

INGREDIENTS

4 cups all-purpose flour, approximately
3 tablespoons sugar
2 teaspoons salt
1 package dry yeast
¼ cup nonfat dry milk
½ cup water
1 cup (2 sticks) butter, room temperature
5 eggs, room temperature

BAKING
TINS

This dough may be used in a variety of forms. See recipes that follow for appropriate tin, sheet, or pan.

BY HAND
OR MIXER
15 mins.

Into a large mixing or mixer bowl, pour 1 cup flour, the other dry ingredients, and water. Beat in the mixer for 2 minutes at medium speed, or for an equal length of time with a large wooden spoon or spatula. Add the butter and continue beating to blend together.

Add a second cup of flour. Mix thoroughly. Add the eggs, one at a time, and the remaining flour, 1/4 cup at a time, beating after each addition.

The dough will be soft and sticky, and it must be beaten until it is shiny, elastic, and pulls away from your hands. Refrigeration to follow will make it firm.

KNEADING
15 mins.

If by hand, grab the dough in one hand, steadying the bowl with the other, and lift a large handful of it above the bowl — about a foot — and throw it back with considerable force. Continue pulling and slapping at the dough for about 15 minutes. Don't despair. It is sticky. In the beginning, it is a mess. But it will slowly begin to stretch and pull away as you work it.

10 mins.

In a heavy-duty mixer, this can be done in about 10 minutes. Begin with the flat beater blade. When all of the ingredients have been incorporated, change to the dough hook, which will seem to turn aimlessly in the batterlike dough, but soon the dough will begin to come away from the sides. Be patient. Continue mixing for a total of 10 minutes.

BY PROCESSOR

To make brioche dough with a food processor, see page 86.

RISING
1½–2 hours

Cover the bowl with plastic wrap and leave at room temperature until dough has doubled in volume, about 1½ to 2 hours.

Note: If cheese, nuts, or fruit are to be added to the dough, do so at this point before the dough is chilled.

CHILL
4 hours or
overnight

Stir down dough (and add other ingredients, if wanted). Place the covered bowl in the refrigerator. The rich dough must be thoroughly chilled before it can be shaped.

SHAPING

See recipes that follow.

BAKING   Time and temperature will vary according to recipe. See instructions that follow in the recipes below.

PROCESSOR BRIOCHE DOUGH

[ONE POUND]

While dough made in the food processor takes about 6 hours or overnight to fully develop, there is only about 15 minutes of actual working time.

One pound of dough will make about 10 *brioches à tête*.

INGREDIENTS   *1 package dry yeast*
1½ tablespoons warm water
2 cups all-purpose flour, approximately
1½ tablespoons sugar
½ teaspoon salt
2 large eggs, room temperature
¾ stick butter, melted

PREPARATION   Insert metal blade in the bowl of the food processor.
6 mins.   In a small bowl or cup, dissolve yeast in the water. Measure 1 cup of flour into the work bowl and add the sugar and salt. Turn machine on and off several times to aerate. Drop in the eggs and process until mixed, about 5 seconds. Add the yeast.
        Add the remaining cup of flour. Start processor and pour melted butter through feed tube in a steady stream. Stop processing after 20 seconds. Dough will be very sticky, like batter. With a spatula, scrape the dough into a buttered mixing bowl. Cover tightly with plastic wrap and put aside at room temperature until almost tripled, about 3 hours.
        Punch down the sticky dough in the bowl with floured hands.

REFRIGERATION   Cover tightly again with plastic wrap and place in the refrigerator
Overnight   overnight to chill and make firm before using.

Note: On occasion, heavy, sticky batters will "lock" the blade on the shaft. Cuisinart suggests: "When stopped, move the handle of the bowl rapidly back and forth — first clockwise, and then counter-clockwise, then clockwise again."

BRIOCHES À TÊTE

[ABOUT EIGHTEEN BRIOCHES]

The lovely *brioche à tête,* with its golden topknot, is as much at home on the French table as the Eiffel Tower is on the Paris skyline. One has done it with a dramatic presence over the city. The brioche does it with butter and eggs.

While *brioche à tête* is now equally at home *à la table* in this country, I found one of the finest examples of this bread aboard the SS *France.* Not only was it delicious in taste, it was also easy to make, thanks to the talent of the chief *pâtissier* aboard, M. Gousse. He thought it was unnecessary to make the small bread in two pieces — to roll a piece of dough for the body and a smaller one for the head and then attach them — when it could be done more simply.

Because brioche dough must be well chilled, plan to make the dough in the afternoon or evening to bake the following day.

INGREDIENTS	*2½ pounds brioche dough, chilled (page 84)* *1 egg beaten with 1 tablespoon milk or cream, to brush*
BAKING TINS	Small fluted brioche or muffin tins, buttered, and a baking sheet on which to place the small tins for the oven.
SHAPING 25 mins.	Remove dough from the refrigerator and divide into 2 or 3 pieces to make work easier. Return all but one to the refrigerator. Slowly work 1 piece into an 18″ roll, 1½″ in diameter. Use a yardstick and press a mark at 1″ intervals. With knife or scraper, cut the 1″ pieces from the long roll. Each will weigh about 2 ounces. Pressing down forcefully, roll each piece into a ball in the cup

of the palm of your hand. Each will be about the size of a large egg.

There are two ways to shape the brioche.

One is to gently rest the side of the palm on one of the balls, not midway, but at the edge so that about a quarter of the dough is on one side of the palm and three-quarters on the other side. Press down and roll the dough back and forth (perhaps 3 times) until there is a small neck, about ¾", connecting the two pieces. Lift the dough by the small end and lower it into the bottom of the fluted tin.

With the fingers still grasping the small piece, force the smaller piece of dough into the larger one, with fingertips pushing to the bottom of the tin. The top of the small piece should now be about even with the top of the larger piece of dough forced up the sides of the tin. If dough becomes sticky, place the balls in the refrigerator to chill.

A second, traditional way is to pinch off one-quarter of each piece of dough, rolling each into a ball, one large and one small. Deeply indent the large ball with the finger. Moisten the indentation with egg white stirred with water. Place the small ball in the indentation, and press down to seal the two together.

If brioches are to be made over a period of time because of a shortage either of tins or oven space, cover the unused dough and leave in the refrigerator until tins and/or oven space are forthcoming.

RISING
1½ hours

Do not cover brioches as they rise at room temperature. Mix egg and milk and carefully brush each piece. This will keep dough moist during the rise as well as give it its golden color when baked.

When the topknot has risen and the finger marks on the body have disappeared, brush again with the egg-milk wash. The brioches are now ready to be baked.

PREHEAT
375°

Preheat the oven to 375° 20 minutes before baking. Also preheat the baking sheet on which the brioche tins will be placed. The heat underneath will give the dough an extra push in the oven.

BAKING
375°
15–18 mins.

Fill the hot baking sheet with tins and place in the oven.

The brioches will be done when the topknots are well raised, and a rich deep brown in color, about 15 to 18 minutes.

FINAL STEP   Ideally, the *brioches à tête* should be served warm from the oven, but they may be reheated later or frozen. They are delicious whenever served.

Suggestion: The top quarter of the brioche can be cut off, put aside, and the center of the brioche carefully removed. I circle the inside with a sharp knife and, with a fork, carefully pick and scrape out the heart. Fill with a fresh egg, bake, and sauce with béarnaise. Cover with the topknot. (I make these by the dozens for family when we vacation.) Also fill with chicken or tuna salad or something similar of choice.
Delicious!

PETITS PAINS AU CHOCOLAT
(*Chocolate-Filled Brioche Rolls*)

[ONE DOZEN BRIOCHES]

To make the soft and delicate chocolate-filled brioche rolls, *petits pains au chocolat*, French *boulangers* wrap brioche dough around a slender stick of chocolate made expressly for this purpose. If this special chocolate is not at hand, a spoonful of chocolate bits will do as well.

INGREDIENTS   *1½ pounds brioche dough*
2 cups semisweet chocolate bits
1 egg beaten with 1 tablespoon milk, to brush

BAKING
SHEET   One baking sheet, greased, Teflon, or lined with parchment paper.

SHAPING
20 mins.   Turn dough onto floured work surface. Press and roll dough into a narrow rectangle, about 24″ long. Cut the length into 2 pieces. Return 1 piece to the refrigerator while working with the other.
With rolling pin and fingers, shape the piece into a length about 36″ long and 4″ wide. Keep a sprinkle of flour on the work

surface so the dough can be moved freely. If the dough becomes sticky, return it to the refrigerator for a brief respite.

When the dough has been rolled — about ¼″ thick — place 1 or 2 tablespoons of chocolate bits in a line 1 inch below the top edge. Leave a ½″ margin at both ends. Lift the front edge of the dough sheet and place over the row of chocolate. Gently roll the length of dough forward until the chocolate center is surrounded with about 2 thicknesses of the dough.

Cut the roll into 5″ lengths with a knife or dough scraper. Pinch seam and ends tightly together, pushing back chocolate bits if they obtrude. Place on the baking sheet, seam down.

Repeat cutting and shaping *petits pains* from length of dough. When finished with the first length, repeat with the second piece of dough.

RISING
45 mins.

Cover *petits pains* and allow to rest at room temperature until risen to double in size, about 45 minutes.

GLAZE

Twenty minutes before bake period, glaze the pieces with egg-milk wash and leave uncovered until they are placed in the oven.

PREHEAT

Preheat oven to 375°.

BAKING
375°
25 mins.

Uncover *petits pains* and place baking sheet on middle shelf of oven. Look at the *petits pains* after 20 minutes. If those on the outer perimeter are browning too fast while those on the inside are not, gently shift them around.

They are baked when a deep golden brown and firm to the touch.

FINAL STEP

Place on metal rack to cool.

Delicious when a bit warm and the chocolate is soft and runny. Place one in the inside pocket of a ski jacket to have warm at the top of the mountain.

9

BRIOCHES CROISSANTS

[TWO DOZEN CRESCENT-SHAPED BRIOCHES]

This recipe combines in a different way two French favorites — the croissant and the brioche. It is brioche dough rolled into a crescent shape for a fine breakfast roll. This recipe was created by M. Raymond Calvel, an outstanding French *boulanger*, a professor in the French national school for bakers in Paris, and a friend.

INGREDIENTS
2½ pounds brioche dough, chilled (page 84)
1 egg beaten with 1 tablespoon milk, to brush

BAKING SHEET
One or 2 baking sheets, ungreased, or lined with parchment paper.

PREPARATION
Remove the dough from the refrigerator. If the full recipe is more than can be shaped and baked at one time, divide the dough and return a portion to the refrigerator to keep chilled.

SHAPING
25 mins.
Roll dough into a rectangle 24″ long by 10″ wide — and about ⅛″ thick, the thickness of a wooden yardstick. Don't rush the rolling. Allow the dough to relax or it will continue to draw back. When the sheet of dough is at least 10″ wide, and thin, let rest for a few minutes before cutting.

Trim the sides of the rectangle with a pastry wheel or sharp knife, and cut the sheet lengthwise into 2 pieces. With a yardstick or ruler, mark a series of 5″ triangles down the length of each piece and cut.

Roll each triangle from the bottom edge toward the point. Stretch the dough slightly as you begin to roll. Stop when the point is toward you and tipped down. Place on the baking sheet and bend ends to form a crescent. Repeat with the other triangles. Place pieces 1″ apart.

RISING
25 mins.
Brush with egg-milk glaze and leave uncovered at room temperature for about 25–30 minutes. Brioche pieces will be raised and slightly puffy.

PREHEAT   Preheat oven to 425°.

BAKING   Brush with glaze again before pieces go into the oven. Croissants
425°   will be baked when a deep golden brown, about 20 minutes. If in
20 mins.   a large oven, croissants may be baked on lower and middle
              shelves. However, midway in the bake period, exchange baking
              sheets so each will have been exposed to the same temperature
              variations.

FINAL STEP   Remove from oven and place on rack to cool. Delicious warm or
              rewarmed. They freeze well.

Bagels and Bialys

BAGELS and bialys traditionally have been found together in the marketplace. Very old forms of baked goods, both are from the same Eastern European Jewish culture and are mentioned in manuscripts as early as the first half of the thirteenth century. Both are solid, chewy, and delicious. While the bagel holds the edge in popularity, the bialy, a dimpled bun with an onion filling, is closing fast. The bagel is cooked first in boiling water to give it its shiny crust and then baked. The bialy is simply baked.

Growing up in a small town in Indiana, far from bialys and bagels, I did not appreciate the enthusiastic following each had until I wrote my first book and failed to mention either. The response was immediate and sustained: "How can the *Complete Book of Breads* be complete without bagels and bialys?" I have since made amends and do so again with these recipes.

LES BAGELS DE JO GOLDENBERG
(Jo Goldenberg's Bagels)

[TEN LARGE BAGELS]

One of the best bagels to be had anywhere is at the large Jo Goldenberg restaurant-deli at 7, rue des Rosiers in Paris. Famous for its food, especially bagels, the deli is a favorite of the more than half-million French Jews who live in Paris. Located less than a mile away from the Cathedral of Notre-Dame and surrounded by four synagogues, the restaurant is well worth the visit.

The Goldenberg bagel can be made as varied as the imagination will allow—onion, sesame seed, poppy seed, white, rye, salted, plain, whole wheat, caraway seed, and on and on.

Bagel lovers are fiercely partisan—water or egg! This recipe is for a water bagel and made with white flour. It is plain, with suggestions as to how it can be glamorized. The egg bagel, on the other hand, is rich with sugar and egg and, if you wish, can be baked without first cooking in simmering water.

The method here for shaping the bagel is an easy one. The professional bagel baker, on the other hand, would roll the dough into a slender length that would go completely around his open hand—plus enough to overlap. He would then roll the bagel back and forth under the palm to seal the ends. It is difficult for an amateur to maintain the same thickness over the whole length of the dough. The easy way to shape a bagel is simply to push a hole through the ball of dough. Twirl it around your index finger and let centrifugal force enlarge it in much the way a pizza cook spins a piece of dough into a larger disk.

Don't use a cookie or doughnut cutter. Tradition frowns on it. If you do, don't mention it when someone praises your perfectly shaped bagels.

Your first effort may not produce a perfect shape but will be delicious nevertheless.

INGREDIENTS   *3½ to 4 cups bread or all-purpose flour, approximately*
1 package dry yeast
2 tablespoons sugar

1 teaspoon salt
1½ cups hot water (110°–130°)
To Boil:
3 quarts simmering water
1½ tablespoons malt syrup or sugar
Glaze:
1 egg white beaten with 1 teaspoon water
Topping:
Of choice, see above

CONTAINER   Four-and-a-half-quart saucepan for simmering water in which to drop the bagels in first stage of their development.

BAKING
SHEET   One baking sheet, greased or Teflon, sprinkled with cornmeal.

BY HAND
OR MIXER
15 mins.   Measure 2 cups of flour into a mixing or mixer bowl; stir in the yeast, sugar, and salt. Pour in the hot water and stir vigorously with a wooden spoon or with mixer flat beater at low speed for 2 minutes. Add the balance of the flour, a small portion at a time; stir by hand. When the batter gets thick and heavy, attach mixer dough hook. If by hand, lift from the bowl and place on the floured work surface.

KNEADING
10 mins.   If kneading by hand, do so with strong 1-2-3 rhythm of push-turn-fold. Add flour if dough is sticky or elastic. Bagel dough must be stiff and smooth. Knead for 10 minutes.

If under the dough hook, knead for 10 minutes at medium-low speed. Add flour if the dough sticks to the sides of the bowl. Bagel dough should be firm and solid when pinched with the fingers.

BY PROCESSOR
5 mins.   Attach the plastic dough blade.

Measure 2 cups of flour, the yeast, sugar, and salt into the work bowl. Pulse to blend. With the processor on, pour the hot water through the feed tube to form a heavy, sticky dough. With the machine running, add small portions of the remaining flour through the feed tube to make a ball of dough that will ride the blade and clean the sides of the work bowl.

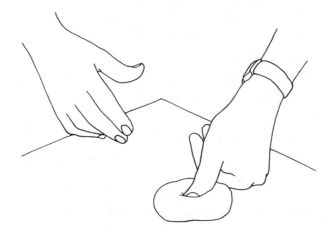

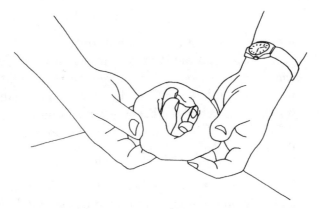

KNEAD
60 secs.

Process to knead for 60 seconds.

Stop the machine, uncover, and pinch the dough. If it is wet, it needs more flour. If not wet, turn from the bowl, dust lightly with flour (to prevent sticking).

FIRST RISING
1 hour

Place the dough in a greased bowl, cover tightly with plastic wrap, and set aside at room temperature until double in volume, about 1 hour.

During this period, prepare the water in a large saucepan. Bring to a boil and add 1½ tablespoons of malt syrup or sugar. Reduce heat and leave at a simmer, with water barely moving.

SHAPING
15 mins.

Turn the dough onto flour-dusted work surface, and punch down with extended fingers. Divide the dough into 10 pieces, 2 to 3 ounces each. Shape each into a ball. Allow to relax for a few minutes before flattening with the palm of the hand.

With the thumb, press through the center of the bagel and tear open with the fingers. Pull the hole open, and spin it around the index finger. It should look like a bagel!

Place bagels together on the work surface.

SECOND
RISING
5 mins.

Cover bagels with waxed paper only until dough is slightly raised, about 5 minutes. A baker calls this "half-proofed." If they go beyond half-proof, the bagels may not sink when first dropped into the simmering water. If by chance the bagels do go beyond this point, no great problem. Proceed as if they sank, even though they are floating. Only a professional bagel maker would appreciate the nuance.

PREHEAT

Preheat the oven to 425° before boiling the bagels.

BOILING
2–3 mins.

The water should be simmering. Gently lift 1 bagel at a time with a large skimmer and lower into the hot water. Do not do more than 2 or 3 at a time. Don't crowd them. The bagel will sink and then rise after a few seconds. Simmer 1 minute, turning over once. Lift out with the skimmer, drain briefly on a towel, then place on prepared baking sheet. Repeat with all of the bagels.

BAKING
425°
25–30 mins.

This is the time to glaze and glamorize the moist bagels with different toppings — salt, onion bits, or sesame, poppy, or caraway seeds. Bake on the middle oven shelf.

When bagel tops are a light brown color, about 25 minutes, turn them over to complete baking. This will keep bagels in a rounded shape without the sharp flatness on one side. Remove from the oven when brown and shiny, about 30 minutes.

FINAL STEP

Place on a metal rack to cool.

Bagels are versatile. In addition to all the other ways to enjoy bagels, slice into 4 thin rounds; bake until dry throughout and begin to brown, about 20 minutes. Remove from oven, butter and salt lightly — return to the oven until the butter soaks into the rounds, about 5 minutes.

BIALYS

[TWO DOZEN BIALYS]

The bialy (pronounced "bi-ale-ee") was brought to this country by immigrants from Bialystok, a city in Poland near the Russian border.

INGREDIENTS

Filling:
2 tablespoons dry onion flakes, soaked
2 teaspoons poppy seeds
1 tablespoon vegetable oil
1 teaspoon salt

Dough:
4½ cups bread or all-purpose flour
5 teaspoons sugar
2 teaspoons salt
1 package dry yeast
1¾ cups hot water (110°–130°)

BAKING
SHEET

Baking sheet sprinkled with cornmeal or lined with parchment paper.

PREPARATION
2 hours

Filling: Soak the onion flakes in water for about 2 hours. Drain and press out the water with a paper towel. If the onion flakes are coarse, mince fine in a food processor or blender. Stir in the poppy seeds, oil, and salt, and set aside.

BY HAND
OR MIXER
10 mins.

Measure 3 cups of flour into the mixing or mixer bowl and add the sugar, salt, and yeast. Stir to blend. Form a well in the flour and pour in the hot water. With a wooden spoon, pull the flour from the sides into the middle and beat until a medium batter. If in a mixer, attach the flat beater and, with the machine running, pour in the water.

Add remaining flour, ¼ cup at a time, until the batter becomes a rough but elastic dough. Attach the dough hook if in the mixer.

KNEADING
10 mins.

Turn the dough from the mixing bowl and knead with strong push-turn-fold strokes; crash the dough down against the work surface occasionally to help develop the gluten. If the dough is sticky, dust with sprinkles of flour. If under the dough hook, the dough will clean the sides of the bowl and form a ball around the hook. If it persists in sticking to the sides, add small portions of flour while the mixer is running. Knead for 10 minutes until the dough is smooth and elastic when stretched.

BY PROCESSOR
5 mins.

Attach the plastic dough blade.

Measure 3½ cups of flour into the work bowl and sprinkle in the sugar, salt, and yeast. Pulse several times to mix well. With the processor running, pour the hot water through the feed tube. Stop the machine, remove the cover, and with a rubber spatula pull all of the dry flour into the center. Pulse. Add 1 cup of flour. Pulse for 3 seconds to blend. With the machine running, add remaining flour, ¼ cup at a time, until the batter becomes a mass that is carried around the bowl by the force of the blade and cleans the sides.

KNEADING
50 secs.

When the dough has formed a ball, knead for 50 seconds. If the dough is slightly sticky when taken from the bowl, dust lightly with flour.

FIRST RISING
1 hour

Place the dough in a greased bowl and set aside to double in volume at room temperature, about 1 hour.

SECOND
RISING
45 mins.

With the fingers or fist, punch down the dough, re-cover, and let double in volume again, about 45 minutes.

SHAPING
12 mins.

Take the dough from the bowl and divide into 4 equal parts. Divide each part into 6 pieces. Roll each piece into a tight ball under a cupped palm. Let the balls rest for 10 minutes under a length of waxed paper or a cloth.

With hard blows of the palm or under a rolling pin, shape each ball into a 4″ circle, about ½″ thick. Place on the prepared pan.

THIRD RISING
30 mins.

Cover the circles with waxed or parchment paper and put aside to rise to slightly *less* than double, about 30 minutes. A baker would say "three-quarter proof."

FILLING
8 mins.

With care not to deflate the outer part of the bialy, push a deep depression in the center with the thumbs. Stretch the dough uniformly outward until the well is at least 1½″ across, and thin on the bottom.

Place about ½ teaspoon of the onion filling in the well.

FOURTH
RISING
25 mins.

Cover the bialys with waxed paper and allow the rolls to rise until almost doubled, about 25 minutes.

PREHEAT

While the dough is rising, preheat the oven to 450°.

BAKING
450°
25 mins.

Place the bialys on the middle shelf of the hot oven and bake until a light brown, about 25 minutes.

FINAL STEP

Place the baked bialys on a metal rack to cool.

A bialy is delicious sliced in half horizontally, buttered, and spread with cream cheese. Or filled as for a sandwich.

KA' ACHEI SUMSUM
(Salted Sesame Bagels)

[ABOUT TWO DOZEN SMALL BAGELS]

A length of butter-rich dough wrapped once around the index finger and baked, the *sumsum* is a small salted sesame bread traditional with Syrian Jews on a Sabbath morning with their coffee.

INGREDIENTS

3 cups bread or all-purpose flour, approximately
1 package dry yeast
1 teaspoon salt
1 cup hot water (110°–130°)
8 ounces (2 sticks) butter or margarine, melted
1 beaten egg, to brush
½ cup toasted sesame seeds, to sprinkle

BAKING SHEET	One baking sheet, greased, Teflon, or lined with parchment paper.
BY HAND OR MIXER 15 mins.	Measure 2 cups of flour into a mixing or mixer bowl and sprinkle in the yeast and salt. Stir to blend well. Pour in the water and the melted butter (warm but not hot). Beat 100 strokes with a wooden spoon or 2 minutes with the mixer flat beater. Add the balance of the flour, ¼ cup at a time, stirring and working in the flour with the hands. If in the mixer, change to the dough hook when dough gets too dense for the flat beater.
KNEADING 8 mins.	Turn the dough onto the floured work surface and knead aggressively with a rhythmic motion of push-turn-fold. If in the mixer, the dough should clean the sides of the bowl and form a ball around the dough hook. It is a rich dough and will soon lose its stickiness. Knead for 8 minutes.
BY PROCESSOR 4 mins.	Attach steel blade. Add 2 cups of flour and the dry ingredients to the work bowl. Pulse to blend. With the machine running, pour the water through the feed tube, and follow with the melted butter. It will be a thick, wet batter. Stop the machine and prepare to add the remaining flour, ¼ cup at a time, through the feed tube, or by removing the cover for each addition. Turn on the processor and add the flour. When the dough forms a rough ball and cleans the sides of the bowl, stop the machine, remove cover, and check consistency of the dough with the fingers. It should be slightly sticky, but if too wet, add 1 or 2 tablespoons of flour and process again. If too dry, add teaspoons of water and process.
KNEAD 60 secs.	Process for 60 seconds to knead. It should be slightly sticky and very elastic when the kneading is complete. Dust the dough with flour before stretching it between your hands to test. If it stretches poorly, that is, breaks apart, return the dough to the processor for a few seconds more.
RISING 2 hours	Cover with plastic wrap and leave at room temperature. (Because of its richness, it takes about 2 hours for the dough to double in bulk in the bowl.)

SHAPING
12 mins.

Divide the dough into 24 equal pieces and roll each into a tight ball. Set aside. Roll the first ball under the palm into a 6″ length. Press the ends into points.

Form the piece into an overlapping circle on the baking sheet. Place the index finger down against the sheet and wrap the length of dough around it, letting the end overlap on the top of the piece underneath. Press the ends gently to join. Repeat for the other pieces, and place 1½″ apart on the baking sheet.

REST
20 mins.

Brush the *sumsums* with beaten egg and sprinkle liberally with sesame seeds. Try poppy seeds on some for an attractive variation. Don't cover during the rest period.

PREHEAT

When putting the breads aside to rest, preheat the oven to 375°.

BAKING
375°
35 mins.

Unlike the conventional bagel that is first cooked in boiling water, these go directly into the oven. They are done when a bright golden yellow and firm when pressed, about 35 minutes.

FINAL STEP

Allow to cool on a metal rack. Delightful served with coffee or tea — or anytime. They keep well in a bread box and also freeze well.

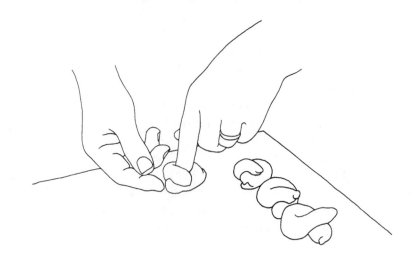

Crackers

I T is essential in making a cracker to roll the dough so thin that when it puffs in the oven, it will look like a cracker and not a fat wafer. The dough can be rolled directly on the baking surface to achieve a thinness not possible if rolled on the work surface and transferred.

Folding the dough — ends into the middle — helps produce tender crackers. Pricking the rolled-out dough with the tines of a fork will keep the crackers from excess blistering during baking.

If the dough should draw back as it is being rolled, walk away from it for a few minutes and then roll again. Eventually, the sheet of dough will be properly thin — thin to the point that it appears fragile. Use a pasta machine if you have one. It will crank out a uniform, wafer-thin strip of dough.

Crackers are more attractive when they are cut into uniform squares or rounds. Measure off parallel lines and cut with a pizza cutter, which

103

will not pull the dough as will a knife. Or use a pastry jagger — a wheel that leaves a border not unlike the cut of pinking shears.

If the crackers are to be salted or covered with seeds, sprinkle from a foot or so above the crackers to get an even distribution. Toss quickly, moving from side to side while you sprinkle.

The baking time will vary slightly for each cracker on the baking tin — faster on the outside and slower in the center. Remove crackers from around the perimeter as they brown and crisp. Brushing the crackers with melted butter or vegetable shortening immediately upon removing them from the oven will keep them crisper longer and create a golden sheen.

Note: While a good cracker can be baked with all-purpose flour, a better cracker can be made with a mixture of three cups of all-purpose flour and one cup of cake flour. The combination of these two flours in a 1 to 3 ratio is very close to the kind of flour used for crackers by commercial bakers.

PLAIN SODA CRACKERS

[ONE HUNDRED CRACKERS]

This is the kind of cracker that turned me into a crackerphile when I was seven years old, hardly tall enough to peek over the top of the wooden cracker barrel in Knox's Grocery. One day, Mr. Knox offered me the pick of a newly opened barrel. It was the beginning of an affair with crackers that has lasted more than three-quarters of a century. I am addicted. Waitresses rush the crackers to safety when I come in the door. My wife hides them I know not where. There are always cracker crumbs in my pockets.

This is a fine basic recipe that can easily be used to make a number of other kinds of crackers with the addition of seeds, herbs, and spices. Cheese, too.

Malt syrup, among the ingredients below, adds a touch of sweetness, flavor, and color, but it does so in such a small way in this recipe that I have made it an option.

INGREDIENTS

1½ cups all-purpose flour, approximately
1 package yeast
½ teaspoon salt, plus extra for sprinkling
¼ teaspoon baking soda
¼ teaspoon cream of tartar
⅔ cup hot water (120°–130°)
½ teaspoon malt syrup, if available
2 tablespoons solid vegetable shortening
2 tablespoons butter, melted, to brush

BAKING
SHEET

One baking sheet to fit the oven, lightly greased or lined with parchment paper.

BY HAND
OR MIXER
6 mins.

Into the mixing or mixer bowl, measure 1 cup flour and the dry ingredients. In a small bowl, combine the hot water, malt syrup, and shortening. Stir to blend and pour the liquid into the dry ingredients; stir vigorously to blend with a wooden spoon or with the mixer flat beater. Add the balance of flour to make a rough mass that can be worked under the hands or with a dough hook. If the dough is sticky, add liberal sprinkles of flour.

KNEADING
4 mins.

If by hand, knead with a rhythmic push-turn-fold motion until the dough is soft and elastic. Add sprinkles of flour to control stickiness. If using a mixer, the dough will form a soft ball around the revolving dough hook and clean the sides of the bowl. Add flour if necessary to firm up the dough. Knead only until smooth, about 4 minutes.

BY PROCESSOR
4 mins.

Attach the steel blade.

Measure 1 cup flour and the dry ingredients into the work bowl. Pulse. Combine the hot water, malt syrup, and shortening, as above. With the processor on, pour the liquid through the feed tube. Add remaining flour, ¼ cup at a time, until the dough becomes a soft elastic mass that will ride on the blade and clean the sides of the bowl, about 4 minutes.

KNEADING
30 secs.

Process to knead the dough for 30 seconds.

REFRIGERATION
1 hour–
overnight

Drop the dough into buttered bowl, cover with plastic wrap, and place in the refrigerator to relax—from 1 hour to overnight. The longer the better, up to 18 hours.

PREHEAT

Preheat the oven to 425° 20 minutes before baking.

SHAPING
10 mins.

With a heavy rolling pin, roll the dough into a rectangle about 18″ x 6″ and no thicker than ⅛″. Fold the dough from the short ends, brushing off the excess flour, to make 3 layers. Roll again— with the rolling pin or through a pasta machine.

Prick the dough with the tines of a fork. Cut the dough along the edge of a ruler or yardstick with a pizza or cookie cutter into desired shapes.

Place the crackers close together on the prepared baking sheet. Sprinkle lightly with salt from 12″ above the crackers to distribute salt evenly.

BAKING
425°
10–20 mins.

Bake on the middle shelf of the oven until lightly browned and crisp, depending on the thickness of the crackers. Inspect the crackers several times during the bake period to make certain those on the outer edge of the baking sheet are not getting too brown. If so, shuffle them—out to in.

FINAL STEP

Brush the crackers with melted butter before removing them from the baking sheet to cool on a metal rack.

VARIATIONS

Sesame-onion crackers: Add to the dough, with the dry ingredients, 4 teaspoons *each* sesame seeds and grated onions.

Herb crackers: 4 teaspoons *each* chopped fresh parsley and chives and ½ teaspoon dried dillweed.

Caraway seed crackers: 4 teaspoons caraway seeds.

Poppy seed crackers: 2 teaspoons poppy seeds.

HAVREMEL FLATBRØD
(Oatmeal Flatbread)

[MAKES 1 POUND]

Decorah, Iowa, considers itself the focus of Norwegian-American life and culture in the United States. A lovely small town on the Iowa River, near the Minnesota state line, Decorah is the home of Norma Wangsness, who lives across the street from the Vesterheim, the outstanding Norwegian immigrant museum. She is considered the town's best cook, and I can vouch for that. I spent hours in her kitchen to learn about Norwegian cuisine, including *havremel flatbrød*, the oatmeal flatbread.

These oven-baked crackers, delightfully crisp and tasty, are served with cheese, spreads, and soups. To add fiber, replace 1 cup of white flour with whole wheat.

Her grandchildren love these and call them "granny crackers."

INGREDIENTS	*2 tablespoons sugar*
	¾ cup melted butter
	½ teaspoon salt
	1 teaspoon baking soda
	1½ cups buttermilk
	3 cups white flour or 2 cups white and 1 cup whole-wheat
	2 cups quick-cooking oats
BAKING SHEET	One baking sheet. Pastry cloth and pastry sleeve for rolling pin.
BY HAND OR MIXER 8 mins.	In a bowl, stir together the sugar, melted butter, and salt. In a separate vessel, add the soda to the buttermilk.
	Alternately add the flour and the buttermilk to the sugar-butter mixture. Stir in the oatmeal.
	If by hand, stir with wooden spoon to blend. If in the mixer, use flat beater blade and mix for 2 minutes. Add sprinkles of flour if needed.
KNEADING 4 mins.	Knead by hand or with the mixer for 4 minutes.

PREHEAT

Preheat the oven to 350°.

SHAPING
20 mins.

To facilitate measuring the amount of dough needed for each piece of *flatbrød*, divide the dough into 2 pieces and roll each into a log. Cut from the log ⅓ cup of dough — and mark remaining length of dough accordingly.

Shape the small piece of dough into a round ball. Flatten it down on the pastry cloth with the palm. Roll paper-thin with rolling pin covered with the pastry sleeve. Roll onto pin and unroll the dough on the baking sheet.

Either cut with pastry cutter into squares before baking or bake and then break into pieces.

BAKING
350°
8 mins.

Place in the oven and bake at 350° for about 8 minutes, or until lightly browned. (The baking time depends on the thickness of the rolled dough.)

FINAL STEP

Slip *flatbrød* off the baking sheet onto a metal rack to cool. (Break the *flatbrød* into pieces now, if necessary.) These may be stored in a covered container for weeks.

CHEDDAR CHEESE CRACKERS

[MAKES ABOUT TWELVE OUNCES OF DOUGH OR FOUR DOZEN ONE-INCH CRACKERS]

Cayenne pepper accents the Cheddar cheese in this cracker — great for a snack or the cocktail tray or the buffet. Or just to eat out of hand.

INGREDIENTS

½ cup (2 ounces) Cheddar cheese
1½ cups all-purpose flour
¼ teaspoon salt
¼ teaspoon cream of tartar
¼ teaspoon baking soda
⅛ teaspoon cayenne pepper
½ teaspoon malt, if available

⅓ cup plus two tablespoons tepid water
2 tablespoons vegetable shortening, room temperature
Salt, to sprinkle
Melted butter, to brush

BAKING
SHEET

One or 2 baking sheets, depending on the size of the oven — greased or lined with parchment paper. If the pan(s) is small, the crackers are baked in 2 batches.

PREPARATION

Shred cheese or cut into chunks if for the food processor.

BY HAND
OR MIXER
8 mins.

Measure 1 cup of flour into a mixing or mixer bowl and add the salt, cream of tartar, baking soda, cayenne pepper, and cheese. Stir to mix well. In a separate bowl, dissolve the malt in the water and add the shortening. Form a well in the center of the flour; pour in the liquid/shortening. If by hand, stir with wooden spoon to blend. The mixture will be quite heavy. If in the mixer, use the flat beater and mix for 2 minutes.

Add remaining flour a few tablespoons at a time to form a dough that can be lifted from the bowl to knead — or left in the mixer bowl under the dough hook.

KNEADING
4 mins.

Knead briefly by hand, adding sprinkles of flour if the dough is wet. In the mixer, the dough will form a soft ball around the revolving dough hook. If dough clings to the sides of the mixer bowl, add light sprinkles of flour. Knead by hand or with the mixer for 4 minutes, until the dough is smooth.

BY PROCESSOR
4 mins.

Attach the steel blade.

Measure all of the flour into the work bowl and add the salt, cream of tartar, baking soda, cayenne, and the cheese chunks. Pulse until cheese pieces are small granules in the flour. In a small bowl, dissolve the malt in the water and add shortening. Turn on the processor and pour the liquid through the feed tube. If the dough does not form a ball, add water by the teaspoon.

KNEADING
25 secs.

When the dough forms a ball and rides with the blade, process to knead for 25 seconds.

REFRIGERATE
1 hour

Place the dough in a small bowl, cover tightly with plastic wrap, and place in the refrigerator to relax for at least 1 hour. The dough can be used immediately or it can be kept tightly wrapped for several days in the refrigerator.

PREHEAT

Preheat the oven to 400° 20 minutes before the bake period.

SHAPING
12 mins.

Divide the dough in half. Keep one half covered. With the hands and a heavy rolling pin, press and roll the dough into a rectangle no longer than the length of the baking pan, usually about 18″, and 7″ wide. The dough should be no thicker than 1/8″. Fold the dough from the ends to make 3 layers. Turn the dough and roll it again into a rectangle.

Lift the dough from the work surface and lay on the prepared bake sheet. Prick the entire surface with the tines of a fork. With rolling pizza cutter or sharp knife, cut the dough into crackers of the desired size. Dough can also be cut with cookie cutters. Sprinkle the crackers lightly with salt.

The crackers will be broken apart after baking.

BAKING
400°
Time: Varies

Bake in the center of the preheated oven until lightly browned and crisp, 8 to 15 minutes, depending on the thickness of the dough. Check the crackers frequently so they are not baked beyond where you want them. I like mine well baked and crisp, which means that often my crackers are almost scorched along the fringes.

FINAL STEP

Remove from the oven and immediately brush with melted butter. Cool on wire rack. Repeat with remaining dough.

The crackers will stay fresh for 3 to 4 weeks if stored in an airtight container.

A RICH CRACKER

[ABOUT THIRTY-SIX CRACKERS]

Milk, butter, and 1 egg go into this dough to make a rich but crispy cracker.

INGREDIENTS
2 cups all-purpose flour, approximately
1 teaspoon salt
½ teaspoon baking powder
¼ cup (4 tablespoons) butter, room temperature
¾ cup milk
1 large egg
Salt, to sprinkle if desired

BAKING SHEET   One baking sheet to fit the oven, lightly buttered or lined with parchment paper. Unless it is a large commercial range and oven, plan to bake the crackers in 2 batches.

PREHEAT
400°

Preheat the oven to 400°.

BY HAND
OR MIXER
8 mins.

Measure 1 cup of flour into a mixing or mixer bowl and add the salt and baking powder. Cut the butter into the flour with a pastry blender or 2 knives. If in the mixer, use the flat beater. Stir the milk and egg together and pour into the flour. Beat the batter with vigorous strokes of a wooden spoon or at medium speed in the mixer.

Add the balance of the flour, ¼ cup at a time, to make a dough that is a soft mass that can be lifted to the work surface or left in the mixer under the dough hook.

KNEADING
4 mins.

Knead for a short period—no more than 4 minutes—with the hands or under the dough hook.

BY PROCESSOR
5 mins.

Attach the steel blade.

Measure 1 cup flour, salt, and baking powder into the work bowl. Pulse. With the processor on, drop in the butter and follow this with the milk and egg. Add the balance of the flour. The dough will form a ball and clean the sides of the bowl. Add sprinkles of flour if the dough is wet.

KNEADING
30 secs.

Process to knead for 30 seconds.

SHAPING
10 mins.

Divide the dough into 2 pieces. Roll each as thin as possible, but you still should be able to move dough to the baking sheet. Place the dough on the sheet, prick the dough with the tines of a fork; cut into squares or rounds. It is better to do the cutting on the baking sheet rather than to cut on the work surface and then try to move the crackers one by one.

Leave the other ball of dough under a piece of plastic wrap while the first batch of crackers bakes.

BAKING
400°
10–20 mins.

If desired, lightly sprinkle the crackers with coarse kosher or sea salt.

Place the baking sheet in the middle of the oven and bake until crackers are a rich brown. The bake time will vary according to the thickness of the crackers, so check every 5 minutes.

When the first batch of crackers is baked, repeat with the remainder.

FINAL STEP

When the crackers are a golden brown and crispy, take from the oven and place on a rack to cool.

Stored in a closed container, the crackers will stay fresh for several weeks. They also freeze very well.

SESAME CRACKERS

[ONE HUNDRED BITE-SIZE CRACKERS]

Both sesame seeds and sesame oil are in these delicious crackers, which are enriched with honey and butter. Baked in long strips, they are broken into bite-size pieces when taken from the oven.

If sesame oil, which has a strong flavor and must be used with caution, is not available, substitute more butter.

INGREDIENTS

2 cups all-purpose flour, approximately
1 cup whole-wheat flour
1 package yeast
2 teaspoons salt
1 cup hot water (100°–120°)
1 tablespoon honey
3 tablespoons melted butter, cooled to lukewarm
1½ teaspoons Oriental sesame oil
Melted butter, to brush
½ cup sesame seeds, to sprinkle

BAKING
SHEET

One baking sheet to fit the oven, lightly greased or lined with parchment paper. Crackers probably will be baked in 2 batches.

BY HAND
OR MIXER
15 mins.

Measure 1 cup each white and whole-wheat flour into mixing or mixer bowl and add the yeast and salt. In a separate bowl, stir together the hot water, honey, melted butter, and sesame oil. Pour the liquid slowly into the flour, beating with strong strokes for 3 minutes with a wooden spoon or at medium speed with mixer flat beater.

Add remaining white flour, ¼ cup at a time, to make a soft dough that can be lifted to the work space, or left in the mixer bowl under the dough hook.

KNEADING
4 mins.

If by hand, knead with an aggressive push-turn-fold rhythm, adding sprinkles of flour if the dough is sticky. Knead only until the dough is smooth.

If in the mixer, knead with the dough hook and add flour, if needed, to form a soft ball around the revolving arm. It will clean the sides of the bowl at the same time. Knead for 4 minutes.

BY PROCESSOR
4 mins.

Attach the steel blade.

Measure ½ cup of white flour into the work bowl and add the yeast and salt. Pulse to blend. Prepare the liquids in a separate bowl, as above. With the processor running, pour the liquid through the feed tube and add the balance of the all-purpose flour. The dough will be a heavy batter. Add whole-wheat flour, ¼ cup at a time, through the feed tube to form a mass that will ride the blade and clean the sides of the bowl. Turn off the machine and allow to stand for 1 minute so the liquid is fully absorbed into the whole-wheat flour.

If the dough is dry and crumbly, add water by the teaspoon, with the machine running. If it is too wet, add either white or whole-wheat flour by the tablespoon. Dough should be slightly sticky.

KNEADING
30 secs.

Process to knead for 30 seconds.

RISING
1 hour

Note: The dough will rise only one time.

Butter a bowl and drop in the dough. Cover the bowl with plastic wrap. Set aside for 1 hour.

PREHEAT

Preheat oven to 375° before starting to roll the dough.

SHAPING
12 mins.

Divide the dough into 2 pieces. Cover one with plastic wrap while pressing the other by hand into a rough rectangle. With a rolling pin or in a pasta machine, roll the dough into a thin rectangle the length of the baking sheet and about 6″ to 8″ wide — as thin as it can be rolled. Be concerned more about its thickness than its length or width.

If the dough pulls back as it is being rolled, step aside for a few moments while it relaxes.

Place the length of dough on the baking sheet, and with a rolling pizza blade or jagger cut into strips about 1½″ wide. Prick (dock) each cracker with the tines of a fork. Brush with melted butter and sprinkle with sesame seeds.

Repeat for the second piece. If the dough is to be held for a second baking, cover with plastic wrap and leave on the work surface.

BAKING
375°
10–20 mins.

Place the baking sheet on the middle shelf of the oven. Bake until a golden brown and dry. Test by pressing with a finger. The bake time will depend on the thickness of the crackers, and may range from 10 minutes to 20. Watch them carefully.

FINAL STEP   With a spatula, lift the sheet of crackers from the pan and place on a rack to cool. Break off the long strips, and then break the strips into one- or two-bite pieces of whatever length desired.

These crackers will keep well for 2 or 3 weeks in a tightly covered container.

KNÄCKERBRÖD
(Swedish Oatmeal Crackers)
[ABOUT ONE HUNDRED CRACKERS]

Rich and oatmeal-flavored with 2 full cups of uncooked rolled oats and butter, *knäckerbröd* is a favorite Swedish cracker. The original Scandinavian recipe called for ½ cup sugar. I thought that too sweet and cut it back to 3 tablespoons.

These are delicious served with cheese and soup and fruit.

INGREDIENTS   *½ cup vegetable shortening*
¼ cup butter, room temperature
3 tablespoons sugar
2 cups uncooked rolled oats, plus oats to sprinkle on pan
3 cups all-purpose flour
2 teaspoons salt
1 teaspoon baking soda
1½ cups buttermilk

BAKING   One large baking sheet (the largest the oven will accommodate),
SHEET   greased and sprinkled lightly with rolled oats. The dough will fill more than 1 sheet, so the balance is held in the refrigerator until the oven shelf is available.

PREPARATION   *Note:* This recipe is so easy to do by hand that I have not included instructions for the mixer or food processor. Although either can be used, it is hardly worth the extra cleanup time.

MIXING
8 mins.

In a large bowl, cream shortening, butter, and sugar until smooth. In a second bowl, combine the oats, flour, salt, and baking soda. Alternately add flour and buttermilk to creamed mixture, blending until stiff—like cookie dough.

REFRIGERATE
1 HOUR

Refrigerate the dough for at least 1 or more hours to stiffen.

PREHEAT

Preheat oven to 375°.

SHAPING
10 mins.
for each sheet

Divide dough into 4, 6, or 8 portions, depending on the size of the baking sheet. Shape each into a ball. Return all but one to the refrigerator to keep chilled.

Place the ball of dough on the prepared baking sheet. Flatten as much as possible with the hands, then use a rolling pin to roll dough to edges of the baking sheet—as thin as possible, no thicker than 1/8". Prick the sheet evenly with tines of a fork.

Using a pastry wheel, knife, or pizza cutter, score dough into 2" squares.

BAKING
375°
10–20 mins.

Bake 10 to 20 minutes or until nicely browned and crisp. As they bake, remove those on the fringes that are browning faster than the others.

FINAL STEP

Allow the crackers to cool 3 minutes on the baking sheet before placing them on a rack. When cooled, break the crackers where they are scored. Repeat with the remaining dough.

Store in container with tight-fitting lid.

LIL'S ICE-WATER CRACKERS

[TWO DOZEN CRACKERS]

Dip a store-bought cracker in ice water, brush with melted butter, and bake. It immediately assumes a different and delicious persona. Puffy, buttery, and done to a deep golden brown, the cracker is especially good with soups and chowders.

This recipe came from Lillian Marshall, an outstanding Kentucky cook and author, who does imaginative things with food. This is one of them.

INGREDIENTS   *24 plain saltine crackers*
               1 quart ice water
               1 stick butter or margarine, melted

BAKING PAN   A shallow pan in which to soak crackers and later in which to bake them.

PREHEAT   Preheat oven to 475°.

PREPARATION   Lay a single layer of saltines in the shallow pan and pour ice water
15 mins.   over them. Let stand about 3 minutes. Carefully remove crackers with a spatula and place on a double layer of paper towels (laid over a linen towel) to drain for 5 to 8 minutes.

               Dry pan and pour half the melted butter over the bottom; spread with fingers. Arrange crackers on pan and drizzle the remaining butter over them.

BAKING   Place in the oven and bake for 15 to 20 minutes. This is a hot
475°   oven, so check frequently. The outside crackers may brown
15–20 mins.   quicker than those on the inside, so shuffle them around. Don't burn them.

FINAL STEP   Serve hot. Enjoy.

ONION POPPY SEED CRACKERS

[FIVE DOZEN SMALL CRACKERS]

A touch of black pepper with onions and poppy seeds gives these crackers a wonderful aroma while baking and a delicious taste when eating. Excellent for cocktails and buffets.

INGREDIENTS

1 medium onion, finely chopped (about 1 cup)
2 cups all-purpose flour, approximately
1 teaspoon baking powder
1 tablespoon sugar
2 teaspoons salt
1/4 teaspoon black pepper, freshly ground
2 tablespoons poppy seeds
1 egg, room temperature
1/3 cup vegetable oil, of choice
2 tablespoons water, if needed

BAKING SHEET

Baking sheet or sheets to fit the oven, lightly greased or lined with parchment paper.

PREPARATION

Chop the onion finely and set aside. It should make about 1 cup.

BY HAND
OR MIXER
6 mins.

Measure the flour, baking powder, sugar, salt, black pepper, and poppy seeds into the mixing or mixer bowl. In a separate bowl, stir together the egg, oil, and the chopped onion. Slowly pour the onion mixture into the flour, stirring vigorously with a wooden spoon to blend well or use the flat beater of the mixer. The dough should be firm. Add more flour if needed.

KNEADING
4 mins.

If by hand, turn the dough onto a floured work surface and knead briefly — only enough to make a smooth dough. Add sprinkles of flour if the dough is sticky.

If in the mixer, attach the dough hook and knead until the dough forms a soft mass around the revolving hook. If the dough does not clean the bowl, add a small amount of flour.

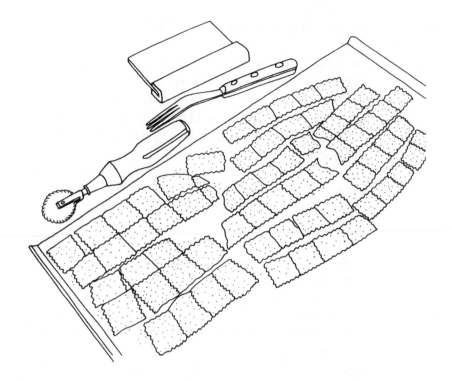

BY PROCESSOR
12 mins.

Attach steel blade.

　　Measure the flour, baking powder, sugar, salt, pepper, and poppy seeds into the processor work bowl. Pulse. Prepare the egg, oil, and onion, as above. With the processor on, pour the liquid mixture through the feed tube. If the dough is dry and crumbly, add 1 or 2 tablespoons of water. If the dough is wet, add 1 or 2 tablespoons of flour.

Note: More flour may be needed since the onions will continue to release juice as the processor runs. Add the final portion of flour by hand rather than in the machine to better judge the texture of the dough.

KNEADING
20 secs.

Process to knead in the machine for 20 seconds and then transfer dough to the work surface to complete the kneading.

REST
30 mins.

Place the dough in a buttered bowl, cover with plastic wrap, and put in the refrigerator to relax for 30 minutes.

PREHEAT

Meanwhile, preheat the oven to 375°.

SHAPING
12 mins.

Divide the dough into 2 pieces. Cover one with plastic wrap while shaping the first batch of crackers.

Press and roll the dough into a rectangle about the length of the baking sheet. Roll the dough as thin as possible without tearing it apart. With the help of the rolling pin, lift and transfer the thin sheet of dough to the baking tin.

With a rolling pizza cutter or jagger, cut the dough into as many crackers as you desire. I do mine freehand because I like the design irregularity, while a ruler or yardstick will give it a professional touch.

Prick (dock) each cracker with the tines of a fork.

Repeat for the second piece of dough.

About sixty 1″ crackers can be cut from the dough.

BAKING
375°
10–20 mins.

Place the baking sheet on the middle or lower shelf of the oven. Bake until a light golden brown, about 10 minutes, but this depends on the thickness of the dough. After 8 minutes, check the crackers to be certain they are baking as you want them. (I like mine crispy and deep brown, which takes longer.)

FINAL STEP

Remove the baking sheet and lift off the crackers with a spatula to cool on a metal rack.

Note: The food processor is ideal for the chore of onion chopping. The more finely the onions are chopped, the more juice they will release, and thus the more flour they will need. If you don't enjoy chopping by hand or in the processor, substitute dehydrated onion flakes and add a little more water.

Le Croissant

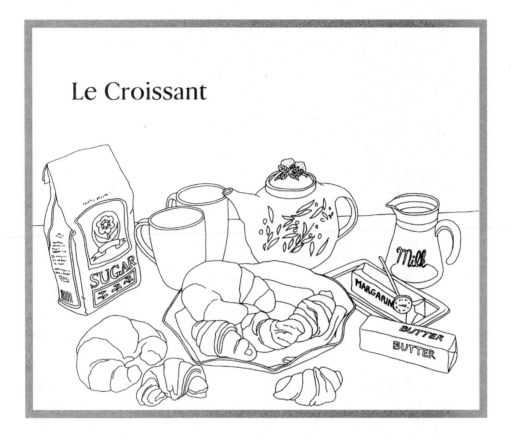

THERE was a time in this country, not so long ago, when the croissant was unknown. Your waiter at breakfast would simply roll his eyes heavenward if you asked for it. The croissant is not mentioned in my well-thumbed encyclopedic book for American bakers written in the 1960s. That has changed dramatically. Today, the croissant is at home everywhere in this country. Cowboys carry croissants on cattle drives and Gloucester fishermen pack them aboard their boats for lunch.

The French croissant is a flaky masterpiece, crescent in shape, that stands proudly alone with nothing in or on it. To the eye, it is beautiful in its golden simplicity. To the palate, it is a myriad of layers crushed into buttery goodness.

To achieve this miracle of baking, the French *boulanger* attends to several aspects of his croissants.

• Butter for layering produces the richest croissant — finer, softer, and with greater keeping ability than one made wholly with margarine. However, a croissant made with margarine is usually more flaky. There is a midpath — half butter and half margarine, which will give excellent results. Margarine alone becomes soft and oily when layered into the dough and must be treated with care.

• Both the dough and the butter (and/or margarine) should be chilled to between 60° and 65°. If it is too cold, the butter will break into rough pieces and tear the dough. If the butter is warm and oily, it will be absorbed into the dough instead of remaining intact in layers.

A small Taylor dial thermometer is handy to check the temperatures of both the butter and dough.

• If, during the rolling process, the butter oozes out from between the layers, chill the dough again. "The cold will correct many mistakes," a *boulanger* in the bakeshop aboard the great passenger ship the SS *France* explained. "Cold is indispensable in making the croissant."

• Place a moist cloth over the dough during rests both in and out of the refrigerator so it will not crust. Wrap it in a damp towel before placing it in the refrigerator overnight after the third and final turn.

• When the rolled dough is bent into the shape of a horseshoe, the tip of the triangle or tongue is placed low on the inside of the croissant, not under. Steam in the oven is not necessary if the croissants are glazed with egg yolks or a mixture of milk and egg. Croissants brushed only with water should also have a broiler pan of water in the oven for additional moisture.

• Croissants should feel springy to the touch and flaky when taken from the oven. The eggs, the dough, and the layers of butter/margarine all contribute to the volume and flakiness of the baked product.

Early on, it was my concern that Americans, in their zest for a new experience, would stuff the croissant with so many odd and unusual fillings that it would be difficult to recall what the true croissant was really like. But, happily, the croissant is so versatile that it has reckoned with these departures to emerge triumphant.

Devoted as I am to the plain croissant, I have departed at times from the path. Grated hard cheese over the dough after it is cut in triangles is a favorite. Try a large dab, perhaps a tablespoonful, of almond paste or frangipane filling or pastry cream spread over the triangle. The possibilities are endless.

THE FRENCH CROISSANT

[TWENTY-FOUR TO THIRTY CROISSANTS]

One of the finest croissants I was ever served was aboard the transatlantic passenger liner the SS *France*. On a round-trip voyage of the ship, I spent several memorable days with her *boulangers* and *pâtissiers* working and observing. Unlike today's one-class cruise ships, the *France* carried first-class and second-class passengers. In the ship's bakery, the croissants for the first-class dining room were made in the traditional crescent shape, while the same croissants destined for the other dining room were not given the quarter-moon shape but left straight. "When we are making hundreds, it just takes less time to shape and we can get more of them on a baking sheet," explained M. Gousse, the *pâtissier*.

This is the SS *France* recipe for its feather-light (1 ounce) croissant.

INGREDIENTS

To Layer:
3 tablespoons flour to blend with butter/margarine
3 sticks butter (³/4 pound) or butter and margarine, equally divided and softened at room temperature

Dough:
4 cups all-purpose flour, approximately
2 teaspoons salt
2 tablespoons sugar
2 packages dry yeast
¹/4 cup warm water
1¹/2 cups milk, warmed to 80°–90°
¹/2 cup half-and-half, warmed
1 egg plus 1 tablespoon water, beaten together, to brush

BAKING SHEET

One or more ungreased baking sheets or trays. Do not use a flat baking sheet or one with open corners unless you form a liner of aluminum foil with ¹/2″ sides to retain butter, should it run.

PREPARATION
2–3 hours

Sprinkle flour over butter and blend together on the work surface. On a length of foil, fashion a 6″ square of soft butter; fold over the sides of the foil to enclose. Place in the refrigerator to chill for 2 to 3 hours.

BY HAND
OR MIXER
5 mins.

While the butter is chilling, prepare the dough.

In a large mixing or mixer bowl, blend 2 cups of the flour with salt and sugar. Dissolve yeast in warm water and add it and the warmed milk and half-and-half to the flour mixture. Stir with a wooden spoon or the flat blade of an electric mixer to thoroughly blend the batterlike dough, about 2 minutes.

KNEADING
5 mins.

Stir in additional flour, ¼ cup at a time, to make a soft but not sticky dough. (It will stiffen when chilled.)

Knead by hand or under a dough hook for 5 minutes to form a solid mass.

BY PROCESSOR
5 mins.

Prepare the butter as above.

Attach the steel blade.

Place 2 cups flour in the work bowl and add the dry ingredients. Pulse to mix. Pour the ¼ cup water, milk, and half-and-half through the feed tube. Pulse once or twice to be certain that all dry ingredients are moistened.

Add the balance of the flour, ½ cup at a time, turning the machine on briefly after each addition.

KNEADING
30 secs.

When the mixture forms a mass and begins to clean the sides of the bowl, knead for 30 seconds. Don't overknead!

REFRIGERATION
1 hour or
more

This begins the process of cooling the dough and at the same time allowing it to rise. Cover the bowl with plastic wrap and place in the refrigerator for at least 1 hour.

SHAPING
10 mins.

Determine that both butter and dough are about the same temperature—65° is ideal. The block of butter should bend but not break (too cold) nor be oily (too warm) when bent slightly. This may mean taking the butter out of the refrigerator an hour or so early to reach workable temperature. Likewise for the dough.

Place the dough on a floured work surface and with the hands press it into a 10″ square. Unwrap the block of butter and lay the block diagonally on the dough. Bring each point of dough into the center, overlapping the edges at least 1″. Press the dough into a neat package. With a heavy rolling pin, roll the dough into a rectangle, approximately 8″ x 18″. This dimension is not critical.

Caution: If the butter seems to be breaking into small pieces under the dough rather than remaining solid, allow the dough/ butter to warm a few minutes. But if the butter softens, becomes sticky, and oozes while making the turns, put the dough back into the refrigerator for several minutes.

First and second turns: Fold the length of dough into thirds, as for a letter. Turn so that the open ends are at twelve and six o'clock. Roll again into a rectangle. This time, fold both ends into the middle and then close, as one would a book. The dough will now be in 4 layers.

Wrap the package of dough in a cloth (an old tea towel is good) that has been soaked in cold water and wrung dry.

REFRIGERATION
1–2 hours

Place the wrapped dough in the refrigerator to relax and chill for 1 or 2 hours.

Third turn: Remove the dough from the refrigerator and place on the floured work surface. Unwrap, roll out, and fold in thirds, as for a letter. This is the final turn before it is rolled out and cut into croissants.

REFRIGERATION
4–6 hours or
overnight

Dampen cloth again and wrap loosely around the dough. Place the package in a plastic bag so moisture will be retained (not pulled out of the cloth). Leave in the refrigerator 4 to 6 hours or overnight.

SHAPING
40 mins.

Have ready the egg wash, a knife or pastry cutter, and a wooden yardstick if you wish the pieces to be cut precisely — otherwise, plan to cut them freehand. You may have or can borrow a French-made croissant cutter that cuts the dough into triangles.

Sprinkle work surface with flour.

Roll the dough until it is a generous 10"-x-38" rectangle, and, most importantly, about 1/4" thick. This is a crucial dimension, since it determines the size and texture of the croissants.

Trim irregularities to make the strip uniform in width. Cut the strip lengthwise to make two 5" pieces. Mark the strip into triangles, 5" wide on the bottom. Using a yardstick as a guide, cut through the dough with a pastry or pizza cutter or knife. Separate the triangles, place them on a baking sheet, and chill for 15 to 20 minutes.

Anytime the butter softens and sticks, place the triangles in the refrigerator until they are chilled again.

Place the first triangle on the work surface, point away. Make a 1″ cut in the base of the triangle to allow it to stretch. Roll the triangle from the bottom to the point, slightly stretching the dough sideways with the fingers as you roll. Place the croissant on the baking sheet. Touch the tip of the point to the pan but do not place underneath the body of the croissant. Bend into a crescent or half-moon shape. Repeat until the sheet is filled. Cover lightly with waxed paper or parchment paper. If there are more croissants to bake than there are pans or oven space, cover the triangles before shaping and reserve in the refrigerator.

RISING
1–2 hours

Croissants will double in volume at room temperature in 1 to 2 hours.

When the croissants are two-thirds raised, remove waxed paper and brush with the egg wash. Leave uncovered for the remainder of the rising time.

PREHEAT

Preheat the oven to 425° 15 minutes before the bake period.

BAKING
425°
22–25 mins.

Place on the bottom shelf. After 10 minutes, move to middle or top shelf for an additional 12 to 15 minutes. (Parisians like their croissants a deep brown, almost burned.) You may wish to take them out earlier if you plan to freeze, reheat, and brown additionally later.

Croissants at the edge of the pan will brown quicker than those inside, so remove them early from the oven and shuffle those remaining. Return to the oven for a few additional minutes.

FINAL STEP

Place the croissants on a rack to cool. Admire — and then take the first delicious flaky bite.

Another way to go: Slice an older croissant horizontally and toast.

Note: While cold butter can be worked into a pliable mass with a metal dough blade or spatula, it is much easier to leave butter at room temperature for 1 or 2 hours to soften and shape into a square before chilling.

BUTTER CROISSANTS

[SIXTEEN CROISSANTS]

Rather than butter spread in layers of dough as for a French croissant, the butter in this delicious croissant is cut into the flour with a pastry blender, as for a baking-powder biscuit. The yeast and other ingredients are then mixed in to make a soft dough that is marbled with pockets of butter that form flaky layers.

I have not made this recipe in the food processor because the whirling steel blade would chop the butter into particles too fine to create a layering effect.

This quick way to make croissants was done by the innovative food staff of *Sunset* magazine, the fine regional publication for the western states, Hawaii and Alaska, and a few like me in the middle of the country.

INGREDIENTS

1 package dry yeast
½ cup warm water (110°)
⅓ cup evaporated milk
1 teaspoon salt
1 tablespoon sugar
1 egg, lightly beaten
2½ cups all-purpose flour, approximately
2 tablespoons butter or margarine (melted and cooled)
8 tablespoons (1 stick) butter, chilled in the refrigerator
1 egg, beaten with 1 tablespoon water, to brush

BAKING
SHEET

Two baking sheets, greased or Teflon. If your oven is limited to 1 baking sheet, refrigerate the second batch of made-up croissants until the oven is ready.

BY HAND
OR MIXER
20 mins.

In a small bowl, dissolve the yeast in water and stir in the milk, salt, sugar, the beaten egg, and ½ cup of flour. Beat by hand to make a smooth batter, then stir in the melted butter. Set aside.

In a large mixing or mixer bowl, using a pastry blender or 2 knives (not the fingers—too warm), cut the chilled butter into 2 cups of the remaining flour until the butter particles are the size of small peas. If in the mixer, use the flat beater blade. Pour the yeast batter over the flour and carefully mix together until the flour is moistened. If it is wet and sticks to the bowl and hands, add sprinkles of flour. *Do not knead.* This is a *mixing* process, not a kneading process, to create a compact ball of soft dough.

FIRST RISING
4 hours–
5 days

Place the ball of dough in a bowl, cover with plastic wrap, and refrigerate for at least 4 hours and up to 4 or 5 days.

SHAPING
15 mins.

Turn dough out onto the floured work surface; press and work it into a ball. Divide into 2 equal parts. Shape 1 part at a time, leaving the remaining dough in the refrigerator.

With a rolling pin, roll the dough into a circle — 16″ to 18″ in diameter. Using a pizza cutter or a sharp knife, cut the circle into 8 equal wedges. It may be necessary to trim snippets of dough at the base of the triangles to make them uniform when rolled into crescents. (After years in the kitchen, I have yet to roll a perfect circle!) Loosely roll wedges from the base to the point.

Shape into a quarter-moon crescent and place on the baking sheet with the tip down but not under.

SECOND
RISING
1½–2 hours

Cover the croissants with waxed or parchment paper and let rise at room temperature to almost doubled in volume, 1½ to 2 hours. (Don't speed their rising by putting them in a warm place.)

PREHEAT

Preheat the oven to 375° 20 minutes before baking.

BAKING
375°
30–35 mins.

Brush the croissants lightly with the egg-water mixture and bake until lightly browned, about 30 to 35 minutes.

FINAL STEP

Serve hot from the oven or cool on racks. To reheat, arrange rolls (thawed if frozen) in a single layer on a baking sheet. Place uncovered in a 350° oven for about 10 minutes.

GIPFELTEIGS
(Swiss Croissants)

[ABOUT TWO DOZEN ROLLS]

A speciality of a small *Bäckerei* in the Swiss village of Wichtrach, two delicate *Gipfelteigs* will fit comfortably on the palm of the hand as compared with one French croissant, to which it is closely related.

If there is one different ingredient in this small bread that contributes so much to its good flavor, it is the *Schweinefett*, country lard, used in making the dough. It imparts a flavor that is difficult to duplicate with any other shortening. It is an option, however, and I have used vegetable shortening in the dough with good results.

While there are 55 layers of dough and margarine when all of the turns have been made, the dough is rolled unusually thin — 1/8″ — before the triangles are cut. While not all of the layers are retained in rolling, enough remain to impart a special texture not found in other croissants. The Swiss baker Herr Rolf Thomas prefers margarine over butter to layer because he feels it allows the special flavor of the lard in the dough to come through. ˛

The preparation of the dough before it is cut into triangles is best done the night before baking, since the layered dough must be thoroughly chilled before the final step.

INGREDIENTS	*3 cups bread flour, approximately* *1 package dry yeast* *2 teaspoons salt* *3 tablespoons sugar* *1 cup hot water (110°–130°)* *3 tablespoons lard or margarine, room temperature* *1/4 pound (1 stick) margarine, room temperature, to layer* *1 egg beaten with 1 tablespoon milk, to brush*
BAKING SHEETS	One or 2 baking sheets, greased or Teflon. (One baking sheet may mean 2 bake periods.)
BY HAND OR MIXER 25 mins.	In a large mixing or mixer bowl, combine together 1½ cups of flour, the yeast, salt, and sugar. Pour the cup of hot water into the bowl. Stir to make a smooth batter. Allow this to stand 5 minutes.

The 3 tablespoons of lard or other shortening, at room temperature, is added to the batter and blended with 25 strong strokes with a large wooden spoon or the flat beater in the mixer bowl. Pour in additional flour, ¼ cup at a time, and stir first with a utensil and then with the hands to make a shaggy mass that cleans the sides of the bowl. If in the mixer, remove the flat beater and replace it with the dough hook.

KNEADING
10 mins.

Lift dough to the floured work surface and knead with a strong push-turn-fold rhythm to develop the dough into a soft, elastic mass. If in the beater, the dough will clean the sides of the bowl and form a ball around the dough hook. Toss down light sprinkles of flour to control stickiness if it develops. Knead for 10 minutes.

BY PROCESSOR
10 mins.

Attach steel blade.

In the work bowl, measure together 1½ cups of flour, the yeast, salt, and sugar. Pulse. With the processor on, pour 1 cup of hot water through the feed tube. Add the lard. Pulse to make a smooth batter. Allow this to stand for 5 minutes.

Turn on the processor and add the remaining flour through the feed tube, a small portion at a time, to make a rough ball that will ride on the blade and clean the sides of the bowl.

KNEADING
50 secs.

Process to knead for 50 seconds.

LAYERING
20 mins.

Knead the margarine with a pastry scraper or spatula to soften and cream. Set aside.

With rolling pin and fingers, roll and stretch the dough into a 8″-x-14″ rectangle. Let it rest 3 or 4 minutes to relax the dough. With the fingers or rubber scraper, spread margarine over dough, leaving an untouched border around the edges.

First turn: Fold and overlap the dough lengthwise in 3 sections —as one would fold a business letter. The rectangle now measures about 10″ x 5″ and is 3 layers deep.

Second turn: Lightly flour the dough and work surface. Turn the dough so the short sides of the rectangle are at six o'clock and twelve o'clock and roll into a new rectangle. Fold again in thirds.

REFRIGERATION
3 hours

Wrap the dough in a double thickness of damp towel so the surface of the dough will not dry out. Slip the dough packet into a plastic bag, lay on baking sheet, and place in the refrigerator, 3 hours or overnight if more convenient.

LAYERING
5 mins.

Third turn: Place dough on the floured work surface. Carefully roll out dough as before and fold in thirds. This is the final turn before rolling dough into a thin sheet.

SHAPING
20 mins.

Sprinkle the work surface with flour so the dough will move easily under the rolling pin. Roll the dough into a long rectangle — about 24″ x 8″ — and ⅛″ thin. Allow the dough to rest before cutting with a pastry wheel or knife or the dough will draw back when cut.

With a yardstick as a guide, trim dough and cut into 2 lengthwise sections 6″ wide. The *Gipfelteig* triangles are 4″ x 6″. Mark each section at 4″ intervals, alternating on the right and left sides of the section, to produce a series of triangles, 6″ x 4″.

Lay the triangles to one side. If there are too many to bake at one time, reserve the surplus in the refrigerator, separated by small pieces of waxed paper.

With a rolling pin, lightly roll triangle back and forth to press it out and make thinner. With a knife, make a small ½″ cut in the center of the base to allow the finished *Gipfelteig* to better hold its crescent shape when rolled. Hold the point under a finger. With the other hand, roll up the dough toward the point. Place on baking sheet. Shape into a crescent. Repeat with the others about 1½″ apart.

RISING
1 hour

Brush each piece with egg-milk glaze and leave uncovered at room temperature for about 1 hour.

PREHEAT

Preheat the oven to 375° 20 minutes before the bake period.

BAKING
375°
25 mins.

Brush pieces again with the glaze. Place the sheet on the middle shelf of the oven. Fifteen minutes later, shift baking sheet front to back and quickly inspect the crescents. They are small and brown rapidly in the final few minutes of baking. If your oven is hotter than it should be, be prepared to take out croissants a few minutes early. Bake for about 10 minutes after inspecting.

FINAL STEP   Remove from the oven and cool on a metal rack. Serve while warm if possible. To freeze, cool first on rack and package airtight. Thaw before returning to 350° oven for 12 minutes.

Flatbreads

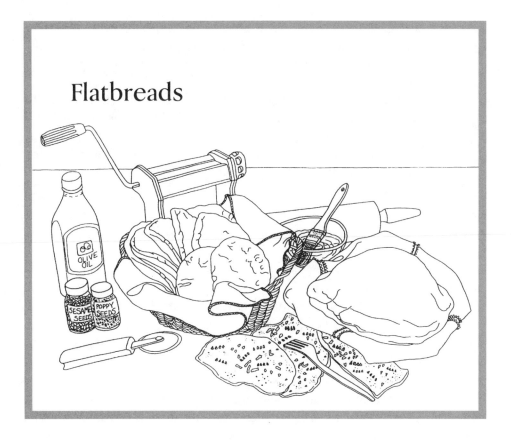

FLATBREADS — some crisp, some soft, some puffed, some not — are a staple in many cultures, ranging from the Near and Middle East to the Scandinavian countries. This selection ranges across the world.

PEDA

[EIGHT PIECES]

Now a favorite bread in this country, pita or *peda* is a flat disk of dough that has been the heart of Middle East cuisine for many years. Known also as a pocket bread, the dough puffs to leave the center hollow. The *peda* can be torn or cut open and filled with meat or other delicacies, or a bit of it can be used as a spoon or as a pusher.

The pieces of dough must be rolled flat before they are placed in a hot (500°) oven. The dough should be rolled to a thickness of a wooden yardstick, or this line of type. The oven heat generates steam inside the *peda* and immediately the dough puffs into a ball. Later, as it cools, the bread will collapse.

The oven must be hot. If it is not, the piece of dough will think it is meant to be a bun and rise slowly but without the all-important pocket in the center.

<table>
<tr>
<td>INGREDIENTS</td>
<td>2½ cups bread flour, approximately
2 teaspoons salt
1 tablespoon sugar
1 package yeast
2 tablespoons cooking oil, olive oil preferred
1 cup hot water (100°)</td>
</tr>
<tr>
<td>BAKING SHEET</td>
<td>One baking sheet. Eight 7″ squares of aluminum foil.</td>
</tr>
<tr>
<td>BY HAND
OR MIXER
5 mins.</td>
<td>Measure 1 cup of flour into a large mixing bowl and stir in the salt, sugar, and yeast. Add oil and hot water. Blend at low speed of electric mixer for 30 seconds, increase to high for 3 minutes, or beat vigorously with a wooden spoon for an equal length of time. Stop mixer. Stir in the balance of the flour, ½ cup at a time. The dough should be a rough, shaggy mass that will clean the sides of the bowl. If the dough is moist, add a small amount of additional flour.</td>
</tr>
<tr>
<td>KNEADING
6 mins.</td>
<td>Turn the dough onto a lightly floured work surface — countertop or breadboard — and knead with a rhythmic 1-2-3 motion of push-turn-fold. Knead for about 6 minutes, or an equal length of time with a dough hook.</td>
</tr>
<tr>
<td>BY PROCESSOR
5 mins.</td>
<td>Insert steel blade.
Place 1 cup flour and other dry ingredients in the work bowl. Pulse once or twice to blend ingredients. Mix oil with hot water and pour through feed tube. Process for 15 seconds. Remove cover</td>
</tr>
</table>

and add remaining flour, $\frac{1}{2}$ cup at a time, until dough forms a ball and rides on the blade. Knead in this fashion for 45 seconds. Dough should be soft and perhaps slightly sticky. Use sprinkles of flour to control stickiness.

Turn from bowl and knead by hand for a moment or two to be certain dough is of the right consistency.

RESTING
20 mins.

Divide the dough into 8 pieces. Roll into balls, cover with towel or waxed paper, and let rest for 20 minutes.

SHAPING
5 mins.

With the palm of the hand, flatten each ball into a disk. Finish with a rolling pin — flattening the dough into a disk about 6″ in diameter and $\frac{1}{8}$″ thick. Their thinness is more important than making them perfectly round. Irregularity adds charm.

Place each round on a prepared piece of foil. Placing the dough on the foil rather than on a baking sheet or stone allows a softer heat to surround the dough. A direct thrust of heat from a baking sheet would form a crust difficult to puff.

PREHEAT

Preheat oven to 500°.

BAKING
500°
8 mins.

Place 2 or 3 of the breads on the baking sheet and place in the oven. Bake for about 8 minutes, or until they are puffed. Repeat with the remaining disks. Place *pedas* under broiler for 2 minutes if browner crusts are desired.

FINAL STEP

Remove the breads from the oven and wrap in a large piece of foil. The tops will fall and there will be a pocket in the center. Serve warm. Or let cool and freeze. Thaw before using. To reheat, stack several in a pile, wrap with foil, and place in a 375° oven for 10 to 15 minutes.

NAAN

[MAKES EIGHTEEN PIECES]

Naan is one of the delicious breads made in India and across the steppes of Central Asia. In India, it is served with a variety of vegetable dishes as well as meat and chicken preparations. While this recipe from northern India is flavored with dehydrated onion, 1 cup fresh onions, chopped fine or grated and cooked until translucent, may be used. It may also be made with mint or garlic in the dough or sprinkled on top after the naans have been brushed with yogurt before putting into the oven.

Naans may be baked in a hot oven or put under the broiler.

Santosh Jain, my friend and teacher in all matters of Indian cooking, gave me this recipe, with lessons to accompany.

INGREDIENTS

2 tablespoons dehydrated onions
2 tablespoons water
3 cups all-purpose flour, approximately
1 package dry yeast
1 teaspoon salt
1 teaspoon sugar
1½ cups milk
3 tablespoons vegetable oil
4 tablespoons plain yogurt (set aside 1 tablespoon to brush)

BAKING
SHEETS

Two baking sheets, greased or Teflon.

BY HAND
OR MIXER
20 mins.

In a small bowl, reconstitute the dehydrated onion in the water. Set aside for a moment.

In a large mixing or mixer bowl, measure 2 cups of flour and dry ingredients. Stir well to blend together. Pour in the milk, add the oil, yogurt, and onions. Beat 100 strokes with a wooden spoon or mix 2 minutes under the flat beater blade. Stop the mixer and attach the dough hook. Gradually work in the remaining flour, sufficient to make a soft mass that cleans the sides of the bowl. The dough will form a soft ball around the hook and clean the bowl.

KNEADING 8 mins.	If by hand, turn the dough onto a floured work surface and knead with a strong push-turn-fold motion for 6 to 8 minutes, until the dough is smooth and elastic. Add sprinkles of flour if the dough is wet and sticky. Knead with the dough hook for 8 minutes.
BY PROCESSOR 4 mins.	Attach steel blade. Measure 2 cups of flour into the work bowl and add dry ingredients. Pulse to blend. Remove the cover and add milk, oil, yogurt, and onions. Turn on the processor and add remaining flour, 1/4 cup at a time, through the feed tube. Sufficient flour will have been added when the batter becomes a mass that cleans the sides and rides with the blade.
KNEADING 1 min.	When the dough forms a ball, process for 1 minute. Stop the machine and feel the dough. If it is dry, add water by the teaspoon, with the machine running. If too wet, add flour.
FIRST RISING 1 hour	Place the dough in a lightly greased bowl, cover, and set aside to rise until double in bulk, about 1 hour.
PREHEAT	Preheat the oven to 450° or ready the broiler by placing the rack 8″ from the flame.
TO SHAPE 8 mins. 20 mins.	Turn the dough onto the floured work surface, roll it into a uniform length, mark, and cut into 16 pieces. Roll each between the palms into tight, solid balls of dough, about the size of golf balls. Cover with waxed or parchment paper and allow them to rest for 20 minutes. By hand and rolling pin, press and flatten each ball into a thin circle no more than 3/16″ thick and about 6″ to 8″ in diameter.
BAKING 8–10 mins.	Arrange the naans on the baking sheet, brush lightly with yogurt, and place on the middle shelf of the oven. Watch carefully. When the naans begin to puff in about 5 minutes, turn them over and bake until they are firm to the touch, about 8 to 10 minutes. Slide them under the broiler for a minute or so to brown the tops lightly.
BROILER 3–5 mins.	This is a fast bake! The naans will be done in less than 5 minutes. (My hot broiler does the job in 3 minutes.) When the tops of the

naans are puffed, turn them over with care. They are quite crispy and have a tendency to slide off the bake sheet.

FINAL STEP   Serve the naans hot or at room temperature.

LAVASH

[TEN TEN-INCH PIECES]

Thin, crisp, and crackly, *lavash* is ideal to serve with soups or broken into small pieces at the buffet table for spreads and dips.

A rolling pin or a pasta machine will press it thin. Then the piece should be spread on the *back of the hands* and stretched ever so gently. Don't be tempted to grab the edges with the fingers and pull because the dough will tear.

The pieces can be sprinkled with sesame or poppy seeds or left plain before they are popped into the oven.

Stored in a sealed carton or bag, the pieces of crackerlike bread will keep indefinitely.

INGREDIENTS   *2 cups bread or all-purpose flour*
               2 cups whole-wheat flour
               1 package yeast
               1 tablespoon salt
               1½ cups hot water (100°–120°)
               ¼ cup milk, to brush
               ¼ cup toasted sesame and/or poppy seeds

BAKING   One or more lightly greased baking sheets. Usually, only 2 breads
SHEETS   fit on 1 sheet, but they bake so quickly 1 sheet can be used
               repeatedly.

BY HAND   In a bowl, place 1 cup each of the 2 flours and add yeast and salt.
OR MIXER   Stir well to blend. Pour in hot water and beat with a wooden
15 mins.   spoon to thoroughly mix for 3 minutes — or 2 minutes with flat

beater if using electric mixer. Add remaining cup of whole-wheat flour and stir vigorously to blend. Add the remaining white flour, 1/4 cup at a time. Don't overload the dough with flour. It should be soft and elastic.

KNEADING
6–8 mins.

Turn the dough onto the work space and knead with a brisk 1-2-3 rhythm — push, turn, fold. If the dough is sticky, add sprinkles of flour. Knead by hand for 6 to 8 minutes. If using dough hook, knead for 8 minutes at medium speed. If the dough does not clean the bowl but sticks to the sides, add sprinkles of flour.

BY PROCESSOR
6 mins.

Insert metal blade.
    Place all of the 2 flours in the work bowl. Add the yeast and salt. Pulse for a few seconds to blend. Pour the hot water through the tube as the machine is running. Stop processor, remove top, and check consistency of dough. If too dry, add a small amount of additional water. If wet, add flour. When in balance, the dough will form a ball and spin around the work bowl on top of the blade.

KNEADING
45 secs.

With the machine running, knead for 45 seconds.

FIRST RISING
1 hour

Lightly grease a bowl . Drop in the dough and turn to coat all sides. Cover with plastic wrap and put in warm place until the dough has doubled in bulk, about 1 hour.

SECOND
RISING
30 mins.

Turn back plastic wrap and punch down the dough with fingers. It will collapse. Cover again and let it rise for an additional 30 minutes.

PREHEAT

Preheat oven to 400°.

SHAPING
12 mins.

Divide the dough into 10 pieces. Roll each into a ball, cover with waxed paper, and let rest for 5 minutes. On a lightly floured work surface, press down the first ball of dough under the palm. Next, roll the dough as thin as possible. Under pressure, it may stick to the work surface, but leave it there for a moment until the dough relaxes. With spatula or dough knife, work the piece loose from the table. Keep the dough dusted with flour as it is rolled.

When the dough has been rolled as thin as possible, lift it in your hands and drape it carefully over the back of your hands. (Take off your rings before doing this.) Slowly stretch the dough, turning it as you stretch.

When it is paper-thin and stretched to its thinnest point without tearing, lay it carefully on the work surface. Cover with waxed paper and proceed to the next piece.

When the second one has been prepared, brush both with milk and sprinkle with choice of seeds — sesame or poppy. These two will be in the oven while the others are prepared.

BAKING
400°
10 mins.

Place the dough pieces on the prepared baking sheet and place in the hot oven. The bake period will be short, so be attentive! Bake for 10 minutes, or until the breads have pulled away from the baking sheet and are beginning to brown. The pieces will not brown uniformly.

FINAL STEP

Put the baked *lavash* on racks to cool. The pieces will do so quickly because they are thin. Store those not immediately eaten in a dry place. Watch for crumbs, as they are very crispy.

Note: To toast seeds, place them on a baking sheet and into a 300° oven for 20 minutes.

Deep-Fried Breads

OR a long time, deep-fried breads—doughnuts, Mexican *sopaipillas*, hush puppies, and fritters—were in a reserved category. "Yes, I must try them someday," I kept telling myself, but for several reasons, I did not. My mother's doughnuts were so nearly perfect I didn't think I could ever achieve such perfection. The oil bothered me. Too hot, the oil smoked and the dough burned. Too cool, the dough absorbed the fat and the result wasn't worth the bother. Hot oil also burns.

Finally, I took the plunge.

First, I bought a quality deep-fat–frying thermometer, a Taylor, with a wooden handle that was always cool to the touch and a metal clip to attach it to the wall of the kettle or skillet or pot or whatever. It took a bit of adjusting to get the silver column in the thermometer to hover right around the 370° to 380° mark, but I never fried more than one batch of two or three doughnuts or fritters at a time so as not to send the temperature plummeting. To stabilize the temperature, the oil was three to four inches deep.

The doughnuts emerged crisp, puffed, and tender — and without a trace of greasiness inside or out. There was a freshness and flavor to these homemade doughnuts and other deep-fried breads that followed that couldn't be achieved by a machine-made product. I was delighted.

Later on, I bought a Crockpot, with an automatic thermostat, whose metal shell, without the heavy ceramic inner bowl, could be adjusted to a precise temperature for deep-fat frying.

Another important consideration for all deep frying is the kind and care of the oil. It can be selected from among numerous unsaturated vegetable oils, including canola (my favorite), corn, soybean, and sunflower. Olive and peanut oil are other choices.

ABOUT DOUGHNUTS IN PARTICULAR

There are essentially two kinds of doughnuts — yeast-raised and cake. Cake-doughnut dough, leavened with baking soda and/or baking powder, is not left to rise but goes directly into the hot fat after a short rest.

They come in many shapes and sizes, ranging from the classic ring (with the "hole" fried separately) to doughnuts filled with a dozen kinds of jellies and jams, rectangles of dough twisted into crullers, and doughnuts dipped in icings and doughnuts dusted liberally with confectioners' sugar or granulated sugar alone or sugar mixed with cinnamon and doughnuts covered with nuts or bright sparkling "sprinkles."

SUGGESTIONS

- Equip your kitchen with a quality doughnut cutter. No $1.50 piece of light tin that leaves strings of uncut dough to tear the doughnut apart when separated. I often use one large and one small of my French *coupe pâte* pastry cutters with razor-sharp beveled edges. A deep-fat–frying thermometer is recommended.
- Keep dough firm enough to handle but not stiff, as for bread. It should be soft and velvety, and may need sprinkles of flour over and under the dough to keep it from sticking to the work surface and the hands. Some recipes call for the dough to be placed in the refrigerator for a short time beforehand to firm it up.

• For turning the doughnuts while they are frying, buy a quarter-inch wood dowel at the hardware store or lumberyard, cut twelve inches long, and whittle a not-too-fine point on one end. Push down one side of the doughnut and it will obediently turn over. A long chopstick will work equally well, but over time, the oil will discolor it.

• When a doughnut is taken from the kettle, place it on brown paper or paper towels to drain. Replace it immediately with an uncooked one to keep the oil at an even temperature. It is an assembly line — one doughnut coming out with a fresh one going in.

• Cruller-type doughnuts can be made with rectangular dough pieces twisted three or four times and fried.

• Twists, on the other hand, are pencil-thin lengths of two ounces of dough twisted as they are rolled between the palms. Push with one hand, pull with the other — and you have a twist. Fold the length in half, pinch the ends together, and allow it to twist by *untwisting*. In the hot oil, they puff and expand into delicious doughnuts.

• To glaze a doughnut, dip it while warm into a thin icing made of confectioners' sugar mixed with milk. Place on a grate for the excess to run off. Hold the ring with the thumb and index finger and carefully lower the doughnut halfway into the icing.

MY MOTHER'S YEAST-RAISED DOUGHNUTS

[ONE DOZEN DOUGHNUTS]

This could be called a beginner's doughnut, for it is an easy one to make.

INGREDIENTS
2½ cups bread or unbleached flour, approximately
1 package dry yeast
3 tablespoons sugar
½ teaspoon salt
½ teaspoon ground nutmeg or mace
½ cup warm water (100°)

(continued on next page)

3 tablespoons vegetable oil
1 large egg, lightly beaten
Vegetable oil for frying
Granulated sugar, or mixed with cinnamon for sprinkling

EQUIPMENT

One deep-frying pan, skillet, or kettle, deep-fat–frying thermometer, doughnut cutter (see Introduction to this section).

BY HAND
OR MIXER
20 mins.

In a large bowl or mixer bowl, stir together 1 cup flour, yeast, sugar, salt, and nutmeg or mace. Shape a well in the dry ingredients. Pour in water, 3 tablespoons vegetable oil, and beaten egg. Stir with wooden spoon or mixer flat beater blade to make a smooth batter. Add flour to make a soft dough — light and velvety, not as solid as for bread.

FIRST RISING
1 hour

Cover the dough with plastic wrap or a pastry cloth and set aside to rise to double in volume, about 1 hour.

SHAPING
25 mins.

Punch down the dough and turn onto the floured work surface. If the dough is sticky, sprinkle with flour. Knead a dozen times. Let stand for 15 minutes to relax the dough. With a floured rolling pin, press and roll the dough into a ½″-thick sheet. Allow the dough to relax a few minutes so that it won't pull back when cut.

Cut the dough with a floured cutter and place rings and the "holes" on a floured pastry cloth or work surface. Press and roll the scraps together and cut more doughnuts. At the same time, a few twists (see Introduction to this section) can be fashioned by pinching off 2-ounce scraps of dough and twisting the dough.

SECOND
RISING
45 mins.

Cover the doughnuts with a cloth or waxed paper or plastic wrap and allow to double in size, about 45 minutes.

PREHEAT
370°–380°

In a deep pan, skillet, or kettle, bring 3″ to 4″ of vegetable oil to 370°–380° over moderate heat. Test with the thermometer.

FRYING
2–3 mins.

With a spatula or carefully with the fingers, slide or drop a test doughnut into the hot oil and fry about 90 seconds on each side, turning once with the doughnut stick or spatula. Break one doughnut open when it has cooled—test and taste for done-ness.

Continue with the balance of the doughnuts, cooking no more than 3 at a time in the oil. Place doughnuts on brown paper or paper towel to drain.

FINAL STEP   When the doughnuts are warm—not hot—roll each doughnut in granulated sugar in a small bowl. Flavor the sugar with ground cinnamon, if you wish. Or sprinkle with confectioners' sugar from a dredge or through a sieve.

Serve warm.

BRIGHAM YOUNG'S BUTTERMILK DOUGHNUTS

[ONE DOZEN DOUGHNUTS]

Brigham Young ate only two meals a day, but they were substantial. At breakfast, he often ate cornmeal mush, hot doughnuts with syrup, cod-fish gravy, and a roasted squab from his pigeon cote. As a cereal, he ate a bowl of popcorn covered with rich milk.

This recipe for the doughnuts is his.

If you are a home baker in the South, you may wish to use the self-rising flour that is so beloved by many southern cooks. If so, delete baking powder, baking soda, and salt from the list of ingredients below.

INGREDIENTS   *1 cup buttermilk*
½ cup granulated sugar
2 teaspoons baking powder
½ teaspoon baking soda
1 teaspoon salt
¼ teaspoon grated nutmeg
2 eggs
2 tablespoons butter, melted
2½ cups all-purpose flour, approximately
Vegetable oil for frying (Young's cooks used lard)
Confectioners' or granulated sugar, to dust

EQUIPMENT

One deep, heavy frying pan or kettle, deep-fat–frying thermometer, doughnut cutter.

BY HAND
OR MIXER
30 mins.

Mix the buttermilk, sugar, baking powder, baking soda, salt, nutmeg, eggs, and butter in a large bowl. Add the flour gradually, using just enough so that the dough is sufficiently firm to handle, yet as soft as possible. Allow it to rest 15 minutes.

SHAPING
10 mins.

Turn out onto a lightly floured board and knead for a few minutes. Roll out about ³⁄₄″ thick. Cut with a floured doughnut cutter or sharp knife into 3″ rounds, cutting out and saving the centers to fry separately.

REST
5 mins.

Place the doughnuts on the lightly floured work surface or pastry cloth and let rest for about 5 minutes.

FRYING
370°–380°
2–3 mins.

Heat oil to between 370° and 380°. Fry doughnuts 2 to 3 minutes, turning one time. Fry the holes separately, as they take less time.

FINAL STEP

Drain on brown paper or paper towels. When the doughnuts have cooled somewhat, dust with confectioners' sugar or granulated sugar.

BEIGNETS
(French Doughnuts)

[THREE DOZEN DOUGHNUTS]

When it is time for coffee in New Orleans's Vieux Carré, it is also time for a *beignet*, the French Quarter's famous doughnut. Part of the fun of it is that it is a small square or rectangle *without* the doughnut hole. It is not to be confused with the *beignet soufflé* made with *pâte à chou* in my *Complete Book of Pastry*. Both are deep-fried and delicious.

To be true to its French roots, I have added a jot of brandy to the list of ingredients.

INGREDIENTS	*3 to 3½ cups all-purpose flour, approximately*
	1 package dry yeast
	1 teaspoon salt
	¼ cup granulated sugar
	½ teaspoon ground nutmeg or mace
	1 cup milk
	¼ cup vegetable shortening
	1 tablespoon brandy
	1 egg
	Vegetable oil for frying
	Powdered sugar for dusting

EQUIPMENT

Heavy skillet or kettle, slotted spoon. Stick for turning (see Introduction to this section).

BY HAND
OR MIXER
20 mins.

In a mixing or mixer bowl, combine 1½ cups of flour, the yeast, salt, sugar, and nutmeg or mace. Heat the milk until warm. Stir milk, shortening, and brandy into the flour with a wooden spoon or mixer beater blade. Beat until it is a smooth batter. Add the egg. Beat for 2 minutes and gradually stir in as much of the remaining flour as you can to make a soft, velvety dough — not stiff as you would for a bread dough. Use sprinkles of flour to keep dough from sticking to hands or the work surface when you turn the dough out of the bowl.

CHILL
1 hour

Cover the dough and chill thoroughly in the refrigerator, about 1 hour.

PREHEAT

Preheat the oil to 370°–380° while the dough is being cut.

SHAPING
10 mins.

Turn the dough onto the floured work surface and roll into an 18″-x-12″ rectangle, about ¼″ thick. With a knife or pizza cutter, cut the dough into a series of 2″ squares or 3″-x-2″ rectangles.

REST
10 mins.

Allow the pieces to rest for 10 minutes before starting to fry.

FRYING
2 mins. each

Drop each piece into the hot oil with the fingers or from a spatula. Fry for about 2 minutes, turning once, until golden. Fry no more than 6 in a batch.

FINAL STEP

Drain on brown paper or paper toweling. When somewhat cool, dust with confectioners' sugar.

Serve warm and be prepared for a rush for seconds and thirds and even fourths!

PERGEDEL DJAGUNG
(Indonesian Spiced Corn Fritters)

[ABOUT TWO DOZEN FRITTERS]

Corn came late to Indonesia, a rice-loving nation, but now is used extensively in its cooking. It is the principal ingredient of this deep-fried fritter — *pergedel djagung* — and is combined with a range of spices and finely chopped vegetables. The light batter is spooned onto the hot oil to become flat golden crisp rounds.

Once I mistakenly doubled the amount of flour in the mixture to make a thick batter that became a fritter about the size of a golf ball — crispy brown on the outside and moist and tender inside.

This adventure in Indonesian cooking came to my kitchen in a recipe adapted from *Pacific and Southeast Asian Cooking*, one of the volumes in the Foods of the World series from Time-Life.

INGREDIENTS

2 cups corn kernels, fresh or frozen
1/2 cup water
2/3 cup all-purpose flour
2 eggs, lightly beaten
1/2 cup chopped scallions, including some of the green tops
1/2 cup finely chopped celery

2 teaspoons salt
¹/₄ teaspoon white pepper
Vegetable oil in which to fry

EQUIPMENT   Heavy skillet or kettle, deep-fat–frying thermometer, slotted spoon.

PREHEAT   While preparing the ingredients, preheat the oil to 370°–380°.
370°–380°

PREPARATION   In the jar of an electric blender or food processor work bowl,
5 mins.   blend the corn and water until it is fairly smooth, but don't make
               it a puree. Leave evidence of the kernels.
                   Scrape this into a large bowl and add all the ingredients except,
               of course, the oil for frying. Mix until well blended. This will be
               a medium batter that is easy to spoon.

FRYING   Spoon about 2 tablespoons of the corn mixture over the hot fat,
370°–380°   allowing enough space so the batter spreads into a flat round
2 mins. each   without touching its neighbor. Fry 2 or 3 at a time for about 2
               minutes, until each side is brown and crisp.

FINAL STEP   Place the fritters on brown paper or paper toweling to drain.

BEIGNETS DE POMMES
(Apple Doughnuts)

[APPROXIMATELY FORTY-EIGHT SLICES]

Apple slices dipped in a batter touched lightly with brandy and deep-fried were a favorite of famed Impressionist painter Claude Monet, at the family dinner table in Giverny, near Paris. (For another Monet favorite, see page 204.)

Sprinkled with sugar and served warm, the *beignets* are golden brown on the outside and pink and soft on the inside. I compare the taste and texture to a slice of delicious apple pie — with a hole in the center.

INGREDIENTS *1 cup all-purpose flour*
2 egg yolks
1 tablespoon brandy
½ teaspoon salt
½ cup of milk, approximately
6 tart apples
Vegetable oil for deep-frying
1 cup granulated or confectioners' sugar, to dust

EQUIPMENT Heavy skillet or pan for frying, deep-fat–frying thermometer.

PREPARATION In a bowl, measure in the flour, and make a well in the center.
25 mins. Pour in the egg yolks, brandy, and salt. With a spatula, gradually
mix in the flour, then add milk to make a smooth but fairly thick
batter. Put the batter aside to rest for at least 20 minutes.
Peel the apples, core, and slice ¼″ thick.

FRYING Stir the batter. Working in batches of no more than 4 or 5, dip the
20 mins. apple rings in the batter and fry, turning occasionally, until golden
brown. Using a slotted spoon or a wire skimmer, lift the *beignets*
to a baking sheet lined with brown paper or paper towels. Keep
the cooked *beignets* warm in a low oven while the rest are frying.

FINAL STEP Sprinkle with granulated sugar or sift confectioners' sugar over the
beignets and serve hot.

SOPAIPILLAS

[EIGHTEEN TO TWENTY-FOUR PUFFS]

A favorite bread at the Restaurante Rancho de Chimayó in the pictur-
esque 400-year-old village of Chimayó, New Mexico, is its *sopaipillas*,
gold puffs served with its highly seasoned food. Hot from the kettle, a
corner of the *sopaipilla* is broken off and filled with honey.

We dined one night in the *restaurante* by the soft light of a kerosene lantern. The ambiance was pleasing. The *sopaipillas* served with the meal were outstanding.

INGREDIENTS

Oil to deep-fry
1¾ cups all-purpose flour
2 teaspoons baking powder
1 teaspoon salt
2 tablespoons vegetable shortening or lard
⅔ cup cold water, approximately

EQUIPMENT

One deep kettle or skillet with 2″ to 4″ vegetable oil or fat. A slotted spoon.

PREHEAT

Preheat oil or fat to 370°–380° while preparing the dough.

BY HAND
OR MIXER
8 mins.

Sift flour, baking powder, and salt into a mixing bowl. Cut shortening into the flour with a pastry blender, crossed knives, or the fingers. The flat beater of the electric mixer is also excellent for this chore. The mixture will resemble coarse meal.

Add water by the tablespoon but only enough to make a stiff dough.

KNEADING
4 mins.

Turn onto a lightly floured work surface and knead until smooth and somewhat elastic. It will be responsive under the hands, but not so much as a fully developed bread dough.

BY PROCESSOR
5 mins.

Attach the steel blade.

Measure the dry ingredients into the work bowl and drop pieces of the shortening over the mixture. Cover and pulse 3 or 4 times to cut the shortening into tiny pieces in the flour. With the processor running, pour in enough water through the feed tube to form a ball of dough that will ride on the blade and clean the sides of the bowl.

KNEADING
40 secs.

When the ball has formed, process to knead for 40 seconds.

RESTING 10 mins.	Place the dough on the work surface, cover with a cloth or a length of waxed or parchment paper, and allow to rest for 10 minutes.
SHAPING 5 mins.	Roll the dough into a rectangle about 12″ by 15″ and very thin — no more than ⅛″ thick. With a pastry wheel or knife, cut into 2″ or 3″ squares.
FRYING 1–2 mins.	Drop 2 or 3 squares of the dough into the hot fat. Turn several times with a slotted spoon so that each *sopaipilla* puffs and browns evenly. Remove and drain on paper towels.
FINAL STEP	Serve immediately with honey.

OLIEBOLLEN
(Dutch Fruit Fritters)

[THIRTY-SIX FRITTERS]

Oliebollen, a delicious fruit-filled fritter, is from the cookbook *Eet Smakelijk (Eat Well and with Taste),* a compilation of recipes put together by the Junior Welfare League of Holland, Michigan. Holland, on the shores of Lake Michigan, is as Dutch as it is possible to be and still be in the United States.

INGREDIENTS	*3½ cups all-purpose flour, approximately* *2 packages dry yeast* *1 teaspoon salt* *½ cup nonfat dry milk* *¼ cup sugar* *1½ cups hot water (110°–130°)* *3 eggs, room temperature* *1 quart or more vegetable oil, to cook fritters* *¼ cup each raisins (light or dark), currants, and chopped candied orange peel*

2 tablespoons grated lemon peel
¼ cup confectioners' sugar, to sprinkle

EQUIPMENT

Deep skillet or small kettle, slotted spoon, turn-over stick (see Introduction to this section).

BY HAND
OR MIXER
15 mins.

Measure 2 cups of flour into a large bowl and add the yeast, salt, nonfat dry milk, and sugar. Stir in the hot water.

In a small bowl, beat the 3 eggs and pour into the flour mixture. The batter will not absorb the eggs immediately, but keep beating with vigorous strokes — or in the electric mixer — until it does. Add more of the remaining flour, a small portion at a time, to make a heavy batter that can be spooned later into the hot fat.

RISING
1 hour

Cover the mixing bowl with plastic wrap and put aside to let rise to double its volume, about 1 hour.

PREHEAT
370°–380°

Heat the skillet and bring the oil to 370°. Stir down the batter with a heavy wooden spoon and work in the raisins, currants, orange peel, and lemon peel.

FRYING
5 mins. each

Drop rounded teaspoons of batter into the hot fat. Cook until puffed and both sides are golden brown — about 5 minutes. (Use a teaspoon for the batter — a tablespoon is too large.) Repeat for all.

FINAL STEP

Place the hot fritters on absorbent paper to drain.

While warm, arrange them on a serving dish and sprinkle liberally with confectioners' sugar. Delicious with coffee or tea.

DOUBLE CORN HUSH PUPPIES

[THREE DOZEN SMALL, TWO DOZEN LARGE FRITTERS]

It is a challenge to introduce hush puppies* without reciting the thrice-told tale of how these corn fritters got their name. But I will try.

While most hush puppies are made chiefly of cornmeal and white flour, this recipe goes a step beyond with the addition of fresh corn kernels, an egg, and shredded Cheddar cheese. Serve small ones with cocktails. Large ones for a fish fry or a barbecue. Try adding 1 tablespoon fresh thyme leaves to go with game, chops, or roast chicken.

Nora Lee Rorie of Monroe, North Carolina, gave this recipe to Sarah Belk, author of *Around the Southern Table*, who gave it to me. Since Sarah does not like to deep-fry, she cooks these fritters in a shallow ⅛″ of oil, a method she finds safer and less costly than deep-frying.

INGREDIENTS
Vegetable shortening or oil for frying
½ cup cornmeal, preferably stone-ground
⅓ cup all-purpose flour
½ teaspoon baking powder
½ teaspoon baking soda
⅛ teaspoon salt
¼ cup finely minced white onion
½ cup fresh whole corn kernels (or thawed frozen corn), parboiled and drained
⅓ cup finely shredded Cheddar cheese
Pinch ground cayenne pepper
1 egg
⅔ cup buttermilk

EQUIPMENT
Heavy skillet, slotted spoon, turn-over stick (see Introduction to this section). The oil is too shallow to use the thermometer, so you must judge when it is hot but not smoking. Test with a small spoonful of batter.

* Of course you knew. Hush puppies were tossed to hunting dogs gathered around the campfire to stop their yapping. One less-than-enthusiastic critic, after a meal of not-very-good fritters, remarked, "Maybe that is still the best use for them."

PREHEAT   Pour ⅛″ to ¼″ oil into the skillet over medium heat while prepar-
                        ing the batter.

PREPARATION   In a bowl, combine cornmeal, flour, baking powder, baking soda,
12 mins.   and salt. Stir in onion, corn, cheese, and cayenne. Make a well in
                        the center. In a small bowl, beat the egg into the buttermilk
                        and pour into the flour mixture. Stir until just combined; don't
                        overmix.

FRYING   Drop the batter into the hot oil by the teaspoon or tablespoon.
3 mins.   Cook for about 3 minutes, turning 2 or 3 times, or until golden
                        brown. Lift out the fritters and place them on paper towels to
                        drain.

FINAL STEP   Serve hot.

Muffins

A MUFFIN is a quick bread baked for a single serving. It is cakelike in texture, with a tender yet coarse crumb. (The English muffin is the exception.) The secret to making a muffin is not to worry about lumps and clumps in the batter. They come with the territory. They are natural and necessary. The less the batter is beaten, the better. A muffin that has been beaten until it is smooth will be tough and flat, with unwanted tunnels running through it.

Here are a baker's dozen muffin recipes ranging from blueberry, lemon zucchini, carrot, corn, and dill to buckwheat as well as *cidre* and *épices*.

156

BLUEBERRY LEMON MUFFINS

[EIGHTEEN LARGE OR THIRTY-SIX SMALL MUFFINS]

One of the treasures of Mackinac Island in Michigan is the blueberry lemon muffin that has been served for years at the turn-of-the-century Iroquois Hotel on the beach.

In the Iroquois kitchen, the pace is unhurried. The only deadline for the kitchen is to have a score or more baskets of warm muffins ready for guests coming down to breakfast on the terrace at water's edge.

The plump blueberries fairly burst through the sides, while inside they are deep purple pools flavored by the lemon zest. When the muffins are done and allowed to cool for a few moments, each is dipped headfirst in melted butter and then in granulated sugar.

INGREDIENTS

1½ cups all-purpose flour
2 teaspoons baking powder
1 teaspoon salt
¼ cup sugar
1 egg
¾ cup milk
⅓ cup vegetable oil
1 cup blueberries, fresh or frozen
½ tablespoon lemon zest

Glaze:
2 tablespoons butter
¼ cup sugar, to glaze

MUFFIN TINS

2 medium (2½″) muffin tins for 18, or 3 small (1½″) muffin tins for 36, greased or Teflon.

PREHEAT

Preheat oven to 400°.

BY HAND
15 mins.

Sift the flour into a mixing bowl and add baking powder, salt, and sugar. In a small bowl, crack the egg and beat with a wire whisk or fork for 10 seconds. Add milk and oil to the egg and stir to blend. Make a well in the flour and pour in the egg-milk mixture. Stir as little as possible to moisten the flour.

Set the batter aside for a moment while mixing the blueberries with the lemon zest.

Fold the berry mix into the muffin mix, again stir gently and as little as possible.

Spoon batter into the tins to three-fourths full.

BAKING
400°
20 mins.

Put muffins in hot oven and set timer for 20 minutes. It may take them an additional 5 minutes to become golden brown. Check at 15 minutes and if they are browning too quickly, place on bottom shelf or cover with a length of aluminum foil or brown paper.

FINAL STEP

When the muffins are baked, cool for 5 minutes. Run a knife around the edges of each. Tilt the tray and gently lift each muffin from its tin.

Dip the top of each lightly in the melted butter and then in the sugar.

The muffins can be held overnight and heated for eating the following day. They can also be frozen, but fresh-baked are best.

Present the muffins in a manner prescribed on a sign in the Iroquois bakeshop: "Arrange the muffins in an orderly manner and serve."

MUFFINS AU CIDRE
(Cider Muffins)

[ONE DOZEN LARGE OR TWENTY-FOUR SMALL MUFFINS]

Autumn, when branches in the orchards hang heavy with apples and cider is in the making, is the time to think of French *muffins au cidre*, muffins made with sweet cider. Cider, of course, is available throughout the year at roadside stands and stores owned by orchardists.

INGREDIENTS

2 cups all-purpose flour
1½ teaspoons baking powder
1 teaspoon baking soda

1 teaspoon salt
1 teaspoon cinnamon
³/₄ cup currants or raisins
1 egg
³/₄ cup sweet cider
5 tablespoons butter, melted (reserve 1 tablespoon to brush)
¹/₄ cup maple syrup
2 tablespoons white or brown sugar mixed with 1 teaspoon cinna-
  mon, to sprinkle

PREHEAT   Preheat oven to 400°.

MUFFIN CUPS   Two dozen 1½″ for small muffins, one dozen 2½″ for medium, greased or Teflon.

BY HAND   Mix together the flour, baking powder, baking soda, salt, and
15 MINS.   cinnamon in a mixing bowl. Stir in the currants or raisins with a fork. In another bowl, beat the egg until lemon-colored and slightly thickened. Add the cider, 4 tablespoons of the melted butter, and maple syrup and beat well. Combine the two mixtures gently with a wooden spoon. Stir to moisten all the ingredients — don't attempt a smooth batter.

BAKING   Spoon the batter into the prepared tins, filling three-fourths full.
400°   Bake small muffins about 12 minutes; the large muffins 18 min-
12–18 mins.   utes. Bake on the middle shelf of the oven.

FINAL STEP   Brush the hot muffins with melted butter and sprinkle with cinna-mon/sugar.
               Serve hot.

BUCKWHEAT AND HAZELNUT MUFFINS

[ONE DOZEN LARGE MUFFINS]

Buckwheat has a long and praiseworthy history in my family that began with my Grandmother Condon's pancakes and, now, these moist, delicately flavored muffins. I spread her pancakes thick with butter and lavished maple syrup over them. Here the butter and the maple syrup are among the ingredients — along with hazelnuts, buttermilk, butter, and eggs. A rich and tasty muffin indeed!

While buckwheat is seldom used in bread baking, it is highly nutritious, with twice the amount of B vitamins as whole-wheat flour, and is low in calories. It is not a true grain, since it is an herb, not a grass. The Dutch brought it from Europe in the 1600s and grew it along the Hudson River. The name is derived from two words — *boc* (beech) and *whoet* (wheat).

Hazelnuts, chopped and toasted, add an unexpected crunchiness to the mixture while not overpowering the curious flavor of buckwheat. Lacking hazelnuts, other nuts may be substituted, of course.

INGREDIENTS	*⅓ cup chopped hazelnuts, or other nuts of choice*
	1½ cups all-purpose flour
	⅔ cup buckwheat flour
	¼ cup rolled oats
	2 teaspoons baking powder
	½ teaspoon baking soda
	1 teaspoon salt
	1 cup buttermilk
	4 tablespoons butter, melted
	¼ cup pure maple syrup
	2 eggs, lightly beaten
MUFFIN CUPS	One dozen standard 2½″ muffin cups, greased or Teflon.
PREHEAT	Preheat oven to 400°.
BY HAND 15 mins.	In advance, chop and toast hazelnuts and set aside. In a large bowl, combine all-purpose flour, buckwheat flour,

rolled oats, nuts, baking powder, baking soda, and salt. In a second bowl, beat together for 10 seconds the buttermilk, melted butter, maple syrup, and eggs. Pour into the flour mixture and stir together with wooden spoon or spatula just until ingredients are blended and moistened. The batter will be lumpy — leave it that way.

Spoon the batter into the tins almost to the top edge.

BAKING
400°
20–25 mins.

Slide the muffin tins into the oven and set the timer for 20 minutes. The tops should feel dry and springy, and a cake tester or toothpick should come out clean. Don't overbake.

FINAL STEP

When the muffins are baked, remove from oven and allow them to cool for 5 minutes. Tilt the tin and lift each muffin from its cup.

Serve warm with butter and preserves for breakfast or tea.

Note: While buckwheat is not often used in making bread, I have several recipes for buckwheat loaves in my *New Complete Book of Breads,* including *Bauernbrot,* a delicious Austrian peasant loaf made with a starter.

MUFFINS AUX ÉPICES
(Spice Muffins)

[EIGHTEEN MUFFINS]

These muffins from France are made with a cluster of spices — nutmeg, cinnamon, ginger, and cloves — plus maple syrup, butter, eggs, and raisins. The recipe calls for white pepper, which is not in every kitchen. A light grinding of black pepper is a substitute.

The French recipe calls for a cup of whey, the vitamin-packed clear liquid that separates from the thicker part of milk in making butter and cheese, which can usually be found in dehydrated form in health-food stores. Mix 3 tablespoons of the powdered whey to 1 cup of water for this recipe. Otherwise, use milk.

INGREDIENTS

2½ cups all-purpose flour
¾ cup rye flour, stone-ground preferred
1 tablespoon baking powder
1 teaspoon baking soda
1 teaspoon salt
1 teaspoon finely ground pepper, white preferred
1 teaspoon grated nutmeg
1 teaspoon cinnamon
½ teaspoon ground ginger
½ teaspoon ground cloves
1 cup raisins or currants
3 eggs, room temperature
½ cup maple syrup
1 cup nonfat milk or whey (see above)
8 tablespoons melted butter

MUFFIN CUPS

Eighteen muffin cups, greased or Teflon.

PREHEAT

Preheat oven to 400° before preparing the batter.

BY HAND
20 mins.

In a large bowl, mix together white and rye flours, baking powder, baking soda, salt, pepper, and spices. Mix in the raisins.

In another bowl, beat the eggs until they are lemon-colored and slightly thickened. Add the maple syrup, milk (or whey), and butter; beat well. Fold in the flour mixture with a spatula or spoon. Do not overmix. The batter will be thick and clumpy.

Spoon the batter into the prepared muffin cups, filling two-thirds full.

BAKING
400°
18–20 mins.

Bake for 18 to 20 minutes or until a toothpick inserted in a muffin comes out clean.

FINAL STEP

Serve hot and bless the French baker who first put together these spices and other good things.

HONEY BRAN MUFFINS

[TWELVE TO EIGHTEEN MUFFINS]

Deep brown and moist, these muffins taste rich because they *are* rich —buttermilk, honey, butter, eggs, brown sugar, bran, nutmeg, either chopped dates or raisins, and, the final touch, chopped walnuts.

I discovered these at The Ark, a restaurant in the village of Oysterville on the shore of Willapa Bay in Washington. It is a remote spot on the Pacific Coast, a few miles from where the Lewis and Clark expedition ended. Piles of oyster shells surround the restaurant, while on the water, oyster boats and crab boats come and go.

Acting together, buttermilk and baking soda lift the muffins. Two teaspoons of orange zest may be substituted for nutmeg.

INGREDIENTS
³/₄ cup buttermilk
¹/₄ cup honey
³/₄ stick butter, melted
2 eggs, room temperature
1 cup packed brown sugar
2 cups sifted cake flour
1 tablespoon baking soda
1 teaspoon salt
¹/₄ teaspoon freshly grated nutmeg or 2 teaspoons grated orange zest
3 cups bran flakes
¹/₄ cup chopped dates or raisins
¹/₄ cup chopped walnuts

MUFFIN TINS   Several muffin tins, greased or lined.

PREHEAT   Preheat the oven to 400° before preparing the batter.

BY HAND
15 mins.   In a large bowl, combine buttermilk, honey, butter, eggs, and brown sugar. Stir well to blend.

In a second bowl, sift the cake flour, baking soda, salt, and nutmeg. Stir in the bran flakes.

Pour the liquid mixture into the flour, and blend well with a wooden spoon or spatula. Quickly stir in the dates or raisins and walnuts. Overstirring can make the muffins tough. The batter will be thick but easily spooned into the tins.

Spoon the batter into the muffin tins to three-quarters full. If only 1 or 2 muffin pans are available, it may be necessary to bake a second time. Place the batter in the refrigerator to reserve.

BAKING
400°
20–25 mins.

Bake in the hot oven for 20 to 25 minutes. Muffins will be a golden brown.

FINAL STEP

Serve, enjoy, and imagine you are lunching at The Ark at the edge of the quiet waters of Willapa Bay.

CARROT MUFFINS WITH BROWN SUGAR

[EIGHT LARGE OR SIXTEEN SMALL MUFFINS]

Bright shreds of carrot and nuggets of dark brown sugar are in this moist muffin that came to my kitchen from White Lily, one of the premier flour companies in the South. This recipe is made with the mill's self-rising flour, but an equal amount of all-purpose flour plus 2 teaspoons baking powder and ½ teaspoon salt can be substituted with excellent results.

If you want the brown sugar completely absorbed into the mixture rather than left in bits to form pools of sugar, dissolve it in the cooking oil before adding to the flour.

INGREDIENTS

1 cup finely shredded carrot
1 cup self-rising flour (or see above)
¼ cup packed dark brown sugar
2 eggs, lightly beaten
¼ cup vegetable oil
1 tablespoon lemon juice

MUFFIN TINS	1 medium (2½″) muffin tin for 8 or 2 small (1½″) tins for 16 muffins, greased or Teflon.
PREHEAT	Preheat oven to 400°.
BY HAND 15 mins.	Shred the carrots and set aside. In a medium bowl, stir together flour and brown sugar. Break up sugar with a pastry blender or rub between the fingers. Make a well in the center of the flour. In a small bowl, lightly beat the eggs and add carrots, oil, and lemon juice. Add all at once to the dry ingredients, stirring just till moistened.
BAKING 400° 15–20 mins.	Fill prepared cups three-quarters full, to near the top. Bake in the hot oven for 15 to 20 minutes, depending on the size of the cups. Insert a toothpick in the center of a muffin. If it comes out clean, it is done.
FINAL STEP	When the muffins are baked, cool for 5 minutes. Run a knife around the edges of each. Tilt the tray and gently lift each muffin from its cup. Muffins can be frozen, but fresh-baked is best.

RED RIVER MUFFINS

[ONE DOZEN MUFFINS]

The fertile Red River Valley in the Canadian province of Manitoba gives its name to an uncommonly good cereal that, in turn, makes uncommonly good muffins. The cereal is a blend of cracked wheat, cracked rye, and whole flax. Its nutty taste and pleasant bite have been known for years to visitors to Canada, but only recently has it been sold south of the Canadian border.

Red River Cereal (see note below)also is the heart of a splendid loaf of pumpernickel bread (see my *New Complete Book of Breads*) that I have been baking for more than two decades.

On occasion, I have added shredded coconut to the muffin mix for a somewhat richer taste.

INGREDIENTS
1¼ cups milk
¼ cup vegetable shortening
¾ cup uncooked Red River Cereal
1½ cups all-purpose flour
4 teaspoons baking powder
l teaspoon salt
½ teaspoon cinnamon
¼ teaspoon nutmeg
½ cup brown sugar
¾ cup raisins
½ cup shredded coconut, if desired
2 eggs

MUFFIN TINS
One dozen medium (2½") muffin tins, greased or Teflon.

PREHEAT
Preheat oven to 400°.

BY HAND
25 mins.
In a medium saucepan, combine milk, shortening, and Red River Cereal. Bring to a boil and cook for 1 minute, stirring constantly. Remove from heat and set aside to cool somewhat. In a small bowl, stir together flour, baking powder, salt, cinnamon, and nutmeg. Stir in brown sugar and raisins, and coconut, if desired.

Lightly beat the eggs together and stir into the cooled cereal. Add the dry ingredients and stir together. If the mixture is too stiff to spoon easily, add 1 or 2 tablespoons of milk. Spoon batter into the tins — fill to a generous three-quarters.

BAKING
400° tops
20 mins.
Set muffin tins on the middle shelf of the hot oven. When the muffins are nicely browned and they are loose in their tins, they are done, about 20 minutes.

FINAL STEP
Remove from the oven. Serve while hot at breakfast or reheat for a later meal. They can be frozen, but fresh is best.

Note: If Red River Cereal cannot be found in your speciality food store or supermarket, query Mille Lacs Wild Rice Corporation, P.O. Box 200, Aitkin, MN 56431, or call (800) 626-3809.

CORNMEAL MUFFINS

[ONE DOZEN MUFFINS]

These are 100 percent corn muffins made wholly with cornmeal, and no shortening except for a small amount used to coat the muffin tins. There is no wheat flour. The taste is all corn.

My neighbor, Fredonna Curry, a fine cook in the tradition of country cooking, said this recipe has been in her southern Indiana family for at least three generations, and perhaps longer. She films the cups with fresh bacon drippings to give the muffins a real down-home flavor. Just before the batter is spooned into the muffin tins, which have been greased and then preheated in the oven, she sprinkles a pinch of cornmeal into each cup. She wants the tins "poppin'" hot to make the pinch of cornmeal sizzle when it hits. This gives her muffins extra crustiness.

INGREDIENTS
*Bacon drippings or other shortening to liberally coat muffin
    cups
1 egg
1 cup buttermilk
1 teaspoon salt
1/2 teaspoon baking soda
Pinch baking powder
1/2 teaspoon sugar
1 1/2 cups white or yellow cornmeal, approximately*

MUFFIN CUPS
One dozen (2½″) muffin cups. Heavy black cast-iron pans are traditional. Others do equally well.

PREHEAT

Preheat oven to 400° and at the same time grease the muffin tins and place in the oven to heat until the shortening just begins to smoke. Watch carefully.

BY HAND
10 mins.

In a small bowl, beat the egg and stir in the buttermilk. Add the salt, baking soda, baking powder, and sugar. Stir in the cornmeal, a portion at a time, until the thick batter is thoroughly blended and smooth. It should be too thick to pour.

BAKING
400°
20–25 mins.

Quickly take the muffin tins from the oven and sprinkle a pinch of cornmeal into each cup. There will be a sizzle when the meal touches the hot fat.

With a spoon, ladle the batter into each cup, three-quarters full. Return to the oven. Bake until the muffins are golden brown, about 20 to 25 minutes.

FINAL STEP

Remove from the oven and serve hot.

If for an informal affair like a fish fry or barbecue, serve right from the muffin tins. Waste no time getting the hot muffins to the table.

SUGARED ORANGE-CURRANT MUFFINS

[TWELVE MUFFINS]

Hot from the oven and dipped in melted butter and then in cinnamon and sugar to give them crusted crowns, these muffins have the good taste of orange peel, nutmeg, coriander, nuts, and currants. Raisins rather than currants are an option.

This recipe is from *Sunset* magazine, the West Coast publication for the family and home, especially the kitchen. Marje Clayton, a muffin devotee for an untold number of years, considers this one of the best.

INGREDIENTS   *3 tablespoons butter or margarine, room temperature*
¹⁄₃ cup sugar
1 teaspoon grated orange peel
1 egg
1¹⁄₂ cups all-purpose flour
1 tablespoon baking powder
¹⁄₂ teaspoon each salt, ground nutmeg, and ground coriander
²⁄₃ cup milk
¹⁄₃ cup each chopped nuts and currants or raisins
¹⁄₂ cup melted butter or margarine
1 teaspoon cinnamon, to mix with sugar
¹⁄₂ cup sugar

MUFFIN TINS   Medium (2¹⁄₂″) tins, greased or Teflon.

PREHEAT   Preheat oven to 375°.

BY HAND
20 mins.   In a small bowl, beat the 3 tablespoons butter and ¹⁄₃ cup sugar until well blended. Beat in the orange peel and egg. In another bowl or on a length of waxed paper, stir together the flour, baking powder, salt, nutmeg, and coriander. Stir dry ingredients with all of the milk into the butter-sugar mixture. Mix well. Stir in the nuts and currants.

     Spoon the thick batter into the prepared muffin cups, filling each about two-thirds full.

BAKING
375°
20–25 mins.   Bake until the muffins are golden and the tops spring back when lightly pressed or a toothpick inserted will come out clean, about 20 minutes.

FINAL STEP   Remove from the pan and dip the top third of each hot muffin in the melted butter, then in the cinnamon/sugar. Serve warm.

LEMON ZUCCHINI MUFFINS

[EIGHTEEN LARGE MUFFINS OR THIRTY-SIX SMALL MUFFINS]

There is lemon zest, lemon juice, and lemon yogurt to give a bright flavor to this muffin made with the versatile zucchini, one of the most fruitful vegetables in the garden.

If basil grows in your garden, you might wish to add 8 or 10 finely cut leaves to further enhance the muffin's flavor.

INGREDIENTS

2½ cups all-purpose flour
1½ teaspoons baking soda
½ teaspoon salt
Dash of nutmeg
4 tablespoons melted butter or margarine
1 cup (8 ounces) lemon yogurt, room temperature
1 egg, room temperature
½ cup sugar
Juice and zest of 1 lemon
1 cup finely grated zucchini
½ cup chopped walnuts

MUFFIN TINS

Medium (2½″) tins for 18, or miniature/small (1½″) tins for 36, greased or Teflon.

PREHEAT

Preheat oven to 425°.

BY HAND
20 mins.

Sift the dry ingredients together onto waxed paper. In a bowl, beat together the butter, yogurt, egg, sugar, lemon juice and zest. Stir in the dry mixture and blend well. Add zucchini and nuts and stir to distribute throughout the batter.

Fill prepared muffin tins three-quarters full.

BAKING
425°
20–22 mins.

Place tins in the middle shelf of the hot oven, and bake for 20 to 22 minutes. Reduce time to 12 to 15 minutes for miniature muffin tins.

FINAL STEP

When the muffins are baked, cool for a few moments. If the muffins do not fall from the tins when overturned, run a knife around the edges of each. Tilt the tray and gently lift each muffin from its cup.

Muffins can be frozen, but fresh-baked is best.

CORN AND DILL MUFFINS

[TWELVE LARGE OR TWENTY-FOUR SMALL MUFFINS]

Speckles of fresh green dill among yellow corn kernels mixed in a golden cornmeal batter is a sure sign that this is an unusual muffin. As well it should be, for it also has butter, egg, cream, and sugar. As for the color of the cornmeal, some like it white and some prefer yellow.

INGREDIENTS

1 cup all-purpose flour
1 cup yellow or white cornmeal
3 tablespoons sugar
1 tablespoon baking powder
1 teaspoon salt
1 egg
1 cup cream, heavy or half-and-half
3/4 cup fresh or frozen whole corn kernels
1/4 cup (4 tablespoons) melted butter
2 tablespoons chopped fresh dill

MUFFIN TINS

Medium (2½") tins for 12 muffins or small (1½") for 24 muffins, greased or Teflon.

PREHEAT

Preheat oven to 400°.

BY HAND
20 mins.

Stir the flour and the cornmeal in a medium bowl and add the sugar, baking powder, and salt. Set aside. Into a small bowl, crack the egg and beat with a whisk. Add cream, corn kernels, melted butter, and dill. Add to the dry ingredients, and stir until well blended.

Spoon batter into the prepared tins, filling each cup three-quarters full.

BAKING
400°
15–18 mins.

Put muffins in the hot oven and set timer for 15 minutes. Test doneness with a toothpick. If it comes out clean, the muffins are done. If not, bake a few minutes longer.

FINAL STEP

Remove tins from oven and allow to cool for 5 minutes before turning out muffins.

Enjoy!

TALOA
(Corn Muffins)

[EIGHT MUFFINS]

I found this recipe for *taloa*, a delicious corn muffin, in a Basque kitchen in the southernmost corner of France where it joins with Spain in the magnificent Pyrénées Mountains. Corn was introduced here more than 400 years ago by Basque crewmen returning with Columbus from the New World. It has been part of the Basque cuisine ever since.

Slice open the *taloa* for a small sandwich, or toast the halves for a different kind of breakfast bread. The Basques sometimes scrape out most of the inside after it is baked, mix it with softened cream cheese, return it to the muffin, and it becomes a *marrakukua*, a delicious, filled surprise for the buffet table or a picnic.

The sprinkle of poppy seeds is not authentic; I thought the texture of the muffins needed a contrasting touch.

This recipe is not as "quick" as most muffins.

INGREDIENTS

1½ cups all-purpose flour, approximately
1 package dry yeast
2 teaspoons salt
2 tablespoons butter or shortening of choice, room temperature

1 cup milk
1½ cups cornmeal (yellow for golden color)
1 egg white, to glaze
2 tablespoons poppy or sesame seeds, to sprinkle

BAKING SHEET	One baking sheet. If not Teflon-coated, dust with cornmeal.
BY HAND OR MIXER 12 mins.	In a bowl, stir together 1 cup white flour, the yeast, salt, butter, and milk. Let stand for a minute or so to allow the yeast to dissolve. Pour in the cornmeal and blend with 25 strong strokes of a wooden spoon or rubber scraper, or 2 minutes with a flat beater. Add the remaining flour, ¼ cup at a time, first with the spoon and then with the hands or under the dough hook to make an elastic ball of dough that cleans the sides of the bowl.
KNEADING 8 mins.	Leave in the mixer bowl if under the dough hook, or, if by hand, turn out on a floured work surface and knead with a push-turn-fold motion until the dough is smooth, soft, and does not stick, about 8 minutes. Avoid making the dough dense with too many sprinkles of flour.
BY PROCESSOR 4 mins.	Use steel blade. Measure 1 cup of white flour into the work bowl and add yeast, salt, butter, and milk. Pulse to make a light batter. Remove cover and add the cornmeal. Replace cover and pulse to blend. With the machine running, add remaining flour through the feed tube to make a dough that will spin with the blade.
KNEADING 45 secs.	Let the machine run 45 seconds to knead.
FIRST RISING 1 hour	Place dough in a greased bowl, cover with plastic wrap, and leave at room temperature until double in volume, about 1 hour.
SHAPING 8 mins.	Turn out the dough and knead for a moment to flatten. Divide the dough into pieces. The muffins can be cut precisely with a biscuit cutter, but I

shape mine by hand — patting each into a muffin about ³/₄″ thick by 4″ in diameter. I like a handcrafted look.

When shaped, place on the prepared baking sheet.

SECOND
RISING
50 mins.

Cover with waxed paper or Teflon sheet and allow to rise for about 50 minutes or until doubled in size.

PREHEAT

Preheat the oven to 400° about 20 minutes before baking.

BAKING
400°
20 mins.

Brush the pieces with egg white (whipped with a bit of water) and sprinkle liberally with seeds of choice.

Bake on the middle shelf for about 20 minutes.

FINAL STEP

Remove from oven and turn the muffins onto a wire rack to cool before serving.

POPOVERS

[A DOZEN OR SO POPOVERS]

Popovers are good to eat. Popovers are unpredictable. There isn't very much to a popover. It is an ungainly-looking device for getting butter, jams, jellies, and honey into the mouth.

The popover owes it all to steam levitation. It is done without yeast or chemicals of any kind. Only steam raises it high, and then lets it drop into a clumsy shape.

There should be at least one popover recipe in every home baker's repertoire. This is a good one.

INGREDIENTS

1 cup bread or all-purpose flour (sift before measuring)
¹/₄ teaspoon salt
1 tablespoon sugar
1 tablespoon butter, melted, or salad oil
1 cup milk, room temperature
2 large eggs

BAKING PANS	Greased muffin pans, heavy cast-iron popover pans, or ovenproof custard cups. Makes 12 popovers in ⅓-cup-size pans, 10 in ½-cup-size pans, or 8 in 5- or 6-ounce glass cups.
PREHEAT	Preheat the oven to 400°.
BY HAND OR BLENDER 1–4 mins.	Blend flour in a mixing or mixer bowl with salt and sugar. Add butter or oil, milk, and eggs, and beat by hand or at medium-high speed in the electric mixer until very smooth. Beat for 3 minutes. Popover batter can also be made in a blender. Combine all of the ingredients and whirl at high speed for 45 seconds. Stop the blender and scrape down the sides after the first 10 seconds.
BY PROCESSOR 2 mins.	Attach steel blade. Measure all the ingredients into the work bowl and pulse 8 or 10 times to blend thoroughly.
FORMING 3 mins.	Fill the cups half full with batter.
BAKING 400° 40 mins. or 375° 50–55 mins.	Bake in the hot oven (400°) for a dark brown shell with a moist interior, 40 minutes. Or bake at 375° for a light popover with a drier interior, 50 to 55 minutes. Be sure to keep the door of the oven closed during the bake period to prevent a collapse under a draft of cold air.
FINAL STEP	Remove popovers from the oven. Turn from the pans and serve while hot. If you like a dry interior, prick the popovers with a skewer or fork. Leave them in a turned-off oven, door slightly ajar, for 8 to 10 minutes.

ENGLISH MUFFINS

[EIGHT TRADITIONAL MUFFINS]

The English muffin in this country is difficult to place because it really is not a muffin but someplace between the English pikelet or crumpet (page 252) and the English fairy cake. The English call it the American muffin. Whichever, it is delicious.

Both agree that it is a sacrilege to cut open an English muffin with a knife. It must be torn apart by hand or separated with forks if it is ever to attain its true splendor of rough peaks and valleys bathed in butter. Even the best muffin, once violated with a knife (no matter how sharp), can never give the taste sensation of one torn apart and toasted.

This recipe is for an English muffin made with batter ladled into an open muffin ring or tin and baked either in the oven or cooked atop the stove on a griddle or skillet. If muffin rings are not at hand, small cans (prepared meats or pet-food cans, for example), open-ended and well scrubbed, work fine.

I have not done this with a food processor because the cleanup of the soft batter is not worth it.

INGREDIENTS	3 cups all-purpose flour, approximately
	1 package dry yeast
	1 tablespoon sugar
	2 teaspoons salt
	1/2 cup nonfat dry milk
	3 tablespoons butter, room temperature
	1 1/2 cups hot water (120°–130°)
	1 egg
RINGS OR TINS	Muffin rings, buttered.
GRIDDLE, SKILLET, OR BAKING SHEET	Electric or soapstone griddle, or heavy skillet for stovetop cooking. Baking sheet for the oven.

BY HAND
OR MIXER
12 mins.

In a large mixing or mixer bowl, measure 2½ cups of flour, yeast, sugar, salt, and dry milk. Stir to blend. Add the butter to the hot water and then to the dry ingredients. Beat for 2 minutes with the mixer flat beater or 150 strokes with a wooden spoon. Add the egg and the remaining ½ cup of flour. Stir to mix well.

FIRST RISING
1½ to 2 hours

Cover with plastic wrap and set aside for 1½ to 2 hours while the batter bubbles and rises to double in volume. It will have a pleasantly sour smell, thanks to the fermentation. In the meantime, butter the rings.

SECOND
RISING
45 mins.

Place the buttered rings on the baking sheet. Stir down the batter and ladle each ring half full. Put aside to rise to the top edge, about 45 minutes. No need to cover.

PREHEAT

While the batter is rising, preheat oven to 400°.

BAKING
400°
25 mins.

Place the rings in the oven. Muffins will not be turned over as they would be on the stovetop griddle or skillet. Bake until a golden brown and springy when tapped down with a finger, about 25 minutes.

GRIDDLE
OR SKILLET
15 mins.

Place the rings on the griddle/skillet with sufficient room between each to lift. With the rings in place, heat the griddle/skillet over a medium-low heat for about 10 minutes.

Stir down the batter and carefully half fill each ring with a ladle or large spoon. Spread the batter evenly. Cook over low to medium heat so as not to scorch.

TURNS
5-min.
intervals

When the batter has risen to the top of the rings, the bubbles begin to show, as in a pancake, and the batter pulls away from the sides, lift off the rings. Turn over. Continue to turn and cook for an additional 10 to 15 minutes, until the muffins are a deep brown and springy when pressed.

FINAL STEP

Remove muffins from the griddle or baking sheet. Cool on metal rack before toasting. Pull apart with the tines of a fork, or the fingers, to toast.

These freeze well and keep for months in the freezer at 0°.

MISSISSIPPI QUEEN SPOON BREAD

[SERVES 6]

In the beginning, spoon bread, a southern favorite, was not in the book until it was served at dinner aboard the big passenger steamboat *The Mississippi Queen* on a week-long Ohio River cruise. It was moist, light, and delicious.

Most spoon breads are made principally with cornmeal, grits, milk, and eggs—however, the steamboat's chef, Keith Bryant, has turned a simple bread into something near-elegant, with shreds of Cheddar cheese, corn kernels, and a hint of garlic. On occasion, he bakes a crab spoon bread by lightly spreading the crab meat on the bottom of the ramekins before pouring the batter.

While spoon breads are often baked in a casserole or a cast-iron skillet, this is baked in individual ramekins to give the bread its own place at the table rather than being spooned onto the plate.

INGREDIENTS
2 tablespoons butter, room temperature, to coat ramekins
½ cup yellow cornmeal
½ cup old-fashioned grits (not instant)
½ cup all-purpose flour
1 tablespoon sugar
1 teaspoon baking soda
1 teaspoon salt
1 cup buttermilk or 1 cup milk mixed with 1 teaspoon cider vinegar
2 eggs, beaten
1¼ cups milk, divided
1 cup (4 ounces) shredded sharp Cheddar cheese
1 cup fresh or defrosted frozen corn kernels
1 small garlic clove, minced

RAMEKINS
Six 1-cup ramekins or custard cups, well buttered. Or, if you wish to bake it as one, a buttered 10″ round cake pan, casserole, or cast-iron frying pan.

PREHEAT
400°
Preheat oven to 400°.

BY HAND
12 mins.

In a large bowl, whisk together the cornmeal, grits, flour, sugar, baking soda, and salt. In a smaller bowl, beat together the buttermilk and eggs and pour into the dry ingredients. Add 1 cup of milk, the cheese, corn, and garlic. Stir just to combine. Don't overmix.

Fill the prepared ramekins not quite to the top. Sprinkle the ¼ cup of milk over the batter.

BAKING
400°
20 mins.

Place ramekins (or casserole) in the oven and bake for approximately 20 minutes or so. (It may be convenient to place the ramekins on a baking sheet for easier handling in and out of the oven.)

Be mindful that the spoon bread is done when the center is barely set — soft and moist and will quiver when lightly shaken — while at the same time, a toothpick inserted in the center will come out clean.

If left in the oven too long, it becomes a muffin.

FINAL STEP

Remove from the oven and let stand for 5 minutes. Serve the spoon bread warm.

Pizza

SINCE the pizza joined the hamburger as one of America's favorite foods, it can now be had in this country anytime, anyplace — no matter time of day nor how remote.

It was less than a quarter of a century ago that the cook's bible, *The Joy of Cooking*, dismissed pizza with one recipe "of one of those Italian pies." The authoritative but snooty *Larousse Gastronomique* gave it one sentence: "a kind of flan . . . made mainly in the Nice region with onions, anchovy fillets and black olives."

There are now dozens of books and hundreds of recipes available to the home cook in this country. I narrowed these down to two basic recipes that I found in France and Italy two decades ago and brought back to my Indiana kitchen. They were first printed in *The Complete Book of Pastry*; the response from readers has been sustained and enthusiastic, so I offer them again.

There is one Italian pizza in particular that is highly esteemed at my table. It is from Sicily, and for this, the dough is allowed to rise three times. It is then partially baked to rise, soft and breadlike, in the oven. It is taken out of the oven, dressed with a wide choice of garnishes, and returned to the oven.

Pissaladière is from France and has cooked onions instead of tomato sauce as its principal topping. It is made with an egg-rich dough that is flavored and enriched by the olive oil in which the onions have been gently cooked.

A fine sauce is essential to an Italian pizza. The recipe for one such is given here. Late summer, when red ripe tomatoes are burgeoning in your garden, or your neighbor's, is the time to lay by a quantity of sauce for the winter months ahead.

Pizza and bread have been baked on the oven floor for several hundred years. The baking stone produces the same result in the home oven. For pizza, this means a crisp and often hard bottom, which many like.

To freeze pizza, partially bake the shell for about 10 minutes. Allow the shell to cool, then spread with cheese and garnishes. Place in the freezer overnight and then wrap for freezer storage. No need to defrost before baking—475° for about 25 minutes, or until crust is brown and crisp and sauce is bubbling.

PIZZA SICILIANA
(Sicilian Pizza)

[SIX LARGE PIECES OR FOUR DOZEN HORS D'OEUVRES]

This handsome rectangle (the shape is peculiarly Sicilian) can be served to 6, or cut into small 2″ squares to be served to a number at a buffet.

INGREDIENTS   Dough:
4½ cups all-purpose flour, approximately
1 package dry yeast

(continued on next page)

2 teaspoons salt
1½ cups warm water (105°–115°)
2 tablespoons olive oil, for dough
2 cups pizza sauce (recipe for homemade sauce follows)

Cheeses:
1 pound mozzarella cheese, grated or cut into small dice
½ cup finely grated Parmesan cheese

Garnishes:
Choice of garnishes (page 185)
¼ cup olive oil or vegetable oil, to sprinkle

BAKING PAN

One 11"-x-16" jelly roll or similar pan with shallow sides, greased or lined with parchment paper.

BY HAND
OR MIXER
10 mins.

Measure 2 cups flour, yeast, and salt into a mixing or mixer bowl. Stir to blend well. Pour in the water and oil. Beat the resulting batter with a wooden spoon or spatula 50 strong strokes or 2 minutes with the flat beater blade at low speed. Gradually add the remaining flour, ¼ cup at a time, with the spoon and then by hand until it can be lifted from the bowl to the floured work surface to be kneaded. If in the mixer, attach the dough hook and continue mixing until the dough pulls away from the sides of the bowl and forms a soft ball around the hook. Be generous with sprinkles of flour if the dough sticks to the bowl.

KNEADING
8 mins.

Knead with the hands for about 8 minutes or under the dough hook until the dough is smooth, shiny, and elastic. If sticky, dust with flour.

BY PROCESSOR
10 mins.

Attach the metal blade.
Measure 2 cups of flour, yeast, and salt into the work bowl. Pulse to blend. With the processor on, pour the water and oil through the feed tube. Add remaining flour, ½ cup at a time, through the feed tube. As the batter thickens into a mass, reduce the amount of flour to a tablespoon at a time rather than suddenly find it has become a hard ball. Stop the machine once or twice to judge by pinching the dough. It should be soft but slightly sticky.

KNEADING 45 secs.	Allow the blade to knead the dough for 45 seconds.
FIRST RISING 1 hour	Place the dough in a greased bowl. Cover with plastic wrap and set aside to rise for about 1 hour.
SECOND RISING 45 mins.	Uncover the bowl and punch down the risen dough. Knead briefly to flatten. Cover and leave for 45 minutes Meanwhile, during the periods when the dough is rising, assemble the pan, the 2 cups of pizza sauce (p. 184) and your choice of garnishes.
SHAPING 5 mins.	Grease the pan. Punch down the dough and place on the lightly floured work surface. With the hands, flatten the dough and push into a rough rectangle. Let the dough rest for a few moments so that it will not draw back. Roll the rectangle slightly larger than the pan. Allow the dough to relax before lifting and placing in the pan. With the palms, press the dough uniformly across the pan and up the sides.
THIRD RISING 30–40 mins.	Cover the dough with a cloth or waxed paper, and put aside to rise until doubled in depth, about 30 to 40 minutes.
PREHEAT	Preheat the oven to 475° about 15 minutes before the dough is ready to be covered with the pizza sauce. Position the baking stone, if it is to be used.
ASSEMBLY	*Working note:* The dough will be covered with the pizza sauce and baked for 10 minutes. It will be removed from the oven and dressed with the desired garnishes, then returned to the oven to finish baking for about 20 additional minutes.
BAKING 475° 10 mins.	Uncover the pan and spread with pizza sauce. Place the pan on the lower shelf and bake for 10 minutes. Remove from the oven and spread with cheese and choice of garnishes. Sprinkle liberally with olive oil and return to the oven.

20–25 mins.   Bake until the sauce is bubbling and the exposed edges of the
                     dough are dark brown and well risen, about 25 minutes.

FINAL STEP   Serve! Enjoy!

A BASIC PIZZA SAUCE

[ABOUT FOUR CUPS]

There are many sauces for pizza, but this one is a well-seasoned sauce
of tomato, with a hint of onion, garlic, and olive oil that can be spread
over any pizza with confidence that it is one of the best. Especially so
when it has been made with fresh-picked tomatoes and simmered on
the stove to fill the kitchen with the enticing fragrance of good things
to come. A summertime project for pleasure in the gray days of winter.

The sauce has a pleasant roughness about it. If you prefer a smoother
sauce, beat it with a wooden spoon or use the blender or food processor.
I prefer it as it comes from the stove.

INGREDIENTS   *4 pounds fresh tomatoes (or 3 1-pound cans)*
               4 tablespoons olive oil
               1 cup finely chopped onions
               1 tablespoon chopped garlic
               1 tablespoon each *basil leaves and oregano, chopped*
               ½ teaspoon each *sugar and black pepper*
               1½ teaspoons salt
               1 6-ounce can tomato paste

SAUCEPAN   One large, heavy saucepan in which to cook the sauce.

PREPARATION   Beforehand, if tomatoes are fresh, drop them into boiling water
10 mins.   for 30 seconds to loosen their skins. Remove from water and slip
               off the skins. Seed, and chop into ½" pieces.
10 mins.   In the heavy saucepan, heat olive oil and drop in the chopped
               onions and garlic. Cook over moderate heat, stirring frequently,
               until the onions are soft and translucent, about 10 minutes.

1 hour   Stir in the tomatoes, basil, oregano, sugar, pepper, salt, and
                  tomato paste. Bring to a boil over high heat, then lower heat and
                  simmer, partially covered, until the sauce is thick, about 1 hour.
                  (Fresh tomatoes should be cooked for an additional 30 minutes.)
                  Taste for seasoning.

FINAL STEP   The sauce may be used immediately, or refrigerated or frozen for
                  a later time.

CHEESES AND GARNISHES

                  Cheese spread over the pizza sauce is the classic foundation for a
                  myriad of garnishes. The amount of cheese here is for the preceding
                  Sicilian pizza.

CHEESE   *1 pound mozzarella cheese, grated or cut into small dice*
                  1/2 cup freshly grated Parmesan cheese

GARNISHES   *Working note*: These garnishes for atop the cheeses are for one of
                  Italy's most popular pizzas. They can be changed or revised at the
                  whim of the chef or his or her guests. Little is sacred in pizza mak-
                  ing.
                      (There was a time when the white button mushroom was the
                  only mushroom readily available in most markets. That has
                  changed, and all for the better. The white has been joined by the
                  oyster, shiitake, crimino, and portobello, as well as dried mush-
                  rooms such as the wood ear.)

                  6 or 8 mushrooms, stemmed, to decorate (depends on variety)
                  1 medium green pepper, seeded and thinly sliced
                  1/2 cup finely chopped onions
                  10 black olives, pitted and quartered

ALTERNATE   Other garnishes for pizzas may include thinly sliced garlic cloves,
GARNISHES   sweet Italian sausage, pepperoni, ground beef, shrimp, anchovies,

prosciutto slices, tiny meatballs, capers, diced hot peppers, and on and on.

These may be used alone or in combination, and with or without one or both of the cheeses.

PISSALADIÈRE
(French Pizza)

[FOUR PIZZAS OR FIFTY HORS D'OEUVRES]

This inspired *pissaladière* came from my sister's inspired kitchen in southern France, in the Alpes Maritimes, where she cooked overlooking shore and sea and, in the distance, the houses and palaces of Monaco.

The onion topping is subtly underscored by the onion flavor of the briochelike dough made with the olive oil in which the onions were cooked. Butter or margarine can be substituted for all or part of the olive oil if the onion flavor in the dough is not wanted.

This excellent dough can be topped with pizza sauce and other garnishes, as for the Italian pizza. But try the onion topping first. It is not overpowering.

The onions are to be prepared first if the olive oil in which they are cooked is used in the dough; hence, the ingredients for the topping are given first.

INGREDIENTS

Topping:
2 pounds onions
1 cup olive oil
1 cup shredded mozzarella cheese
16 anchovy fillets
24 black olives, halved
½ teaspoon each salt, oregano, cumin, and fennel (optional)
1 cup freshly grated Parmesan cheese

Dough:
2 packages dry yeast
¼ cup water

2½ cups bread or unbleached flour, approximately
1 teaspoon salt
6 tablespoons olive oil (in which onions were cooked)
2 eggs

EQUIPMENT
Selection of tart pans and flan rings. The dough can also be baked in a square or rectangular baking pan if it is to be cut into hors d'oeuvres. A baking stone for the oven, if available.

PREPARATION
30 mins.
Topping: Chop onions and cook gently in 1 cup olive oil in a covered skillet or saucepan over low heat until translucent and soft, about 15 minutes. Uncover, turn up the heat slightly, stirring frequently, until onions have turned a dark brown color (but are not burned), about 15 to 20 minutes. Remove from stove and drain off the olive oil. Save if wanted for dough. Onions may be refrigerated until needed.

BY HAND
OR MIXER
10 mins.
In a small bowl, dissolve the yeast in the water. Measure 1 cup of flour into a large bowl or mixer bowl and add the salt. Stir in the 6 tablespoons olive oil drained from the cooked onions, and follow this with the dissolved yeast. Beat with a wooden spoon or spatula or mixer flat beater blade. Stir in the eggs. If in the mixer, attach the dough hook. Add remaining flour, ¼ cup at a time, to make a rough mass, soft but not sticky, and turn onto a floured work surface.

KNEADING
8 mins.
This is a rich dough that is easy to work by hand. Use a dough scraper to occasionally lift the dough off the work surface and slam it down hard to help form the gluten. If in the mixer, mix at a low speed until the dough cleans the sides of the bowl and forms a soft mass around the hook. Add small amounts of flour if the dough does not come away from the bowl and is sticky when pinched. Knead for 8 minutes.

BY PROCESSOR
10 mins.
Attach the metal blade.
In a small bowl, dissolve the yeast in the water, as above, and set aside for the moment.
Measure 1½ cups flour and the salt into the work bowl. Pulse to blend. With the machine on, pour the dissolved yeast down the

feed tube. Follow this with the olive oil and eggs. Pulse several times to blend well. With the motor running, add remaining flour, ¼ cup at a time, to form a rough mass that will clean the sides of the bowl. A ball will form and travel on the top of the spinning blade.

KNEADING
45 secs.

Allow the blade to knead the dough for 45 seconds.

RISING
1–1½ hours

Place the dough in a greased bowl, cover with plastic wrap, and put aside to rise until doubled in bulk, about 1 to 1½ hours.

PREHEAT

Preheat the oven to 425° with baking stone in place, if wanted.

SHAPING
15 mins.

When the dough has risen, punch down, knead briefly, and divide into the number of pieces needed. Roll dough into thin (³/₁₆″) rounds and place in the pans. Push dough to the edges.

Distribute onions over the dough. Sprinkle with mozzarella cheese. Arrange anchovies in spokes radiating from the center. Decorate with olive halves, sprinkle with salt, herbs, and Parmesan cheese.

BAKING
425°
20 mins.

Place pans on the middle shelf of the hot oven. The pizzas will be done when bubbling and golden, about 20 minutes.

FINAL STEP

Serve hot! Enjoy!

Rolls

The most remembered taste at the table is often the smallest object to be served—the roll. Whether at dinner, brunch, buffet, or picnic, the sight and aroma of a basket of delicately shaped rolls send the signal that other good things are certain to follow.

These favorite recipes range from the classic dinner roll in all of its shapes to Claude Monet's *petits pains*, tiny hedgehog rolls from London, honey rolls from Africa, rye sandwich rolls from France, and a dozen others.

189

DINNER ROLLS

[A BASIC DOUGH — TWELVE TO EIGHTEEN ROLLS]

My mother's dinner rolls won blue ribbons at the Indiana state fair and accolades always from those around her dinner table. For years, I looked for a dinner roll superior to Lenora's — without truly believing I would succeed. I did not. It pleased me to always come back to the following recipe for what my mother simply called her "yeast rolls."

Here are 8 of the best-known shapes for dinner rolls — Parker House, bowknots, rosettes, butterhorns, crescents, cloverleafs, fan-tans, and pan rolls.

Perhaps the one shape most often made with this dough is the Parker House roll, known also as the pocketbook roll, which first appeared more than a century ago at Harvey Parker's Boston hotel.

INGREDIENTS	*1 package dry yeast*
	¼ cup milk, room temperature
	1 egg, room temperature
	2 tablespoons sugar
	¼ cup mashed potatoes, homemade or instant
	3 tablespoons butter, softened
	¼ teaspoon salt
	1½ to 2 cups all-purpose flour, approximately, plus sprinkles
	2 tablespoons butter, melted, to brush

BAKING SHEET, MUFFIN PANS, AND/OR CAKE PAN

Baking sheet or sheets for Parker House, bowknots, rosettes, butterhorns, and crescent rolls. Cloverleafs and fan-tans are placed in muffin tins, while pan rolls are set in 8″ or 9″ cake pans. Select the proper ones and grease.

PREPARATION

In advance prepare the mashed potato, whether from fresh potato or dehydrated flakes. It will be used at room temperature.

BY HAND OR MIXER 15 mins.

In a small container, dissolve yeast in milk.

In a large bowl or mixer bowl, blend the egg and sugar. Add potato, butter, and salt. Mix together either with a wooden spoon or mixer flat beater. Add 1 cup of flour and the yeast. Beat 100 strokes or 1 minute in the mixer. Gradually add remaining flour, ¼ cup at a time, first with the wooden spoon and then by hand as the dough becomes firm. If in the mixer, attach the dough hook.

Work the flour into the moist ball until it cleans the sides of the bowl and has lost much of its stickiness. Under the dough hook, the dough will clean the sides of the bowl and form a mass about the revolving hook.

It is an easy dough to work because of its high butterfat content.

KNEADING
8 mins.

If by hand, turn the soft dough onto a floured work surface and knead with a strong push-turn-fold motion until it becomes smooth and velvety under the hands. In the mixer, if the dough sticks to the sides of the bowl during kneading, add sprinkles of flour. Knead 8 minutes.

BY PROCESSOR
3 mins.

Attach the steel blade.

The sequence of adding ingredients varies from above. Measure ¾ cup of flour into the work bowl and add the dissolved yeast, sugar, and salt. Pulse to blend. With the processor running, pour the milk through the feed tube, and add the egg, potato, and the butter. Add remaining flour — 1 tablespoon at a time — either by taking off the cover or using the feed tube, until the batter becomes a rough mass of dough. If the ball of dough does not clean the sides of the bowl, add small portions of flour.

KNEADING
1 min.

When the dough has formed a ball, process for 1 minute to knead. Stop the machine and test the dough with the fingers. If it is too dry, add water by the teaspoon. Too wet, add flour. The dough should be very elastic when stretched between the hands. If not, return to the work bowl and process for a few more seconds.

FIRST RISING
1¼ hours

Return the dough to the bowl, stretch a length of plastic wrap across the top, and leave at room temperature until dough has risen to double in volume, about 1¼ hours.

SHAPING

The dough can be made into one shape of dinner roll or divided among the various shapes, as desired.

PARKER
HOUSE
20 mins.

(12 to 14 pieces)

Dust the work surface with flour. Roll the dough into a circle, about ⅜″ thick. Cut with a 2½″ or 3″ biscuit cutter. Place a light rolling pin in the center of the small rounds of dough. Carefully roll toward each end to create a valley through the center of the round. The center will be about ⅛″ thick, while the ends will be thicker. Or you may press the rounded handle of a knife into the dough to achieve the same results. Keep the rolling pin or knife handle dusted with flour as you work. Carefully brush each round with melted butter. This will allow the baked roll to open as a pocket.

Fold over the round of dough so the cut edges just meet. Pinch with the fingers to seal and press the folded edge (the hinge) securely. Place each about ½″ apart on a baking sheet as completed. Repeat with the remainder of the dough, as desired.

BOWKNOTS
AND
ROSETTES

(12 pieces)

Dust the work surface with flour. With the palms, roll dough into a 12″ rope. Divide the rope in 12 pieces. Roll each into a slender 8″ rope. For a bowknot, tie each into a simple knot. For a rosette, bring one end up and through the center of the knot, bring the other end over the side and under. Place on a baking sheet 1″ apart; press ends to the sheet to keep them from untying.

BUTTERHORNS
AND
CRESCENTS
20 mins.

(8 to 10 pieces)

Dust the work surface with flour.

Roll the dough into an 8″ circle. Let the dough relax for 3 or 4 minutes before cutting into 8 or 10 wedges with a pastry wheel or knife. Roll up the wedge, toward the point, pulling and stretching the dough slightly as you roll. For butterhorns, place each on the baking sheet, with points under. For crescents, roll wedge in the same manner, but curve each into a crescent as it is placed on the baking sheet.

CLOVERLEAFS
20 mins.

(6 pieces)

Dust the work surface with flour. With palms, roll the dough into a 16″ rope. If the rope draws back, allow it to relax for 3 or 4 minutes before proceeding. Cut length into 18 pieces. Shape each into a small ball between the palms; place 3 side by side in each muffin cup.

FAN-TANS
20 mins.

(12 pieces)

Dust the work surface with flour. Roll dough into an 8″-x-16″ rectangle — twice as long as it is wide. If the dough pulls back, let it relax for a few minutes. Brush with butter. With a pastry wheel or knife, cut the dough across the narrow width into five 1½″ strips. Stack the 5 strips and cut stack into 12 pieces. Place each in a 2½″ muffin cup, with the cut side of the dough up.

PAN ROLLS
15 mins.

(12 pieces)

Dust the work surface with flour. With the hands, roll dough into a 12″ rope. Cut into 12 pieces. Shape each into a tight ball under a cupped palm. Arrange in the pan.

SECOND RISING 30 mins.	Brush tops with melted butter, cover with waxed paper, and leave at room temperature until rolls have doubled in size, about 30 minutes.
PREHEAT	Twenty minutes before the bake period, preheat oven to 400°.
BAKING 400° 12–25 mins.	Place rolls in the oven and bake until a golden brown, about 12 to 15 minutes.
FINAL STEP	Remove from the oven and immediately brush with melted butter. Place on metal rack to cool. Delicious served warm from the oven.

EARL GREY TEA ROLLS

[THIRTY-TWO SMALL ROLLS]

Named for a British nobleman, Earl Grey tea, a fragrant orange pekoe tea with a bergamot flavor, gives these delicate rolls a subtle, spicy flavor. Tiny green specks of zest of 2 limes add color and a touch of piquancy.

This recipe is adapted from one in *The Book of Breads*, by Judith Jones and Evan Jones, whose work I greatly admire.

INGREDIENTS	*1 bag (1 tablespoon) Earl Grey tea* *1 cup boiling water* *2 tablespoons sugar* *1 package dry yeast* *2½ to 3 cups all-purpose flour, approximately* *2 tablespoons butter, room temperature* *1 teaspoon salt* *Zest of 2 limes* *Soft butter to brush*

195   ROLLS

BAKING SHEET	One baking sheet, greased or Teflon.
BY HAND OR MIXER 35 mins.	Beforehand, put the tea in a small, warm bowl or pot and pour the boiling water over it. Let steep, covered, for 15 minutes. Lift out the bag and cool.

Pour the sugar and yeast in a mixing or mixer bowl and blend in the lukewarm tea. Add 1 cup of flour and stir to make a light batter. Add the butter, salt, and lime zest. Stir in more flour to thicken the batter. Beat by hand with 50 strong strokes, or under the mixer flat beater for 2 minutes until the batter is thoroughly mixed. Add the balance of the flour, ¼ cup at a time, blending first with a wooden spoon and then by hand or with the dough hook.

When the dough has formed a rough, shaggy mass, place it on the floured work surface to knead or leave in the mixer under the dough hook. If the dough is sticky, add sprinkles of flour. |
| KNEADING 8 mins. 5 mins. | When sufficient flour has been added, the dough under the hook will clean the sides of the bowl and not stick. The dough will be soft and elastic. Knead for 8 minutes by hand or 5 minutes in the mixer. |
| BY PROCESSOR 5 mins. | Insert the steel blade.

(The order of adding ingredients will differ from above.) Mix lukewarm tea and yeast in a small bowl. Stir to dissolve and set aside for the moment. Place 2 cups of flour, sugar, butter, salt, and lime zest in the work bowl. With the machine running, pour the tea mixture through the feed tube. Next add tablespoons of flour to form a rough, shaggy mass that cleans the sides of the bowl and rides the blade.

Stop the machine, remove the cover, and pinch the dough to determine if it is wet and needs flour. If dry and not soft and elastic, add 1 or 2 tablespoons of water as the machine is running. |
| KNEADING 1 min. | With the machine running, knead for 1 minute. |

FIRST RISING
45 mins.

Place the dough in a greased bowl, cover with plastic wrap, and let stand at room temperature while it doubles in bulk, about 45 minutes.

SHAPING
10 mins.

Roll the dough into a length and divide into equal parts in successive steps — 2-4-8-16-32 — and roll the pieces between the palms into tight little balls, each not much larger than a golf ball. Place the balls about 1″ apart on the baking sheet.

SECOND
RISING
30 mins.

Cover lightly with a towel or a length of parchment paper for about 30 minutes.

PREHEAT

Preheat the oven to 375° 20 minutes before baking.

BAKING
375°
20 mins.

Bake until nicely browned, about 20 minutes.

FINAL STEP

Remove rolls from the oven and brush with soft butter. Served warm is best.

CHEESE TWISTS

[ONE DOZEN TWISTS]

There is a rich and satisfying taste that comes from bread made with cheese and it is especially so with these twists. Because of the high butterfat content of this light and golden dough, it is soft, pliable, and easy to work. Not at all sticky.

INGREDIENTS

3 cups all-purpose flour, approximately
2 packages dry yeast
½ teaspoon salt
⅔ cup warm water

1 (5-ounce) can evaporated milk
1 tablespoon butter, room temperature
1½ cups (6 ounces) sharp Cheddar cheese, grated
1 egg white and 1 tablespoon water, stirred together to brush
2 tablespoons poppy seeds, sesame seeds, or grated Parmesan cheese
  to sprinkle

BAKING
SHEET

One large baking sheet or 2 small, greased or Teflon, depending on size of oven.

BY HAND
OR MIXER
12 mins.

In a large bowl or mixer bowl, combine 2 cups flour, yeast, and salt. Heat the water, milk, and butter until very warm (120° to 130°); stir into dry ingredients. Stir in the cheese and add remaining flour, ¼ cup at a time, to form a soft dough that will clean the bowl and, if in the mixer, form a ball around the dough hook.

KNEADING
6–8 mins.

If by hand, turn the dough out onto a floured work surface and knead with a strong push-turn-fold motion until it is smooth and elastic, about 8 minutes. If under the dough hook, knead for 6 to 8 minutes in the mixer bowl.

BY PROCESSOR
5 mins.

Attach the steel blade.
    Measure 2 cups of flour, the yeast, and salt into the work bowl. Pulse to blend. Heat the water, milk, and butter as above and, with the processor on, pour into the work bowl. Add the cheese and remaining flour, ¼ cup at a time, processing after each addition, until the dough is no longer wet but soft and slightly sticky. Process until the dough forms a mass and cleans the bowl. If sticky to the touch, add 1 or 2 tablespoons of flour.

KNEADING
50 secs.

Let the dough spin with the blade for 50 seconds to knead.

FIRST RISING
20 mins.

Let the dough rest on the floured work surface, covered with waxed or parchment paper, for 20 minutes.

SHAPING
15 mins.

Divide the dough into 12 equal pieces for a plump roll or 18 pieces for a slender roll. Roll each piece to a 14″ rope, and rest for 5 minutes before proceeding. Lay a length of dough across the work surface in front of you. Twist the length—pushing forward on one end, pulling back on the other. Quickly pinch the ends together. Lift and let it twist by *untwisting*. Place on a baking sheet.

PREHEAT

Preheat the oven to 375° 20 minutes before baking.

SECOND
RISING
30 mins.

Cover and let rise until doubled in size, about 30 minutes.

BAKING
375°
15–18 mins.

Brush with the egg mixture. Sprinkle with poppy or sesame seeds or Parmesan cheese, if desired. Bake at 375° for 15 to 18 minutes or until a delicate brown. The bottom of the twist should be a deep brown and have a solid feel when tapped with a finger.

FINAL STEP

Remove from the baking sheet and let cool on wire racks. These will stay fresh for several days. If frozen, thaw before reheating in a 350° oven for 15 minutes.

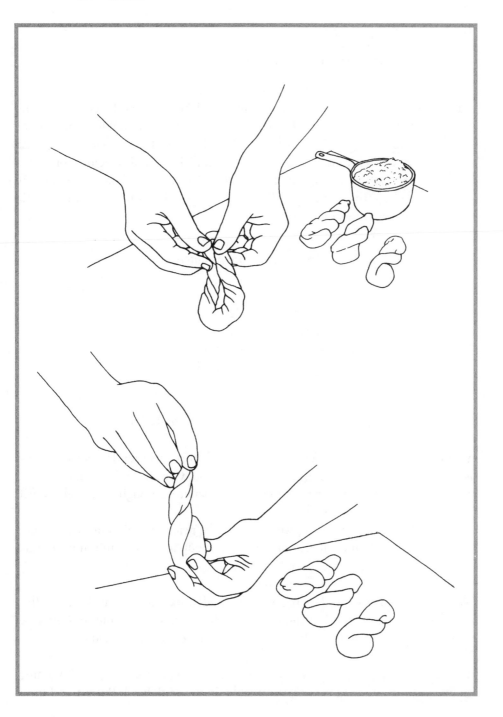

EGG SHELL ROLLS

[ONE DOZEN LARGE, TWO DOZEN SMALL ROLLS]

This recipe is from a half-century-old booklet developed by General Mills for commercial bakers. It is equally comfortable in the home kitchen. Egg whites, whipped to a light peak, produce a thin, crisp paper-shell crust that will keep the rolls fresh and delicious for a long period of time. Store in a bread box or paper sack. Don't place them in a plastic bag or they will quickly lose their crispness. If this should happen, reheat the rolls.

INGREDIENTS	*3 to 4 cups bread flour, approximately*
	1 package yeast
	2 teaspoons salt
	1½ cups hot water (100°–120°)
	1 tablespoon sugar
	2 tablespoons vegetable shortening
	½ teaspoon malt extract (optional)
	2 egg whites
BAKING SHEET	One 11″-x-17″ baking sheet, greased or Teflon.
BY HAND OR MIXER 15 mins.	In a large bowl or mixer bowl, mix together 1½ cups of flour, yeast, salt, and water. Stir to blend. Cream the sugar and shortening together and drop into the batterlike dough. Add malt extract, if available.
	Beat the egg whites to a light peak and fold into the mixture. Add the balance of the flour, ½ cup at a time, until it becomes a shaggy mass, moist and stringy.
KNEAD 6–8 mins.	Turn the dough onto a floured work surface and knead with a strong push-turn-fold motion by hand for 8 minutes or 6 minutes with a dough hook. Dough will be elastic and smooth.
BY PROCESSOR 5 mins.	Place 2 cups of flour and the yeast, salt, water, sugar, shortening, and malt extract, if available, in the work bowl. Pulse 3 or 4 times

to blend the ingredients. Set aside for a moment. Whip the egg whites and add to the work bowl. Pulse to blend.

Add remaining flour, ½ cup at a time, pulsing each time to blend the ingredients. Add the last cup of flour with care so that the dough doesn't suddenly turn into a hard ball.

KNEADING 50 secs.	When the dough cleans the sides of the work bowl and rides in a ball on top of the blade, knead for 50 seconds. Dough will be soft and elastic.
FIRST RISING 1–1½ hours	Place the dough in a greased bowl, cover tightly with plastic wrap, and place in a warm spot (80°–90°) to double in size.
SHAPING 10 mins.	For small rolls, cut the dough into 1-ounce pieces, about the size of a golf ball. For larger rolls, cut the dough into 2- or 3-ounce pieces. Roll tight balls under the palm. Press down hard as you roll the dough. Place the rolls on the baking sheet, taking care to allow sufficient room between each so they will not touch during rising. If they do, they will not brown overall as they should.
SECOND RISING 45 mins.	Cover rolls and put in a warm place until double in volume, about 45 minutes.
PREHEAT	Preheat oven to 400° 20 minutes before baking.
BAKING 400° 25–30 mins.	Place baking sheet on the middle shelf of the oven. Baking time will be between 25 and 30 minutes, depending on the size of the rolls. Rolls will be done when a golden brown.
FINAL STEP	Place crispy rolls on rack to cool. Serve immediately or store in a paper sack to preserve crust. If rolls should lose their crispness, reheat in 300° oven for 15 minutes. Rolls may be frozen. Thaw and reheat.

YEMARINA YEWOTET DABO
(Ethiopian Honey Rolls)

[SIXTEEN ROLLS]

There was a time, not so long ago, when Ethiopia was an Eden — "a land of bread and honey" — before drought and strife changed the face of the land. The breads were baked with flours milled from grains harvested from across vast fields of wheat, sorghum, and millet. The honey was from a myriad of hives of both wild and domestic bees, a beekeeping culture lost in antiquity.

This Ethiopian recipe, rich with honey and delicately flavored with spices, was for a traditional round loaf, but I fashioned the dough into rolls — easier to share with a friend or to set aside for a later occasion.

The choice is to bake them in muffin tins for uniformly shaped rolls or fashioned freehand into rolls not always perfect in shape. Both equally delicious.

INGREDIENTS	*4 cups all-purpose flour, approximately*
	2 packages dry yeast
	1 tablespoon ground coriander
	½ teaspoon ground cinnamon
	¼ teaspoon ground cloves
	1 teaspoon salt
	1 cup milk, room temperature
	½ cup honey
	1 egg, room temperature
	5 tablespoons butter, melted (reserve 1 tablespoon to brush later)
BAKING SHEET OR MUFFIN TINS	One baking sheet, greased or Teflon, or 16 muffin cups, buttered.
BY HAND OR MIXER 15 mins.	In a large bowl or mixer bowl, mix together 2 cups of flour, yeast, coriander, cinnamon, cloves, and salt.

In a small bowl, stir together — with a wire whisk or hand electric mixer — the milk, honey, egg, and 4 tablespoons melted butter.

When blended, pour the milk mixture into the flour and beat

into a batter; 100 strokes by hand or 2 minutes in the mixer with the flat beater blade. If you are using the mixer, attach the dough hook. By hand or mixer, add the remaining flour, ¼ cup at a time, until a rough, shaggy dough is formed.

KNEADING
8 mins.

Turn the dough onto a floured work surface, or leave in the mixer with the dough hook attached. Knead the dough for 8 minutes. If it is sticky, add sprinkles of flour. This is a rich dough that will become a soft, elastic mass that will not stick to the hands or to the sides of the bowl. The dough will form a ball around the hook as it revolves.

BY PROCESSOR
5 mins.

Attach the steel blade.

Measure 2 cups of flour into the work bowl and add the dry ingredients. Pulse to blend. Pour in the milk mixture. Pulse 4 or 5 times to blend the ingredients into a batter. Let the mixture rest for a minute to allow the yeast to dissolve in the wet batter. Add 1 cup of flour and process. Add the balance of the flour through the feed tube, ¼ cup at a time, until the dough forms a ball that rides the blade, and at the same time cleans the sides of the bowl.

KNEADING
45 secs.

Process for 45 seconds to knead.

FIRST RISING
1½–2 hours

Place the ball of dough into a lightly greased work bowl, cover with plastic wrap, and put aside to double in volume, about 2 hours. This is a rich dough and is slow to rise.

SHAPING
10 mins.

Knead once or twice to deflate the dough and then roll into a long cylinder. With a yardstick in hand, mark and cut 16 pieces. Each should weigh about 2½ ounces. Either roll each piece under the palm of the hand into a tight, round ball or, with the fingers, draw the dough into a ball by pinching the dough at the bottom to pull it together in one smooth piece.

Place on the baking sheet or in the prepared muffin cups.

SECOND
RISING
1 hour

Brush the rolls with melted butter and cover with waxed or parchment paper, and put aside to double in size, about 1 hour.

PREHEAT   Preheat the oven to 375° about 20 minutes before baking.

BAKING   With a razor blade or sharp knife, make a ¼″ cut across the tops
375°   of the freestanding rolls, but not those in the muffin tins. Brush
35 mins.   with melted butter.
                       Place the baking sheet or muffin tins in the moderately hot
                   oven and bake until the tops are crispy and golden brown, about
                   35 minutes.

FINAL STEP   Remove the rolls from the oven and cool on a wire rack.
                       Thin slices of the rolls make excellent toast. The rolls may be
                   frozen for several months at 0°.

PETITS PAINS
(Monet's Bread Rolls)

[TWELVE SMALL BREADS]

When we visited the celebrated exhibition of Claude Monet's paintings
in Chicago, I realized how passionate Monet was about good food and
good living. At his house and gardens at Giverny, outside Paris, he
entertained his fellow Impressionists—Renoir, Pissarro, Degas, and
Cézanne—as well as Rodin, Whistler, Maupassant, Valéry, and a host
of other celebrities.

Monet kept journals to bring home recipes for dishes he had enjoyed
in his travels or had come across in Paris, as well as recipes from his
friends.

Jean Millet, who painted *The Gleaners*, gave Monet this recipe for
petits pains.

INGREDIENTS   *½ cup milk*
                   2 teaspoons sugar
                   ½ teaspoon salt
                   1½ tablespoons butter

2 cups all-purpose flour, approximately
1 package dry yeast
½ cup water
1 egg, lightly beaten
1 egg yolk mixed with 1 tablespoon milk, to brush

BAKING
SHEET

One baking sheet, greased or Teflon.

BY HAND
OR MIXER
10 mins.
20 mins.

In a small saucepan, heat milk and sugar to a simmer but do not boil. Remove from heat, add salt and butter. Stir together and set aside to cool. Meanwhile, in a mixing or mixer bowl, stir together ¾ cup flour and the yeast. Add ½ cup water and stir to make a batter. Cover and leave in a warm place for 20 minutes, by which time the mixture will be light and spongy.

Lightly beat the egg and add to the milk mixture when it has cooled. Beat the milk into the sponge with a wooden spoon or mixer flat beater blade. Add the balance of the flour, a tablespoon at a time, until the dough is a rough mass, though slightly sticky, that can be worked by hand or in the mixer.

KNEADING
6 mins.

Sprinkle flour on the work surface and knead the dough by hand or leave in the mixer under the dough hook for 6 minutes. Add sprinkles of flour if the dough remains sticky. The dough will become smooth and velvety.

BY PROCESSOR
15 mins.

Note: Several steps will be done before processing begins. Heat the milk and other ingredients, as above. Make a batter of flour, yeast, and water, as above. Blend the 2 mixtures and set aside for a moment.

Place the balance of the flour in the work bowl. With the processor running, pour the blend of mixtures through the feed tube. The dough should become a ball that cleans the sides of the bowl and rides on the steel blade.

KNEADING
45 secs.

When the dough becomes a unified mass and cleans the bowl, knead for 45 seconds. Remove the cover and test the dough. Turn from the bowl, sprinkle with flour, and work into a ball.

SHAPING	To divide the dough into precise pieces, roll it into a length 12″
15 mins.	to 14″ long. With a sharp knife, divide the dough into a dozen

SHAPING
15 mins.

To divide the dough into precise pieces, roll it into a length 12″ to 14″ long. With a sharp knife, divide the dough into a dozen equal parts. First, roll each piece into a tight ball pressed hard between the palms or under the palm against the work surface. If the dough is sticky, dust with flour.

Gently roll each ball into a tiny baguette 4″ long and 1″ thick.

FIRST RISING
45 mins.

Place the pieces on the prepared baking sheet and cover with a towel, waxed paper, or parchment. Set aside to rise for 45 minutes or until puffy when pressed lightly with a finger.

PREHEAT

Preheat the oven to 400° 20 minutes before baking.

BAKING
400°
15 mins.

Brush each with the egg-milk mixture. Bake until the crust is a golden brown, about 15 minutes.

FINAL STEP

Remove the rolls from the oven and slip them off the pan onto a metal cooling rack.

Freeze well.

WHOLE-WHEAT ICEBOX ROLLS

[MAKES TWO TO FOUR DOZEN ROLLS, DEPENDING ON SIZE]

The beauty of icebox rolls is that the dough is there when you want it —in the refrigerator ready to shape and bake at a moment's notice, a perfect treat for the unexpected guest. And also ideal for a working spouse to make on the weekend and then to serve hot and crusty any or every night of the week. The dough will keep for up to 7 days, well covered, in the refrigerator.

While this recipe is most often made with all white flour, the inclusion of 1 cup of whole-wheat along with 3 cups of white gives the rolls a wheaty taste and a light speckled crust, rather like a pretty young girl with a bridge of freckles across her nose.

This is a small recipe that easily can be doubled or tripled for more rolls.

INGREDIENTS	*1 cup whole-wheat flour*
	3 cups bread flour, approximately
	1 package dry yeast
	1 teaspoon salt
	1 tablespoon sugar
	1½ cups warm water
	2 tablespoons butter, melted
	1 egg, beaten lightly

BAKING
SHEET

One baking sheet, lightly greased or Teflon. On occasion, I have baked a lot of these rolls in 1½″ muffin cups for crusty small rolls — so appealing that it is possible to eat 3 or more at a sitting.

BY HAND
OR MIXER
15 mins.

Measure 1 cup of whole-wheat flour and 1 cup of white flour in a large bowl or mixer bowl and add the yeast, salt, and sugar. With a wooden spoon or mixer flat blade, stir to blend. Add the water, butter, and egg. Stir with vigor for 2 minutes.

Stir in the balance of the white flour, ½ cup at a time, first with the spoon and then by hand. If in the mixer, remove and clean off the flat blade and exchange it for the dough hook. The dough will be a shaggy mass that cleans the sides of the bowl.

KNEADING
8–10 mins.

If using the mixer, knead under the dough hook. Add sprinkles of flour if the dough continues wet or slack. If by hand, turn the dough onto a floured work surface and knead with a rhythmic motion of push-turn-fold. The dough will become soft and elastic. Occasionally, break the kneading rhythm by throwing the dough down hard against the work surface to help develop its elasticity. Knead for 8 to 10 minutes.

BY PROCESSOR
8 mins.

Attach the steel blade. (The short plastic dough blade is not effective with small quantities such as this.)

Measure the whole-wheat and 1 cup white flours and the dry ingredients into the work bowl. Pulse to blend. In a small bowl, stir together the water, butter, and egg. With the machine running, pour the liquid through the feed tube. Add the remaining white flour, a small portion at a time, through the feed tube to form a shaggy mass that cleans the sides of the bowl and spins with the blade.

KNEADING
45 secs.

With the processor running, knead the dough for 45 seconds. The dough may be slightly sticky when first turned from the bowl. If so, dust lightly with flour while patting it into a ball.

FIRST RISING
1 hour

Place the dough in a greased bowl, cover tightly with plastic wrap, and leave at room temperature until it has risen to about twice its original size, about 1 hour.

REFRIGERATE

Punch down the dough, replace the plastic wrap, and store in the refrigerator until ready to use. It will keep for a week to 10 days.

TO SHAPE
12 mins.

To make the rolls, pull and cut off as much dough as you think you will need. Cut into pieces and roll between your hands into balls. Place apart on a greased baking sheet if you want a crusty roll or close together if you want soft ones.

SECOND
RISING
2 hours

Cover lightly with waxed or parchment paper and let rise until double in volume, about 2 hours. Because the dough is taken from the refrigerator and is cold, it will take somewhat longer for the rolls to rise.

PREHEAT

Twenty minutes before the bake period, preheat the oven to 425°.

BAKING
425°
15–20 mins.

Bake for 15 to 20 minutes until golden brown — and freckled.

FINAL STEP

Place on rack to cool before serving.

GÂTEAUX AU POIVRE
(Pepper Cakes)

[FOUR DOZEN LITTLE CAKES]

The pepper cake of Limoux, a small town in southern France, is not a cake but a tiny, twisted, golden wreath of yeast-raised dough, speckled with pepper and formed around the finger. It is most often served as an hors d'oeuvre or snack with drinks or coffee or tea.

Since pepper is the most important single ingredient in these small *gâteaux*, grind it fresh if you can. If a grinder is not part of your *batterie de cuisine*, buy a fresh container of ground pepper at a large market where there is a fast turnover on the spice shelves.

The rolls must be petite and delicate. Allow them no time to rise before you put them in the oven and bake them just long enough to be a shade beyond golden.

Don't expect perfection the first time. Not until the third batch did I succeed in making a truly delicate, pencil-thin strand. And it was not before the fourth batch that I succeeded in making a perfect round-the-finger wreath.

INGREDIENTS

2½ cups all-purpose flour, approximately
1 level teaspoon dry yeast (not packet, but teaspoon)
2 teaspoons freshly ground pepper
1 teaspoon salt
⅔ cup warm water (105°–115°)
1½ sticks (6 ounces) butter, room temperature
1 egg or egg yolk stirred with 1 teaspoon water, to glaze

BAKING
SHEET

One baking sheet, greased, Teflon, or lined with parchment paper.

BY HAND
OR MIXER
10 mins.

In a large bowl or mixer bowl, measure 1½ cups of flour; add the yeast, pepper, and salt. Pour in the water and mix by hand for 50 strokes or with the mixer flat beater for 1 minute to thoroughly blend the ingredients. Drop in butter cut into several small pieces to make mixing easier. Work butter into the flour until it is wholly absorbed. Add remaining flour (about 1 cup) until dough forms a smooth, buttery mass.

KNEADING
5 mins.

If by hand, turn the dough onto a floured work surface and knead. It will be an easy task because of its high butter content — but if it seems too moist or too sticky, toss down several liberal sprinkles of flour and work them in. If in the mixer, attach dough hook and add small portions of flour if dough sticks to the bowl. Knead for 5 minutes.

BY PROCESSOR
4 mins.

Attach the steel blade.

Measure 1½ cups of flour into the work bowl and add the yeast, pepper, and salt. Turn on the machine and slowly pour the water through the feed tube. Stop the machine and add the pieces of butter. With the machine running, add remaining flour, ¼ cup at a time, through the feed tube until the heavy batter becomes a dough. The dough will become a ball that cleans the bowl as it rides on the blade.

KNEADING
45 secs.

Process the dough for 45 seconds to knead. The dough will be slightly sticky when it is turned out of the work bowl, but light sprinkles of flour will make it manageable.

PREHEAT

Preheat the oven to 425°. (This dough goes directly into the oven after shaping, so whatever leavening effect there is takes place in the oven. A vigorous rising might tear the delicate wreaths apart.)

SHAPING
20 mins.

The dough will weigh about 1½ pounds. Divide it into 6 or 8 pieces and begin rolling them into long strands no thicker than a lead pencil — or even thinner. First roll each piece into a rough cylinder. Lay both hands on the center of the roll and move the dough back and forth across the work surface, slowly spreading the hands apart to make the roll longer and thinner. But don't force the dough to spread because it may tear. Be firm when you push *down* on the roll with the hands. You can't collapse it.

When 1 strand seems to be resisting, move on to another. Return to the first and continue the motion. When the strand gets so long that the ends get tangled (more than 18″), cut in two. Be certain the strands are rolled pencil-thin.

Twist 2 slender strands together. The double strand will-try to unwind when you lay it down, so press the ends to the work surface until they relax in the twisted position. Go on to the next pair.

When all of the strands have been paired, hold the tip of the index finger against the work surface. Wrap the dough around the finger to form a small wreath. Allow enough additional length so that the ends can be pinched together (about 5 inches overall) and cut with a knife or scissors. Make certain the strands don't untwist before overlapping and pinching together.

Place on baking sheet ½″ apart. Repeat for all the double strands. When all *gâteaux* have been made, brush with the egg-water glaze. For an extra peppery taste, sprinkle a bit of ground pepper over the glaze.

BAKING
425°
22 mins.

Move the sheet directly to the hot oven. No rest period or rising. Look at the cakes after 15 minutes. If those along the outside edges of the sheet are browning too quickly, push them to the center and move center cakes to the outside.

Cakes will bake dry with little moisture left in them.

FINAL STEP

Remove from the oven and let cool on a metal rack. They will remain fresh for several weeks in an airtight container. They will freeze nicely for several months.

PETITS PAINS À LA POMME DE TERRE
(Potato Rolls)

[SIXTEEN ROLLS]

There is pleasant euphony in the French words that describe these plump and tender rolls made with mashed potatoes. The potato does not stand alone, of course. It is joined by honey, egg, and butter.

INGREDIENTS

1 cup mashed potato, homemade or instant, cooled to room temperature

1 cup water (saved from boiling potatoes or from the tap)

4½ cups all-purpose flour, approximately

1 package dry yeast

2 teaspoons salt

¼ cup honey

1 egg

2 tablespoons each soft butter and vegetable oil

Melted butter to brush

BAKING SHEET

One baking sheet, lightly greased or Teflon.

BY HAND
OR MIXER
15 mins.

Prepare the mashed potatoes and reserve the water in which they were boiled. Use tap water otherwise.

In a large bowl or mixer bowl, measure 2 cups of flour and add yeast and salt. Stir to blend. In a small bowl, beat together water, honey, and egg and pour into the flour. Stir to make a batter. Add the mashed potato, butter, and oil. Beat 100 strokes with spatula or wooden spoon or 2 minutes with the flat beater blade. Gradually stir in remaining flour, ½ cup or less at a time, until the dough forms a mass that can be lifted from the bowl or cleans the sides of the mixer bowl.

KNEADING
6–8 mins.

If by hand, turn the dough onto the floured work surface and knead with a strong push-turn-fold motion until it is soft and elastic, about 6 to 8 minutes. Add sprinkles of flour if the dough is slack or wet. If in the mixer, attach dough hook to knead. Add flour, a tablespoon at a time, if necessary to clean the bowl and form a ball around the dough hook. Stop the machine occasionally to pinch the dough to judge its elasticity. It must not stick to the fingers when tested.

To judge if the dough needs flour and further kneading, rest the ball of dough on the work surface and slap your open palm down hard against the dough. If your hand leaves a clear impression and the dough does not stick to the hand, enough flour.

BY PROCESSOR
5 mins.

Use the steel blade for this small amount of dough.

Measure 2 cups of flour into the work bowl and add yeast and salt. Pulse to mix. In a small bowl, stir together the water, honey, and egg. Turn on machine and pour the mixture through the feed tube. Stop the machine, remove cover, and add butter, oil, and mashed potato. Pulse to blend. Measure remaining flour into the work bowl until the dough cleans the sides of the bowl and forms a ball that rides on the blade.

KNEADING
50 secs.

Leave the machine running to knead for 50 seconds. The dough may be slightly sticky, so sprinkle liberally with flour when you take it from the work bowl.

FIRST RISING
1½ hours

Place the dough in a bowl, cover tightly with plastic wrap, and put aside at room temperature until light and doubled in size, about 1½ hours.

SHAPING
8 mins.

Turn the dough onto the floured work surface. Knead it lightly 3 or 4 times. Roll the dough into a long piece about 16″. With a sharp knife, cut pieces that weigh about 2 ounces, about the size of an egg when rolled into a ball.

REST
15 mins.

Cover the cut pieces and let them rest for 15 minutes.

SHAPING
15 mins.

The rolls can be shaped in two ways. One is to roll the pieces of dough under the palm into balls.

My preference for this particular roll is to hold the piece of dough in the fingers of one hand while, with the fingers of the other hand, pulling down the edges to stretch a smooth, seamless skin over the dough held between the thumb and forefinger.

SECOND
RISING
45 mins.

Cover the rolls with waxed paper or plastic wrap and leave to rise until doubled in volume, about 45 minutes.

PREHEAT

While the rolls are rising, preheat the oven to 400°.

BAKING
400°
25 mins.

Brush the rolls with melted butter and place in the middle of the oven. Bake for about 25 minutes. If the rolls are browning unevenly, turn the sheet around.

FINAL STEP   When the rolls come from the oven, brush again with melted
                  butter. Served warm or cold, these rolls are delicious. They will
                  keep frozen for several months at 0°.

ORANGE TIFFIN ROLLS

[ONE DOZEN MEDIUM OR TWO DOZEN SMALL ROLLS]

If you are invited to tiffin on your next visit to India, do go. You are
being invited to a luncheon and the rolls to be served may well be these
delicious orange-flavored rolls.

Two oranges—juice and zest—and a portion of currants are the
heart of this roll, the recipe for which I found in an old cookbook.
The light orangy aroma of tiffin rolls baking—and being served—is a
delight.

INGREDIENTS   *2 oranges or sufficient to make $1/3$ cup each juice and zest, plus*
                        1 orange for juice for icing
                   3 cups all-purpose flour, approximately
                   1 package dry yeast
                   $1^1/2$ teaspoons salt
                   $1/3$ cup sugar
                   $1/2$ cup milk
                   $1/2$ stick (4 tablespoons) butter or margarine, room temperature
                   2 egg yolks
                   $1/3$ cup currants

                   Icing:
                   Juice of 1 orange stirred into $1/2$ cup confectioners' sugar

MUFFIN TINS   For medium rolls, $2^1/2''$ greased muffin tins with total of 12 cups,
                   or 24 $1^1/2''$ cups for small.

BY HAND   Zest oranges and squeeze for juice. Set aside.
OR MIXER   In a large mixing or mixer bowl, measure $1^1/2$ cups of flour and
20 mins.   dry ingredients. Stir with a heavy wooden spoon or mixer beater

blade. Pour in ⅓ cup of orange juice, zest, and milk. Blend. Stir in the butter and egg yolks with vigorous strokes by hand or 2 minutes in the mixer. Add the currants. Beat until well blended into a heavy batter. Add the remaining flour, ¼ cup at a time, and beat well to form a shaggy mass.

KNEADING
10 mins.

If in the mixer, attach dough hook and knead to form a smooth, elastic body of dough, about 8 minutes. Sufficient flour will have been added when the dough forms a ball around the hook and cleans the sides of the bowl. If by hand, knead with a strong push-turn-fold motion, occasionally lifting the dough into the air and crashing it down against the work surface. It will become smooth and elastic.

BY PROCESSOR
12 mins.

Attach the steel blade.
    Prepare the orange juice and zest, as above.
    Measure 1½ cups of flour and dry ingredients into the processor work bowl. Pulse to blend. With processor running, pour ⅓ cup of orange juice, zest, and milk through the feed tube. Stop. Uncover the bowl and scrape down the sides with a spatula. Drop in the butter, egg yolks, and currants. Start the machine and add the remaining flour, ¼ cup at a time, to form a rough, shaggy dough that cleans the sides of the bowl and rides on the blade.

KNEADING
1 min.

Process to knead for 1 minute.
    Stop the machine, uncover, and pinch the dough to determine if it is soft, moist but not wet. Turn from the bowl and dust lightly with flour to prevent sticking.

FIRST RISING
1–1½ hours

Place the dough in a greased bowl, cover with plastic wrap, and let stand at room temperature while it rises to double in bulk, about 1½ hours. It is a rich dough and slow to rise.

SHAPING
10 mins.

Roll the dough into a long cylinder and divide into equal parts in successive steps — 2-4-8-16 and so on. Shape into balls and drop into the prepared muffin cups. The dough should fill a cup liberally, about three-quarters when pressed into the sides.

If you choose, the rolls can be baked directly on a greased baking sheet without the muffin cups.

SECOND RISING 1 hour	Cover the rolls with waxed or parchment paper and set aside to rise to double in volume, about 1 hour.
PREHEAT	Preheat the oven to 400°.
BAKING 400° 12–15 mins.	Remove the paper covering the rolls and place tins on the middle shelf of the oven. Bake 12 to 15 minutes or until the rolls are lightly browned. While the rolls are baking, mix together the confectioners' sugar and as much orange juice as needed to make an icing that will drip slowly from a spoon. Not too runny.
FINAL STEP	When the rolls have cooled to warm, drizzle the crown of each with a spoonful of icing. The icing will flow down the sides in patterns. The rolls may be frozen and then iced after reheating.

GRANDMOTHER SPURGEON'S CINNAMON ROLLS

[MAKES ONE DOZEN LARGE OR EIGHTEEN SMALL ROLLS]

This roll came from Edmonds, Washington, a lovely small city on Puget Sound, where a fine cook, Jerilyn Brusseau, was given the recipe by her grandmother when she opened a bakery-deli. Grandmother's roll has been the *pièce de résistance*, the cornerstone, of the café for two decades.

    Two flours — all-purpose white and whole-wheat — are used in making the rolls.

    When the dough is cut into 12 pieces to fit into one 9″-x-13″ baking pan, the rolls will bake to about 3″ thick. For a thinner roll, cut the dough into 18 pieces and place in 2 pans.

INGREDIENTS

Dough:
1 cup whole-wheat flour
2½ cups all-purpose flour, approximately
1 package dry yeast
⅓ cup sugar
2 teaspoons salt
¼ cup nonfat dry milk
1 cup warm water
3 tablespoons butter, room temperature
2 eggs
½ cup currants or raisins

Filling:
1½ cups (3 sticks) butter
3 cups dark brown sugar
2 tablespoons cinnamon
1½ cups chopped walnuts

BAKING
PANS

One 9"-x-13" metal or ceramic baking pan (not glass, which tends to caramelize sugar too quickly). For thinner rolls, use 1 additional 8"-x-8" pan.

BY HAND
OR MIXER
10 mins.

In a large mixing or mixer bowl, measure the 1 cup of whole-wheat flour, 1½ cups all-purpose flour, dry yeast, sugar, salt, and dry milk. Blend. Pour the water into the flour-yeast, and stir to make a light batter. Add the butter and eggs. Beat with a spoon or the mixer flat blade until the butter and eggs are absorbed.

Add the currants or raisins. Add the balance of the white flour, ¼ cup at a time, to form a dense mass that can be lifted to the work surface, or left in the bowl under the dough hook. The dough should be smooth, satiny, and somewhat resilient.

KNEADING
8 mins.

If by hand, spread flour on the work surface and turn the dough onto it. Knead with a strong push-turn-fold motion, using only as much flour as necessary to make a smooth, elastic dough that is not sticky. If using the mixer, knead with the dough hook. Knead by hand or mixer for about 8 minutes.

BY PROCESSOR
5 mins.

Attach the short dough blade.

Measure 1 cup whole-wheat and 1 cup white flour into the processor work bowl. Add yeast, sugar, salt, and dry milk. Pulse to blend. Pour in the water. Pulse. Remove cover and stir in butter and eggs. Process for 30 seconds. Add currants.

With machine running, add additional flour, ¼ cup at a time, through the feed tube to form a rough mass that will clean the sides of the bowl.

KNEADING
40 secs.

Keep the machine running and knead dough for 40 seconds.

FIRST RISING
45 mins.

Shape the dough into a ball and place in a large greased bowl, turning over to grease the top. Cover with plastic wrap. Let rise in a warm place until double in bulk, about 45 minutes.

FILLING
5 mins.

While the dough is rising, melt the butter in a small pan. In a small bowl, stir together brown sugar and cinnamon.

SHAPING
15 mins.

Turn dough onto a large floured board. Roll out to a 24"-x-20" rectangle. Brush liberally with melted butter. Cover the dough with the sugar-cinnamon mix and then sprinkle on the nuts.

Roll rectangle tightly from the long side (filling may be slightly runny and dough will be soft). Make certain the seam is on the bottom. Shape with hands to make a cylinder uniform from end to end.

With a sharp knife, cut roll into 12 or 18 equal portions. Place in the 1 or 2 baking pans, cut side down.

SECOND
RISING
30–40 mins.

Cover pan(s) with waxed paper or plastic wrap and let rise until almost doubled in size, about 30 to 40 minutes.

PREHEAT

Preheat oven to 350° while rolls are rising.

BAKING
350°
35 mins.

Place in the 350° oven and bake until browned and the filling is bubbly, about 35 minutes.

FINAL STEP   Take from the oven and immediately invert onto serving platters
or baking sheet, allowing the syrup to drip from the bottom of the
pan onto the rolls.

The dripping is the secret of these successful rolls, Jerilyn explained.

GERMAN SOUR CREAM TWISTS

[THIRTY-SIX LARGE OR SEVENTY-FIVE SMALL TWISTS]

Rich with sour cream, butter, and eggs, this crispy, flaky, sugar-crusted
delicacy can be made any size, large for breakfast or small one-bite
pieces for a buffet or tea service.

INGREDIENTS   *3½ to 4 cups all-purpose flour, approximately*
1 teaspoon salt
1 package yeast
1 cup sour cream, room temperature
1 egg, room temperature
2 egg yolks, room temperature
½ cup (1 stick) butter, room temperature
½ cup margarine or other solid shortening
1 teaspoon vanilla
1 cup sugar, to coat twists

BAKING   Depending on size of oven: 1 large baking sheet, or 1 or 2 small
SHEET   pans, lightly greased or lined with parchment paper.

BY HAND   *Note:* This is a dough rich in fat and easy to work, but it will not
OR MIXER   be as elastic as other yeast doughs. It will rise and become puffy
8 mins.   nevertheless.

Measure 2 cups of flour into a mixing or mixer bowl and add
salt and yeast. Stir to blend. In a saucepan, heat to lukewarm and
stir together the sour cream, egg, egg yolks, butter, and shortening.
Add the vanilla.

If by hand, form a well in the flour and pour in the liquid to make a thick batter. Beat vigorously with a wooden spoon. Add remaining flour, ¼ cup at a time, to form a rough shaggy mass that can be lifted to the work surface to knead.

If in the mixer, attach the flat beater, turn to medium speed, and pour in the liquid. Beat for 2 minutes. Attach the dough hook. Add flour, ¼ cup at a time, to create a dough that is soft and forms around the dough hook as it revolves.

Note: The dough will be quite buttery and be filmed with considerable oil. Light sprinkles of flour will keep it manageable.

KNEADING
5 mins.

If by hand, begin to work with a dough blade, spatula, or putty knife — turning and folding the dough. Then use the hands. Knead for 5 minutes.

If under the hook, knead for 5 minutes. Add sprinkles of flour if the dough is wet with oil.

BY PROCESSOR
5 mins.

Attach plastic dough blade.

Measure 2½ cups of flour into the work bowl and add the salt and yeast. Pulse. Prepare the sour cream, egg, egg yolks, butter, shortening, and vanilla as above.

With the machine running, pour the lukewarm liquid through the feed tube to form a thick batter. Add the remaining flour, ¼ cup at a time, until a rough ball of dough forms and rides with the blade. The dough will clean the bowl as it spins.

KNEAD
30 secs.

Process the dough to knead for 30 seconds.

FIRST RISING
1½ hours

Note: The dough is so buttery that there is no need to grease the bowl beforehand.

Place the dough in the bowl, cover with plastic wrap, and set aside to double in bulk, about 1½ hours.

SHAPING
10 mins.

Remove the dough from the bowl and form into a ball. Liberally sprinkle sugar on the work surface and on the ball of dough. Roll out the dough to 16″ x 8″, occasionally sprinkling on sugar. Fold the dough in half lengthwise and then into quarters. Roll out the dough again into a rectangle 16" x 8" x ½". Sprinkle liberally with sugar.

Rather than use the rolling pin, I often press and shape the dough under the palms of the hands.

The twists may be made large or small. With a pizza cutter or knife held against a yardstick, cut the rectangle into lengths — 1" wide for the large twist, and ½" for the smaller ones. Cut each strip into 4" or 3" pieces.

Twist each piece and place 1 inch apart on the prepared baking sheet. If the pieces resist twisting, let them rest for a few minutes and twist again.

SECOND RISING 1 hour	Cover the twists with parchment or waxed paper and set aside to become puffy and raised, about 1 hour.
PREHEAT	Preheat oven to 375° about 20 minutes before the bake period.
BAKING 375° 25 mins.	Uncover the twists and sprinkle liberally with sugar. Place in the oven and bake until lightly browned, about 25 minutes.
FINAL STEP	Immediately lift the twists from the baking sheet with a spatula — otherwise, the sugared bottoms will stick and never part from the pan in whole pieces. Place on a metal rack to cool.

BOLILLOS
(Mexican Rolls)

[ABOUT SIXTEEN ROLLS]

Bolillos, crisp-crusted rolls split on top and tapered at both ends, are among the most popular wheat breads in Mexico. They're much like French bread rolls, though not as light.

A shallow pan of water in the oven plus a water-filled atomizer keeps the breads in a cloud of steam during the early stages of oven-spring when the dough first begins to rise. This allows the rolls to develop and expand fully before a crisp crust forms.

INGREDIENTS

2 cups water
1 tablespoon sugar
2 teaspoons salt
2 tablespoons butter or margarine
1 package dry yeast
3½ cups bread flour, approximately

BAKING SHEET

Depending on the size of your oven, one 14"-x-18" baking sheet, greased or Teflon, may be sufficient. Shallow pan or the oven's roasting pan. Atomizer to spray water into hot oven.

BY HAND
OR MIXER
18 mins.

Combine water, sugar, salt, and butter in a small saucepan and warm over low heat, stirring to melt butter. Pour into a mixing or mixer bowl, stir in yeast until dissolved. Add 2 cups of flour and beat 100 strokes by hand or 2 minutes with the flat beater blade to make a light batter. Gradually beat in additional flour, ½ cup at a time, to make a stiff dough.

KNEADING
8 mins.

Knead the dough by hand or with the mixer dough hook for about 8 minutes. Add sprinkles of flour if the dough gets sticky. To test the elasticity of the dough, place the ball of dough on the work surface. If it slumps and does not hold its shape, it needs flour. Or slap your palm down against the dough. If your hand makes an impression but does not stick, it has enough flour. Or if it feels like a baby's bottom.

BY PROCESSOR
5 mins.

Attach steel blade.
    Heat ingredients in saucepan, as above. Stir in yeast. Set aside for the moment. Place 2 cups of flour in the processor work bowl and, with the machine running, pour the liquid through the feed tube.
    Add remaining flour, ¼ cup at a time, until a rough mass is formed that cleans the sides of the bowl and whirls with the blade.

KNEADING 1 min.	Process to knead for 1 minute.

SHAPING 10 mins.	Punch down dough and divide into 16 pieces of equal size — about 2 ounces each. An easy way to do this is to roll the dough under the palms into a 16" cylinder. With a yardstick or ruler, mark off the dough and cut with a sharp knife into 16 pieces. Form each into a tight, smooth ball. Shape into an oblong by rolling and gently pulling from the center to the ends until it is 4" to 5" long — the center thicker than the ends. If the dough pulls back, allow it to relax for a minute or two. Place the rolls 3" apart on the prepared baking sheet.

SECOND RISING 45 mins.	Cover *bolillos* with parchment or waxed paper and put aside to rise to almost double in volume, about 45 minutes.

PREHEAT 400°	Before turning on the oven to preheat to 400°, place a shallow pan — a roasting or broiler pan will do fine — on the bottom of the oven or the first rack. Later, it will hold water for steam.

BAKING 400° 30–40 mins.	Five minutes before putting the rolls in the oven, pour $\frac{1}{2}$ glass of water into the heated pan, and do so with care. The resulting rush and splatter of steam can hurt. I use a small, long-handled saucepan to reach into the oven. At the same time, fill the atomizer with hot water. With a razor blade or a very sharp knife, slash each roll about $\frac{1}{2}$" deep and about 3" long in the top.

Place them on the middle shelf of the 400° oven.

Two minutes later, spray the interior of the oven lightly with the atomizer. Do this a second time 5 minutes later, before the crust begins to brown. The tray of water should be empty by this time — no more spraying — to allow the crust to crisp.

Midway in the bake period and again near the end of it, turn the baking pan around, front to back, to equalize the thrust of the heat. Bake for 35 to 40 minutes or until they are a golden brown. Turn over one roll and tap the bottom crust with a forefinger. A hard, hollow sound means the roll is baked. If not, return to the oven for an additional 5 to 10 minutes.

FINAL STEP   Cool on a metal rack. *Bolillos* will keep well for 2 or 3 days before they lose their crispness. Reheat before serving. They can be kept frozen at 0° for several months.

BUTTERY BATTER PAN ROLLS

[ONE DOZEN ROLLS]

Melted butter is beaten into the dough. Melted butter is spread over the bottom of the baking pan or muffin cups. Melted butter is drizzled over the dough.

Buttery, perhaps sinfully so, but no need to eat the whole pan at one sitting. Share them, though after one bite that may become difficult to do. Margarine may be used rather than butter, but it will not be as rich.

INGREDIENTS   *3 cups all-purpose flour, approximately*
2 packages dry yeast
1 teaspoon salt
2 tablespoons sugar
¼ cup nonfat dry milk
1¼ cups warm water (105°-115°)
1 egg
1 stick (8 tablespoons) butter, or margarine, melted

BAKING PAN   One 9″-x-9″ baking pan, or muffin tins for a dozen.

BY HAND   In a large bowl or mixer bowl, measure 2 cups of flour and add
OR MIXER   dry ingredients—yeast, salt, sugar, and dry milk. Stir in warm
15 mins.   water, egg, and 4 tablespoons of melted butter and beat 150 strong strokes with a wooden spoon or 2 minutes under the mixer flat blade. Gradually beat in additional flour, ¼ cup at a time, to make a smooth batter. Be careful not to add so much flour that the batter becomes dough.

BY PROCESSOR   Use steel blade.
5 mins.   Measure 1½ cups of flour into the work bowl and add the 4
dry ingredients. Pulse to blend. Pour in the warm water. Pulse.
Remove cover and add the egg and 4 tablespoons melted butter.
With the machine running, add the flour, ¼ cup at a time, to
make a smooth batter.

FIRST RISING   Cover with plastic wrap and put aside to rise in a warm place
1 hour   until doubled in volume, about 1 hour.

SHAPING   This is a thick, tenacious batter—beyond pouring—that usually
10 mins.   requires a tablespoon in one hand and a spatula in the other to
lift and place a spoonful of dough.
                   Baking pan: Pour half of the remaining butter into the pan,
tilting it side to side to coat the bottom. Beat down the batter and
drop spoonfuls to make 12 rolls. Drizzle the remaining melted
butter over the dough.
                   Muffin tin: Spoon about 1 teaspoon melted butter into each
muffin cup. Fill three-quarters with batter. Drizzle each with
butter.

SECOND   Let rise in a warm place until almost doubled, about 30 minutes.
RISING
30 mins.

PREHEAT   Twenty minutes before baking, preheat oven to 425°.

BAKING   Place baking sheet or muffin pan on middle shelf of the 425°
425°   oven. Bake for 18 to 20 minutes until a rich golden brown.
18–20 mins.

FINAL STEP   Ideally, serve warm from the oven. No need to pass the butter.
                   Equally good reheated. Can be frozen at 0° for months.

HEDGEHOG ROLLS

[SIXTEEN ROLLS]

There is no more wonderful place to find this baked delight for children — the "hedgehog" roll — than in the great food halls at Harrods, London's famous department store. This is its recipe for the storied little creature of so many English tales, here made with currant eyes and crusty spines. For grown-ups, too.

INGREDIENTS	*5 cups bread flour, approximately*
	2 packages dry yeast
	1½ teaspoons salt
	2 tablespoons sugar
	1 teaspoon nutmeg, freshly grated
	¾ cup nonfat dry milk
	2 cups water, tepid
	1 egg, room temperature
	2 tablespoons butter or margarine, room temperature
	48 currants
	1 egg and 1 tablespoon cream or milk, lightly beaten, to glaze
BAKING SHEET	One or 2 baking sheets, depending on oven size, buttered or Teflon. Hedgehogs need space to grow, so provide ample room on the pan.
SPECIAL EQUIPMENT	Pair of sharp, pointed scissors to snip hedgehog spines.

BY HAND
OR MIXER
12–15 mins.

Measure 2 cups of flour into a large bowl or mixer bowl and add dry ingredients — yeast, salt, sugar, nutmeg, and dry milk. Stir in the 2 cups of water. Add egg and butter or margarine. Beat vigorously 100 strokes with wooden spoon or 2 minutes with beater flat blade. Add remaining flour, $1/4$ cup at a time, to bowl and continue beating to form a dough mass that can be lifted from the bowl and placed on the work surface to knead.

Replace beater blade with dough hook and add flour if needed to form a mass that forms around the hook and cleans the sides of the mixer bowl.

KNEADING
6–8 mins.

Knead by hand or dough blade for 6 to 8 minutes or until the dough is smooth and elastic. Properly kneaded, the dough will stretch between the hands 6″ to 8″ before tearing.

BY PROCESSOR
8 mins.

Insert short plastic blade.

Place 3 cups of flour in the work bowl and measure in the dry ingredients. Pulse. Measure in the water, egg, and butter or margarine through the feed tube. Turn on the processor. (Initially, the short blade may not pull all of the ingredients from around the edges. If it does not, open cover and scrape in with a rubber spatula.) Add remaining flour, $1/4$ cup at a time, to form a mass that cleans the bowl and rides the blade.

KNEADING
1 min.

Knead with the processor running for 1 minute. If the dough sticks to the sides of the machine, add sprinkles of flour through the feed tube. Turn the dough from the work bowl into a greased bowl to rise.

FIRST RISING
45–50 mins.

Cover bowl with plastic wrap and put aside to double in volume, about 45 to 50 minutes in a 70° kitchen.

SHAPING
20 mins.

Under the palms, roll the dough into a long cylinder and cut into 16 even-sized pieces. A convenient way to do this is to mark off the pieces with a yardstick or ruler alongside.

Shape each into a ball and put aside to relax the dough as you roll the other pieces. Shape into an oval. Press one end slightly flat, then pinch in the sides to make the hedgehog face. Place the roll on the baking sheet. Glaze with the egg-milk wash. With the face *away from you*, snip the dough with scissors, held at a 45° angle, about ½" deep in a random pattern over the body to make spines. Dip the scissors in water frequently so the points don't stick to the glaze. Press two currants on the face to make the eyes, and one for the nose.

PREHEAT   Preheat oven to 425°.

REST   Cover hedgehogs with a length of waxed paper and let rest for 15
15 mins.   minutes while oven heats.

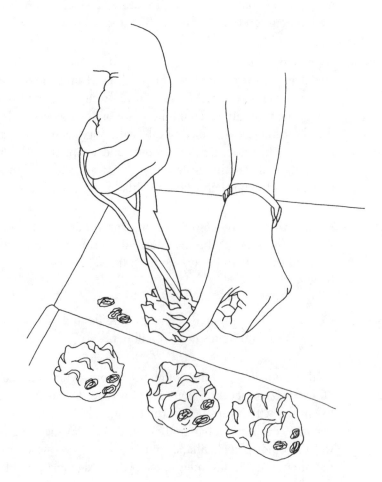

BAKE
425°
25 mins.

If the hedgehogs appear too fat or squat before putting them in the oven, gently press in their sides. Bake on the middle shelf of the hot oven. Midway through the bake period, turn the baking sheet end for end to equalize the heat on the rolls.

FINAL STEP

Collect the hedgehogs onto a metal rack to cool. Children love them warm or cold or just as companions on a study desk.

BREADSTICKS

[SIXTEEN TO TWENTY BREADSTICKS]

Breadsticks can be long or short, slender or chubby, flavored with salt or cheese or seeds or nothing at all. They can be crunchy and crisp on the outside while soft-textured on the inside. They don't have to be pencil-straight to be good. An S curve here and there adds charm. Try a small knot at one end or a hook in the other, or a squiggle in the middle. The long breadsticks — 16″ to 20″ — add a sense of adventure to a simple spaghetti dinner. Twelve-inch sticks served with butter are a delicious accompaniment to an apéritif. Salty ones go great with a schooner of brew.

Make them as long and as spindly as you wish. The skinnier they are and the longer they remain in the oven, the crispier they will be.

INGREDIENTS

3½ cups all-purpose flour, approximately
1 tablespoon sugar
2 teaspoons salt
2 packages dry yeast
¼ cup olive oil (plus extra to brush baking sheet and sticks)
1¼ cups hot water (120°–130°)
1 egg white beaten with 1 tablespoon water, to brush
Kosher salt, sesame seeds, poppy seeds, or others of choice

BAKING SHEET

One large 14″-x-18″ baking sheet or 2 smaller ones, depending on oven size. Brush the sheets with oil.

BY HAND
OR MIXER
10 mins.

In a large bowl or electric mixer bowl, stir together 1½ cups of flour, the sugar, salt, and yeast. Add oil and then gradually stir in hot water. Beat by hand or with the mixer flat beater until the batter is smooth, about 2 minutes. Change to the dough hook. Add remaining flour ½ cup at a time to make a soft dough that can be lifted from the bowl and put on a floured work surface or, if in the mixer, the dough cleans the bowl and forms a mass around the dough hook. Add sprinkles of flour if the dough is sticky.

KNEADING
8 mins.

Knead by hand or under the dough hook to make a dough that is soft and elastic, about 8 minutes. Add sprinkles of flour if needed.

BY PROCESSOR
5 mins.

Attach the metal blade.

In the work bowl, measure 1½ cups of flour and the sugar, salt, and yeast. Pulse to blend. With the processor running, pour the olive oil and water through the feed tube. Add the balance of the flour, ¼ cup at a time, until a mass is formed that clears the sides of the bowl and rides on the blade.

KNEADING
45 secs.

With processor on, knead for 45 seconds.

REST
15 mins.

Place the dough on the floured work surface. Cover the dough with waxed paper or plastic wrap and let rest for 15 minutes.

SHAPING
15 mins.

Brush the baking sheet(s) with olive oil.

Shape the dough into a log and, with a knife, cut it into as many pieces as you want breadsticks, usually 16 to 20. Roll each piece of dough under the palms and, at the same time, pull and shape with the fingers. If the dough resists, let it rest while shaping the others.

The breadsticks can be straight or the ends formed into hooks, loops, S curves, and knots.

REST
15 mins.

Place them on the prepared baking sheet about 1″ apart and brush with oil. Let them rest uncovered for about 15 minutes.

PREHEAT

While the breadsticks are resting, preheat the oven to 375°.

BAKING
375°
45 mins.

With a soft brush, paint each stick with the egg-white wash. Sprinkle with salt or seeds or whatever of choice. Place the baking pan(s) in the oven and bake for about 45 minutes until crisp and golden. Turn the pan(s) front to back halfway through baking to ensure even browning. If 2 pans are used, switch shelves at the same time.

FINAL STEP

Cool completely on wire racks before serving or storing in airtight containers.

Breadsticks placed in plastic bags can be frozen at 0° to keep for several months.

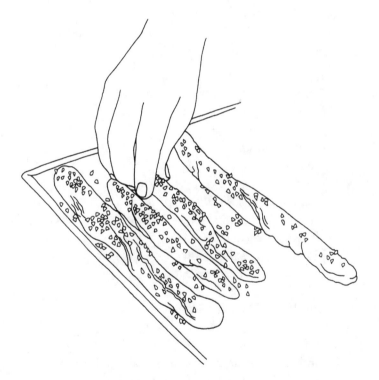

PAINS À SANDWICH
(Rye Sandwich Rolls)

[ONE DOZEN ROLLS]

Unlike rye rolls and breads made with a sponge that takes several days to develop, this French sandwich roll can be done in a day with the same good rye flavor but without the piquancy that comes with fermentation over time.

The ratio of white flour to rye is 2 to 1 to produce a less dense crumb. To bake a larger number of rolls (as for a tailgate party or a Boy Scout picnic), simply double, triple, or quadruple the amount of ingredients.

Preparation by the food processor is not included because the rye dough is too heavy for most machines.

INGREDIENTS
4 cups all-purpose flour, approximately
2 cups rye flour, stone-ground preferred
2 packages dry yeast
1 tablespoon salt
2 teaspoons caraway seeds
2 cups water
1/3 cup molasses, unsulfured preferred
3 tablespoons each melted butter and vegetable shortening
Melted butter, to brush
1 egg and 1 teaspoon water, mixed to glaze
Caraway seeds to sprinkle

BAKING SHEET   One 11″-x-17″ baking sheet.

BY HAND
OR MIXER
15 mins.
In a large mixing or mixer bowl, blend together 2 cups of white and 1 cup rye flours, the yeast, salt, and caraway seeds. Add the water and stir with a wooden spoon or mixer flat beater blade. Stir to blend in the molasses and melted shortenings. Add the remaining 1 cup of rye flour. With 200 strokes of the spoon or 2 minutes with the mixer blade, thoroughly mix together all of the ingredients added thus far. Attach the mixer dough hook.

The heavy batter will be sticky and not very responsive (rye is like that), but it will become so with additional white flour. Add the remaining white flour ¼ cup at a time until the dough forms a mass that can be lifted onto the floured work surface or under the dough hook until the dough cleans the sides of the bowl and forms around the hook.

KNEADING
8 mins.

Knead the dough by hand or in the mixer until it is smooth, about 8 minutes. If the dough is sticky, add sprinkles of flour.

FIRST RISING
2 hours

Place the dough in a buttered bowl, cover with plastic wrap, and put aside to rise at room temperature until dough has doubled in bulk, about 2 hours.

Rye dough is never as elastic as a white flour dough. Hence it takes longer to rise.

Note: At this stage, the dough can be refrigerated overnight if baking the rolls later is more convenient.

SHAPING
15 mins.
10 mins.

Turn the dough onto a floured work surface and divide into 12 equal pieces. Cover the cut pieces and let them rest for 15 minutes.

For a round bun-shaped roll, shape the dough into a ball, rolling it under the palm. Let it rest while shaping the other pieces. Flatten the ball with the palm to a thickness of ¾″ to 1″. Place on the baking sheet.

For a long roll, flatten the piece to form an oval about 6″ long and roll the oval under the palm, pinching the ends and seams closed.

SECOND
RISING
1 hour

Brush with melted butter. Cover with waxed or parchment paper. Put aside to double in size, about 1 hour.

PREHEAT

Preheat oven to 375° twenty minutes before baking.

BAKING
375°
40 mins.

Brush the rolls with the egg wash and sprinkle with caraway seeds. Place rolls on the baking sheet, allowing as much room as possible between them, or place them ½″ apart so they will be joined together when they rise in the oven. Bake about 40 minutes or until the bottom of a roll feels hard and sounds crusty when tapped with the fingertip.

FINAL STEP   Turn onto a wire rack to cool. These can be frozen for several months at 0°.

ONION ROLLS

[ABOUT SIXTEEN ROLLS]

The tantalizing aroma of onion carries from the kitchen when these crescent-shaped rolls are baking. Layered with onion flakes and poppy seeds stirred together with a small quantity of olive oil, the rolls are as delicious as their bouquet and golden brown crust suggest.

Breads enriched with onion have been popular in many cultures since ancient Egyptians gave them a mystic value. This recipe updates that popularity.

INGREDIENTS   Dough:
3½ cups bread or unbleached flour, approximately
1 package dry yeast
⅓ cup nonfat dry milk
2 teaspoons salt
1½ cups hot water (120°–130°)
1 tablespoon butter, room temperature
1 egg, room temperature

Filling:
¼ cup dried onion flakes (see Note)
¼ cup water
2 tablespoons poppy seeds
2 tablespoons olive oil (other oil may be substituted)
1 egg, lightly beaten with 1 tablespoon milk or cream, to glaze

BAKING SHEET	Two baking sheets, greased or Teflon.

BY HAND
OR MIXER
15 mins.

Place 2 cups of flour in mixing or mixer bowl and stir in yeast, dry milk, and salt. Pour in the water. Stir to a light batter and add butter and egg. Blend with 50 strong strokes with wooden spoon or 2 minutes with a flat beater blade in the mixer.

KNEADING
8 mins.

Add remaining flour, ¼ cup at a time, and work into a rough mass by spoon and hand or under the dough hook. If the dough is sticky, add sprinkles of flour. The dough will be soft and elastic. Knead for about 8 minutes.

BY PROCESSOR
5 mins.

Attach steel blade.

Measure 2 cups of flour and dry ingredients into the work bowl. Pulse to blend. With processor running, pour hot water through feed tube. Stop machine, remove the cover, and add the butter and egg. Blend with the processor on. Add remaining flour through the feed tube ¼ cup at a time, to form a rough, shaggy mass that cleans the sides of the bowl and rides on the blade.

KNEADING
1 min.

Process to knead for 1 minute. Stop the machine, uncover, and pinch the dough. If it is wet beyond stickiness, add sprinkles of flour. Turn from the bowl onto the work surface, dust lightly to prevent sticking. Knead into a ball.

FIRST RISING
1 hour

Place the dough in a greased bowl, cover with plastic wrap, and let stand at room temperature while it rises to double in bulk, about 1 hour.

In a small bowl, mix together the onion flakes and water to reconstitute the onions, about 5 minutes. Stir in the poppy seeds and olive oil to make a wet but solid mixture with no excess oil gathering on the bottom of the bowl. Set aside.

SHAPING
30 mins.

Roll the dough into a cylinder 16″ long, and with a knife or dough blade divide into 16 equal parts—by measurement or weight. Shape each piece into a tight, compact ball between the cupped palm and work surface or between the palms. Press hard! Light sprinkles of flour if sticky.

Cover the balls with plastic wrap or waxed paper to rest for 15 minutes.

Flatten the first ball under the palm and, with a rolling pin in hand, roll into an oval — 6″ in length by about 4″ at its widest, and no more than ¼″ thick. With the fingers of one hand, stretch the dough slightly as you roll. If the dough resists and pulls back, put it aside for a moment to relax and move to the next piece.

When the oval is rolled thin, spread a heaping tablespoon of the onion mixture not quite to the edges of the dough. Press the mixture into the dough with the tines of a fork.

With the fingers, roll the dough from the bottom to the top, stretching the dough as it is rolled. The center will be thicker and taper evenly to each side. Press the end against the roll to seal it.

SECOND
RISING
40 mins.

Shape each into a crescent and place on the baking sheet 1″ apart. Cover with waxed paper or a cloth and let rise until almost double in volume — about 40 minutes.

PREHEAT

Preheat the oven to 375°.

BAKING
375°
20–25 mins.

Brush the tops with the egg glaze and bake for about 20 to 25 minutes or until golden brown on top. The underside should be nicely browned as well.

FINAL STEP

Place on a metal rack to cool.

Note: One and a half cups peeled fresh onions, chopped or finely grated and sautéed until soft and translucent, may be used instead of onion flakes and water.

KOULOÚRIA
(Greek Sesame Seed Rings)

[MAKES TWELVE TO FOURTEEN RINGS]

Kouloúria, golden rings covered thickly with sesame seeds, are sold in Greece by street vendors and in bakeshops across the country. Similar in texture to a soft pretzel, the ingredients are few but rich with flavor. The dough is unleavened except for the action of the beaten eggs, so it is not put aside to rise but goes directly into the oven.

INGREDIENTS
¹/₃ cup sesame seeds, to be toasted
3¹/₂ cups all-purpose flour, approximately
1 teaspoon salt
4 eggs (reserve 1 for glaze)
¹/₄ cup olive oil
¹/₄ cup water

BAKING SHEET
One baking sheet, greased or Teflon.

BEFOREHAND
Toast the sesame seeds in a skillet until they turn brown and you can hear them snap, crackle, and pop. Some may wish to leap out of the skillet, so choose one with high sides. Or use the oven, see below.

PREHEAT
Preheat the oven to 375°. You may wish to toast the sesame seeds in the oven during this period, for about 15 minutes. Don't let them burn. Stir or shake them occasionally.

BY HAND
OR MIXER
15 mins.
Measure 2 cups of flour into a large bowl or mixer bowl, and add salt. In a small bowl, briskly beat 3 eggs with a fork or whisk to light yellow and then stir in olive oil and water.

Pour the egg mixture into the flour and beat with a wooden spoon or mixer flat beater blade for 2 minutes. Add remaining flour ¹/₄ cup at a time to form a dough that can be lifted from the bowl to a floured work surface or, if in the mixer, attach the dough hook. If the dough continues wet and sticky, add sprinkles of flour.

KNEADING
6–8 mins.

Knead by hand or under the dough hook for 6 to 8 minutes until the dough is elastic and smooth.

BY PROCESSOR
5 mins.

Attach the steel blade.

Measure 2½ cups of flour and salt into the work bowl. In a small bowl, mix together the eggs, olive oil, and water, as above. With the processor on, pour mixture through the feed tube. Add remaining flour, a small amount at a time, to form a mass that will clean the sides of the bowl and ride the blade.

KNEADING
45 secs.

Knead for 45 seconds. If the ball of dough should stick to the sides, add several teaspoons of flour. When finished, place the dough on a floured work surface.

SHAPING
20 mins.

Allow the dough to rest for 10 minutes before rolling a length under the palms to be cut into 12 to 14 equal pieces. Again allow the dough to rest a few minutes. Roll each piece into a rope about ½" thick. Bend the length into a ring. Pinch the ends together and place on the baking sheet. Continue with the others.

Rather than make tight, plump rings, I often shape the pieces into horseshoes. Equally good to eat.

Beat the remaining egg and glaze each ring or horseshoe. Sprinkle generously with the sesame seeds.

BAKING
375°
25–30 mins.

Place baking sheet in the middle shelf of the oven. Bake until golden brown, about 25 to 30 minutes.

FINAL STEP

Cool on a metal rack.

Take a bite and be transported, *kouloúria* in hand, to Athens, about to step aboard the funicular to the top of Lycabettus Hill.

KAISER ROLLS

[TWELVE ROLLS]

Two things in particular are needed to make the classic kaiser roll. The first is egg and egg white among the ingredients for color, taste, and texture. The second is a hot but moist oven — steam from a pan under the rolls, or a spray into the oven from a water-filled atomizer.

While kaiser rolls sold in retail stores across the country are uniformly stamped out in the five-petal-blossom shape by a machine, the kaiser in the kitchen will likely have a home-crafted appearance but, properly formed or not, the rolls are tender-crusty and delicious. Dusting with rye flour as the rolls are being shaped will keep the "petals" separated rather than melding into one piece.

While not traditional, another way to give the bun its five-petal design is to make curved cuts radiating from the center with a razor blade, *lame*, or a very sharp knife.

Poppy seeds, onion, and salt encrusted on the top of the kaiser is traditional.

INGREDIENTS

3½ cups bread or unbleached flour, approximately
1 package dry yeast
2 teaspoons sugar
2 teaspoons salt
1 cup hot water (120°–130°)
½ teaspoon malt extract, if available
1 egg
1 egg white
1 tablespoon vegetable shortening
Rye flour, for dusting
Poppy seeds, about ⅓ cup to sprinkle on baking sheet

BAKING SHEET

One baking sheet, greased or lined with parchment paper. Pan for water. Atomizer to spray oven interior.

BY HAND
OR MIXER
8 mins.

Measure 1 cup of flour into a mixing or mixer bowl and add the yeast, sugar, and salt. Stir to blend well. Pour in the hot water and malt extract. Mix for 1 minute with wooden spoon or mixer flat beater until a smooth but heavy batter results.

Add the egg, egg white, and shortening. Beat together until the mixture is smooth. If with the electric mixer, remove flat beater and continue with dough hook. Add remaining flour, ¼ cup at a time, until the dough is a solid but soft mass that can be lifted from the bowl — or left under the dough hook.

KNEADING
10 mins.

Knead the dough with a strong push-turn-fold motion, adding liberal sprinkles of flour if the dough is wet. If in the mixer, the dough will clean the sides of the bowl and form a ball around the dough hook. If, however, it continues to cling to the sides, add sprinkles of flour. The dough should be firm.

BY PROCESSOR
4 mins.

Measure 2 cups of flour into the work bowl and add the yeast, sugar, and salt. Pulse to blend. With the machine running, pour the hot water and malt extract through the feed tube. The dough will be a thick batter. Drop in the egg, egg white, and shortening. Pulse 7 or 8 times to blend completely. Add remaining flour, 1 tablespoon at a time, until the dough forms a ball and rides the blade. If dough is wet and sticks to the sides of the bowl, add flour by the tablespoon, with the machine running.

KNEADING
60 secs.

When the dough cleans the sides of the bowl, knead for 60 seconds. Uncover the bowl; pinch the dough to determine if it is soft but firm when kneading is completed.

FIRST RISING
1 hour

Place the dough in a greased bowl, cover tightly with plastic wrap, and set aside to double in bulk, about 1 hour.

SECOND
RISING
45 mins.

Uncover the bowl and punch down the dough with the fingers. Re-cover bowl and allow to double in volume again, about 45 minutes.

SHAPING
15 mins.

Place the dough on a floured work surface and roll it into a long cylinder. With a sharp knife, cut 12 pieces from the length.

Shape the pieces under a cupped palm into smooth rounds. Allow to relax for 5 minutes.

Flatten each roll with the hand and rolling pin to about ⅜" thick. Dust lightly with rye flour.

FOLDING
15 mins.

If using the traditional way to make the classic kaiser, place your thumb in the center of the piece of flattened dough. With the forefinger (or fingers of the other hand), lift up a section equal to about one-fifth of the dough — fold the portion over your thumb. With the side of the hand, hit the dough against your thumb firmly. Move your thumb clockwise. Pick up the second piece and repeat this action.

Repeat for a total of 5 times, but don't hit the last section, twist it into the center where your thumb was.

The entire procedure may be viewed as assembling the spokes of a wheel.

CUTTING

If using an alternative way, make 5 deep circular cuts from the center of each bun with a razor blade, *lame*, or a sharp knife. The dough should be firm to resist tearing.

Sprinkle the baking sheet liberally with poppy seeds. As each roll is shaped, place it *facedown* on the sheet. Yes, facedown.

THIRD RISING
40 mins.

Cover the rolls with a length of waxed or parchment paper, and leave at room temperature to rise — to slightly less than double in size, about 40 minutes.

PREHEAT

In the meantime, prepare the oven by placing a pan under the shelf. Twenty minutes before the bake period, preheat oven to 400°. Five minutes before the rolls are to go into the oven, pour ½ cup of hot water in the pan to form steam and provide a moist environment for the rolls.

BAKING
400°
25 mins.

Be certain hot water is in the pan. Uncover the rolls, turn them right side up.

Place the rolls on the middle shelf of the hot oven. Two minutes later, lightly spray the interior of the oven — not directly on the rolls. Repeat once more early in the bake period, but not after the rolls begin to brown.

Midway through the bake period, turn the sheet around so that the rolls are exposed equally to temperature variations in the oven. They are done when crispy brown and hard to the tap of a finger.

FINAL STEP   Remove the rolls from the oven. If, after the rolls have cooled, they are not as crisp and crusty as you like, put them back into a hot oven for 10 minutes. Do the same later for reheating the rolls.

Serve warm. These are delicious just spread with butter.

Scones, Crumpets, Baps, and Friends

THIS chapter is a medley of the best of English and Scottish small breads, as well as a *pogácsa* from Hungary, a *petit pain à la crème* from France, and a cream scone from the Rock Hill Bakehouse in Upstate New York.

THE SCONE AND BANNOCK

The Scottish scone and bannock are simply made and are seldom embellished with more than raisins or currants or, occasionally, caraway seeds. In modern usage, the bannock is the large round scone, about the circumference of a dinner plate. When the bannock is cut into wedges before being baked, or when the dough is cut into small rounds, you have scones.

In the United States, the scone has grown apart from its Scottish cousin, just as the U.S. croissant, stuffed with everything considered edible, has grown away from the original and plain unadorned French croissant. In this country, anything seems to go for the scone. Walnut, whole wheat, Cheddar and dill, blueberry, chocolate chip, and cheese are just a few of the flavors.

In his delightful and highly informative *The Afternoon Tea Book*, Michael Smith has laid down guidelines for success in baking and eating scones:

- Preheat both the oven and the baking sheet or griddle.
- Handle the dough very gently, especially when kneading.
- Don't twist the cutter when stamping out the scones or they will bake lopsided.
- Scones are best eaten brought straight from the oven and certainly within an hour of baking. However, they do well frozen and reheated.
- Leftover scones are excellent when split and toasted.

Smith writes: "You must present your guest with half slices of scones already buttered. The jam is added with the tip of a tea knife in small amounts as you go along and not spread over the whole surface in a manner considered inelegant in those circles where people know about such manners as tea-table etiquette."

MRS. MACNAB'S SCONES

[SIXTEEN SMALL SCONES]

King Frederick of Prussia rode often from Balmoral Castle, Scotland, where he was a guest, to relish the small tea cakes baked by Mrs. Macnab, near Ballater. While it is not possible to impart her lightness of touch, Mrs. Macnab's recipe in other hands does produce a delicious scone, white and soft on the inside, brown and crisp on the outside.

INGREDIENTS

2 cups all-purpose flour, approximately
1 teaspoon each salt and baking soda
2 teaspoons cream of tartar
3 tablespoons butter, room temperature
1 egg, room temperature and lightly beaten
½ cup buttermilk, room temperature
½ cup currants or raisins (more if you wish)

BAKING SHEET

One baking sheet, greased or Teflon.

PREHEAT

Preheat the oven to 375°.

BY HAND
OR MIXER
10 mins.

Measure the flour, salt, baking soda, and cream of tartar into a mixing or mixer bowl. Stir with a wooden spoon or with the mixer flat beater. With the fingers or with the flat beater, rub the butter into the dry ingredients.

In a small bowl, stir together the egg and buttermilk. Pour the liquid gradually into the flour. If it is too moist and sticks to the hands or flat beater, add sprinkles of flour. Stir in the currants. If the mass is too thick, it may be necessary to attach the dough hook.

KNEADING
2 mins.
or less

If by hand, turn the dough onto a lightly floured work surface, but knead and work as little as possible to achieve a soft, pliable ball. If under the dough hook, knead at low speed for no more than 2 minutes.

PROCESSING
2 mins.

Note: The food processor works almost too fast for this recipe since it may knead the dough too much before it can be turned off. But try it.

Attach the steel blade.

Measure the flour and dry ingredients into the work bowl. Pulse to blend. Drop in the butter and cut into the flour with several pulses. With the machine running, pour the egg-buttermilk mixture through the feed tube. At the moment it has been absorbed, stop the machine.

Turn dough onto the floured work surface and work in the currants with a kneading action. Add sprinkles of flour if the mass is sticky.

SHAPING
10 mins.

Divide the dough into 4 equal parts. Flatten each with the knuckles, not the rolling pin, into a round disk, about 6″ in diameter and ½″ thick. Prick each a dozen times with the tines of a fork. With the moist edge of a kitchen knife, cut into quarters. Lift each onto the baking sheet.

BAKING
375°
15 mins.

Bake in the moderate oven until they are a lovely tan. Don't scorch.

FINAL STEP

Remove scones from the oven. Serve while hot at breakfast, tea, or brunch. I have frozen these, but they are much better freshly prepared.

LONDON'S CREAM SCONES

[ONE DOZEN SCONES]

The London of the recipe title is not the city but Wendy London, who, with her husband, Michael, are two of the most accomplished bakers in the country. He is the master of big and hearty loaves of French and sourdough breads; she, the more delicate breads and pastries, including this cream scone. They began all of this in the Rock Hill Bakehouse, which actually is the kitchen-porch of a 200-year-old redbrick farmhouse near the small town of Greenwich in upstate New York. Their fame has spread and so have a number of bakeries across the country who are baking "the London way."

This is one of the finest breads in the Londons' bakehouse. It is tender, soft, and rich. *Very* rich. Start with thick cream (almost a cup), add milk, ½ cup of sugar, 2 sticks of butter, and speckle with currants. Unlike dough for other scones, this dough is chilled before cutting and then returned to the refrigerator for at least 2 hours or overnight to relax.

To give these scones the touch of elegance they deserve, cut them from the dough with a fluted cutter that is a favorite of pastry makers.

Razor-sharp, the crinkle-cutter cuts cleanly without smearing the dough and leaves a handsome scalloped edge. They are equally good, of course, cut with ordinary biscuit or cookie cutters.

INGREDIENTS

2 cups all-purpose flour, approximately
½ cup cake flour (Softasilk is a good choice)
½ cup sugar
2 teaspoons salt, preferably sea salt
1 tablespoon baking powder
2 sticks butter, chilled
¾ cup heavy cream, chilled
¼ cup milk, chilled
¾ cup currants
1 egg beaten with 1 teaspoon cream, to glaze

BAKING
SHEET

One baking sheet, greased or Teflon. Pastry blender.

BY HAND
OR MIXER
15 mins.

In a large bowl, mix the dry ingredients together by hand or in the mixer bowl with the flat beater blade. Cut the chilled butter into small ½" cubes and drop them into the flour one at a time. By hand, use a pastry blender to chop the butter into small pieces resembling crumbs or coarse meal. In the mixer, set at slow speed to reduce the butter to crumbs. Don't overmix or it will turn into a dough. It must remain dry.

Add cold cream, milk, and currants. Mix until the dough cleans the bowl and is well blended. Do not knead. Mix only as for pie dough. Turn out onto the floured work surface. If the mix is still cold, thanks to the chilled ingredients, it can be rolled and cut right away. If not, and the dough has become sticky, cover with plastic wrap and place in the refrigerator for 1 hour. Push and shape the dough into a smooth, solid mass, adding sprinkles of flour to control the stickiness.

BY PROCESSOR
15 mins.

Insert metal blade.

The mixture must be done in quick, short bursts to keep the particles intact, *not* blended into a solid mass.

Measure the dry ingredients into the work bowl. Pulse to blend.

Uncover the bowl. With sharp knife, cut the 2 sticks of butter into cubes and scatter them over the flour. Cover the bowl and pulse to cut the butter into small particles like bread crumbs. Pour the liquid through the feeder tube, at the same time pulsing the processor. Stop the machine immediately when the dough forms a ball and cleans the sides of the bowl. Do not knead. The dough will be soft and quite moist when it is removed from the work bowl. Add sprinkles of flour if necessary to make it easier to work. Place the dough on the floured work surface. Spread the currants over the dough and work them into it by hand, otherwise the whirling blade would cut the currants into tiny black bits.

SHAPING
10 mins.

With a rolling pin or by hand, flatten the dough into a sheet 1″ thick. Use a ruler to check the thickness to keep the scones uniform.

Dip the cutter in flour and cut out the scones. Place on the baking sheet. Work the scraps together and roll flat and cut. Brush the scones with the wash. Cover the baking sheet tightly with plastic wrap or place it in a plastic bag and refrigerate for 1 or 2 hours or overnight until the dough has relaxed.

PREHEAT

Preheat oven to 400°.

BAKING
400°
20–25 mins.

Lightly brush each scone again with egg glaze. Place the baking sheet on the middle shelf of the oven and bake to light golden in color, about 25 minutes. To test, gently open one to be certain it has properly baked. Check the bottom, which should be a deep brown.

FINAL STEP

Treat the scones gently when they first come from the oven, for they are fragile when hot. Place them on a metal rack to cool. Scones keep nicely for a day or so. Freeze if for a longer period, then thaw and reheat.

Serve with butter and jam or eat plain as is. Delicious.

SOUR SKONS

[ONE LARGE SCONE TO SERVE EIGHT]

The base for this delicious caraway-flavored *skon* from the Orkney Islands, north of the Scottish mainland, is a cupful of oatmeal soaked in buttermilk for 2 or 3 days.

I copied down the spare 2-sentence recipe in a Scottish kitchen: "Soak up some oatmeal in buttermilk for a few days, then take it and beat it up with flour into which you have stirred a little baking soda, sugar to taste (don't over-sweeten), and a few caraway seeds." The second sentence said: "Lay it on the griddle." End of recipe.

I have made this *skon* with currants rather than caraway seed. Equally delicious.

INGREDIENTS	*1 cup oatmeal*
	1 cup buttermilk
	1 teaspoon each *sugar and baking soda*
	¹/₂ teaspoon each *salt and caraway seeds*
	1¹/₄ cups all-purpose flour
GRIDDLE OR BAKING SHEET	Heavy griddle or baking sheet, ungreased.
PREPARATION 2–3 days	Two or 3 days beforehand, measure oatmeal into a small bowl and stir in buttermilk. Cover with plastic wrap and set aside to soak. Stir once each day.
BY HAND OR MIXER 5 mins.	On bake day, stir down the soaked oatmeal. In a separate mixing or mixer bowl, stir together the sugar, baking soda, salt, caraway seeds, and flour.
	Pour the wet mixture into the dry ingredients. Blend by hand or with the flat beater until the oatmeal is absorbed into the flour. The dough should be firm enough to lift from the bowl. If it is wet, add sprinkles of flour. If dry, add a teaspoon or two more buttermilk.
PROCESSING 5 mins.	Attach the steel blade.
	Note: The dough is only to be mixed thoroughly, not kneaded at length — so pulse the processor sparingly.

Measure all of the dry ingredients into the bowl. Pulse to blend. Drop large tablespoons of the oatmeal mixture through the feed tube, pulsing after each addition. When the mixture has been absorbed by the flour, stop the processor and feel the dough. If wet, add flour. When turned from the work bowl, it will be slightly sticky, so dust with flour.

SHAPING
5 mins.

Pat the dough into a circular loaf, about 8″ in diameter and ¾″ thick.

GRIDDLE

While the dough is resting, heat the griddle.

BAKING
Hot
30 mins.

Test the griddle with a sprinkle of flour. If the flour turns a deep brown within 10 seconds the griddle is ready for the scone. Lay the scone on the griddle and, with a knife, score the top into 8 pie-shaped pieces, cutting lightly into the dough, no more than ¼″ deep.

Bake for 5 minutes and turn to bake 5 minutes on the other side. Reduce the heat to medium and bake 30 minutes. During the bake period, turn the scone every 10 minutes. Insert a wooden toothpick into the scone to test for doneness. When it comes out clean and dry, the scone is done. If moist particles stick to the probe, leave on the griddle for another 10 minutes and test again.

OVEN
425°
30 mins.

The scone can be baked in the oven. Arrange scone on the baking sheet, score as above, and place in the oven until it tests done, about 30 minutes.

FINAL STEP

Lift the scone off the griddle with a spatula. Place on the metal rack to cool somewhat before serving. Break along the scored lines, and serve.

CHERRY-STUDDED SCONES

[ONE NINE-INCH BANNOCK, TO BE DIVIDED INTO SIX OR EIGHT WEDGES]

To a Scot, this scone, because of its size, would be a bannock, but when it is cut into wedges, the wedges become scones. The dark sweet cherry, meaty and moist, is ideal for this two-layered scone, with the fruit sandwiched between.

INGREDIENTS

³/₄ cup sweet cherries, pitted and finely chopped
¹/₄ cup all-purpose flour
¹/₂ cup whole-wheat flour
2 tablespoons sugar
3 teaspoons baking powder
¹/₂ teaspoon salt
¹/₂ teaspoon cinnamon
¹/₃ cup vegetable shortening, or butter, or margarine, chilled
¹/₂ cup buttermilk
2 eggs

BAKING SHEET

Baking sheet, sprinkled lightly with flour.

PREPARATION
5 mins.

Wash, pit, and finely chop sweet cherries sufficient to make ³/₄ cup. One pulse in a food processor does it nicely.

PREHEAT

Preheat oven to 400°.

BY HAND
8 mins.

In a large bowl, mix the white and whole-wheat flours, sugar, baking powder, salt, and cinnamon. Cut the shortening into the flours with a pastry blender or fork until rice-size.

In a small bowl, stir together the buttermilk and 1 egg (the other egg will be used for glaze). Add all at once to the dry ingredients. Stir together just long enough to moisten. The less stirring and mixing, the better.

PROCESSOR
5 secs.

Attach the steel blade.

Process the dry ingredients and shortening until coarsely crumbled, about 5 seconds.

Proceed as above.

SHAPING
5 mins.

Divide the dough in half. Pat one piece into a 9″ circle on the lightly floured baking sheet. Spread the chopped cherries evenly over the top. Shape the second piece and, with care, lift and cover the cherries. Press down gently.

With a knife, lightly score the scone into 12 or 16 wedges. Beat the remaining egg and brush the top layer.

BAKING
400°
20 mins.

Bake in the 400° oven for 20 minutes or until a golden brown.

FINAL STEP

Remove the bannock from the oven and place on a cooling rack; when cool, cut into wedge-shaped scones. Delicious served with honey, butter, whipped cream cheese — or alone.

CRUMPETS AND PIKELETS

[EIGHT CRUMPETS OR TWENTY-FOUR PIKELETS]

The English crumpet and the pikelet are made with the same yeast-raised batter that honeycombs each with a myriad bubbles. The crumpet is cooked in metal rings set on a hot griddle or heavy skillet. The pikelet is made with the same batter, but not as thick, and is spooned onto the hot surface as one would a pancake.

Baking soda is combined with the yeast-raised batter at the last moment before cooking to fill them with so many holes and channels that one can often see straight through a crumpet held to the light. Both are delicious served hot from the griddle or toasted, slathered with butter and spread with a jam or jelly of choice.

Scots, too, love their crumpets, and this is the way one cook describes her way of making them: "Put a griddle on a bright clear fire and rub with suet. To have light, pretty crumpets the fire must be brisk and the griddle hot, so that they will rise quickly. Before they get dry on top they should be turned. Do this quickly, and a lovely golden-brown skin as smooth as velvet will be formed, and a delightfully light crumpet produced."

For crumpets, metal rings are needed to contain the batter while it cooks. Use English crumpet rings, flan rings, open-topped cookie cutters, or well-washed tuna or pet-food cans with tops and bottoms removed.

Crumpets may also be baked (see below).

The recipe below makes a batter for a pikelet. For a crumpet, add ½ cup of flour — or a bit more — to thicken to a heavy batter.

INGREDIENTS

1½ cups bread or all-purpose flour (½ cup additional flour if for crumpets)
1 teaspoon salt
1 package dry yeast
⅓ cup nonfat dry milk
1½ cups warm water (80°–100°) (to add later)
¼ teaspoon baking soda
¼ cup water
1 egg white, lightly beaten

SPECIAL
EQUIPMENT

A griddle or heavy skillet for pikelets. For crumpets: Four or more 3″ to 4″ round metal rings, described above.

BY HAND
OR MIXER
6 mins.
30 mins.

For pikelets: Stir 1½ cups of flour, salt, yeast, and dry milk into a medium bowl. Pour in the warm water and beat with a wooden spoon or mixer blade 6 minutes to make a smooth batter.

Cover with cloth and leave at room temperature for about 30 minutes or until the mixture has risen and is bubbly. Mix the baking soda in the cold water and beat it into the batter. Fold in the beaten egg white thoroughly to produce a batter the consistency of thick pouring cream. It will be stringy.

For crumpets, blend in approximately an additional ½ cup of flour to make a heavier batter. If desired, some pikelets can be made first, then the appropriate amount of flour added to thicken for crumpets.

It may call for minor adjustments either in the amount of water or of flour to get a thick batter that must be spooned — beyond pouring.

BY PROCESSOR

Mixing the batter by hand or in the mixer is so easy that it seems hardly worthwhile to unlimber the processor.

COOKING
20 mins.

For cooking on the stovetop, lightly grease the griddle, hot plate, or heavy skillet and heat over medium-low heat until a drop of water sizzles immediately on contact.

Pikelets: Put a tablespoon of batter on the hot surface and cook until the top of the pikelet is almost dry. Turn over with a spatula and cook until the other side is lightly browned.

Crumpets: Place greased rings on the hot surface. Half fill the rings with batter. As they cook, the crumpets will rise and fill with holes. Cook until surface of crumpet is almost dry, about 10 to 12 minutes. Don't scorch the bottoms. Lift one to check how it is doing.

Turn the crumpets over to brown lightly. At this point, they will slip easily from the rings.

PREHEAT

If the crumpets are to be baked, preheat the oven to 400°.

BAKING
400°
25 mins.

Place the rings on the prepared griddle or skillet, fill to three-quarters, and put in the oven for 15 minutes or until lightly browned. Remove rings, turn over the crumpets, and return to the oven for 10 minutes.

FINAL STEP

Serve the pikelets hot from the pan. The crumpets are best split in half with fingers or forks — not sliced with a knife — and toasted.

Both are ideal vehicles for lots of butter and jam and jelly. They also freeze nicely.

BAPS

[EIGHT ROLLS]

The bap — the traditional breakfast roll of Scotland — is a puffed-up bun with a deep impression right in the middle where the baker's thumb has been pressed to keep the bun from blistering. The bap is brushed with milk twice before it goes into the oven to give it a rich sheen. Break the bap apart, spread with butter and jam.

Delicious.

INGREDIENTS	*2 cups all-purpose flour, approximately*
	1 package dry yeast
	¼ cup nonfat dry milk
	½ teaspoon salt
	1 teaspoon sugar
	2 tablespoons lard or vegetable shortening, room temperature
	¾ cup hot tap water (120°–130°)
	¼ cup fresh or evaporated milk, to brush

BAKING SHEET   One baking sheet, greased or Teflon.

BY HAND
OR MIXER
10 mins.

Measure flour into a mixing or mixer bowl and stir in the yeast, dry milk, salt, and sugar. With the fingers, rub the lard into the dry ingredients or attach the flat beater blade and mix until the flour resembles bread crumbs. Gradually pour in the water, stir, and work the flour into a soft ball of dough. Attach the dough hook, if in the mixer. Sprinkle more flour if the dough is sticky, or a bit more water if it is too dry to hold together.

KNEADING
6 mins.

Knead until the dough is smooth and elastic, about 6 minutes. Sprinkle with flour to control the stickiness.

BY PROCESSOR
8 mins.

Attach the steel blade.

Measure the dry ingredients into the work bowl. Drop pieces of the shortening over the flour and pulse to cut the shortening into small granules. With the processor on, pour the water through the feed tube. The dough will form a mass and ride on the blade to clean the sides of the bowl. If it does not — too wet — add small portions of flour.

KNEADING
45 secs.

Knead the dough in the processor for 45 seconds.

FIRST RISING
45 mins.

Place the dough in a bowl, cover with plastic wrap, and put aside until the dough has doubled in size, about 45 minutes. (Don't leave the dough in the processor bowl to rise. It will be a mess to get out later.)

SHAPING   Turn the dough out onto a lightly floured work surface and knead
10 mins.   for a minute or two. Divide the dough into 8 equal pieces. Let it
                 rest for 5 minutes before shaping the baps. Make an oval of each
                 piece—about 3″ long, 2″wide, and ½″ thick. Place on the baking
                 sheet and brush with milk.

SECOND   Cover the baps with waxed or parchment paper and set aside for
RISING   about 20 minutes.
20 mins.

PREHEAT   While the baps are rising, preheat the oven to 400°.

BAKING   Brush the baps with milk for the second time. Moisten a thumb
400°   and press it all the way down into the center of each bap. Bake
18–20 mins.   until a lovely golden brown, about 20 minutes.

FINAL STEP   Delicious served toasted, slathered with butter and spread with a
                 jam or jelly of choice.

PETITS PAINS À LA CRÈME À LA MODE ANCIENNE
(Old-Fashioned Cream Scones)

[EIGHT SCONES]

The French recipe for these cream scones calls for *crème fraîche*, a cream thicker than ours that has a tart edge. While our thick cream will do almost as well in this recipe, it is not difficult to make the French version. Add 1 tablespoon of buttermilk to 1 cup of heavy cream, shake to mix, *uncover*, and leave at room temperature for 1 or 2 days until it thickens. Use it directly in this recipe or cover and refrigerate. It will keep for a week or 10 days.

Traditionally, scones are cooked on a griddle or baking sheet set directly on the burner of the stove. To cook this way, sprinkle flour over the scones, heat the griddle or baking sheet over low heat, and cook the scones until they are puffed and golden—turning them once or twice.

This will take about 25 minutes. Baking in the oven is my preference, however.

The dried fruits in the recipe are optional.

INGREDIENTS	*1⅓ cups all-purpose flour, approximately*
	2 teaspoons baking powder
	⅛ teaspoon salt
	2 tablespoons butter, chilled
	¼ cup dried cherries or cranberries (optional)
	2 eggs
	1 tablespoon honey
	¼ cup crème fraîche *or heavy cream*
	1 egg mixed with 1 teaspoon cream, to brush

BAKING SHEET	One large baking sheet, buttered or Teflon.

PREHEAT	Preheat oven to 400°.

BY HAND	Sift the flour, baking powder, and salt into a large mixing bowl.
15–18 mins.	Cut in the butter with a pastry blender or 2 knives until the mixture resembles coarse meal. Stir in the dried fruit.

In a separate bowl, beat the eggs, and add the honey and *crème fraîche*. Beat this mixture well, pour it into the flour mixture, and combine gently, using 2 forks. Turn out the dough on a heavily floured work surface, coat your hands with flour, and gather the dough together, patting gently until it forms a mass.

If the dough is wet and doesn't form a mass after a minute or two, sprinkle with flour. Knead very gently; just a couple of turns. Cut the dough into 2 pieces, pat and roll each half into a ball. Flatten each ball into a circle about ⅓″ thick. Cut each circle into quarters with a sharp knife or pizza cutter.

BAKING	Gently lift each wedge with a spatula and place on the baking
400°	sheet. Brush the tops with the egg-cream mixture. Bake for 15
15 mins.	minutes or until the scones are puffy and golden brown.

FINAL STEP	Take from the oven and invite the neighbors in for tea.

POGÁCSA
(Hungarian Cheese Scones)

[THREE DOZEN COCKTAIL-SIZE PIECES]

Served in Hungary for breakfast, lunch, and as a snack, *pogácsa* is to be found in many Hungarian folk tales. Storytellers call them *hamuba sült pogácsa* — "biscuits baked in ashes." When a farmer returns from the fields at the end of the day, the children expect something to be left over from his midday meal, usually a *pogácsa*. This treat is called *"madár láttá"* — "seen by the birds."

My friend Hungarian-born Judith Goldinger is an outstanding baker and she gave me the recipe with these words: *jé étvágyat!* The French would translate it as *bon appétit!*

While these scones are made with cheese, they may be made plain and sprinkled with sugar or cracklings or spread with butter. They may also be decorated with slivered almonds or sprinkled with poppy or sesame seeds.

INGREDIENTS
1½ cups bread or all-purpose flour
1 teaspoon salt
1 package dry yeast
6 tablespoons butter
¼ cup milk
¼ cup sour cream
1 egg yolk
½ cup Parmesan or Romano cheese (reserve 2 tablespoons to sprinkle)
1 egg, beaten with 1 tablespoon milk, to brush

BAKING SHEET
One large baking sheet, greased, Teflon, or lined with parchment paper.

BY HAND
OR MIXER
10 mins.
Measure 1 cup of flour into the mixing or mixer bowl and add the salt and yeast. In a small saucepan, stir together the butter (cut into chunks), the milk, sour cream, and egg yolk. Place over low heat to warm to the touch. Do not let simmer or it will cook the egg.

Pour the liquid into the flour and blend by hand or with the mixer flat beater for 2 minutes to make a smooth batter. Add remaining flour, ¼ cup at a time. Mix vigorously with a wooden spoon or dough hook. The dough will be smooth and soft. Transfer the dough to a floured work surface, if by hand, or leave in the bowl under the dough hook.

KNEADING
8–10 mins.

The dough should be soft but not sticky. If sticky, add sprinkles of flour. Knead for 8 to 10 minutes until the dough is velvety and responsive under the hands.

BY PROCESSOR
8 mins.

The sequence differs from above.

Heat the butter, milk, sour cream, and egg yolk in a medium saucepan until warm. The butter need not be completely melted. Measure 1 cup of flour into the work bowl and sprinkle in the salt and yeast. Pulse to blend.

With the processor running, slowly pour the liquid in a stream through the feed tube. Add remaining flour, 1 tablespoon at a time, through the feed tube until the dough becomes a ball riding on the blade and which cleans the sides of the bowl.

TO KNEAD
45 secs.

Once the dough forms a ball, process for 45 seconds. If dough is dry and hard, add water by the tablespoon. If the dough is wet and sticks to the sides of the bowl, add flour by the tablespoon and process for a few more seconds.

ADD CHEESE
4 mins.

Turn the dough from the bowl, and knead for a few moments to be certain the dough has the proper consistency.

Shape the dough into a flat oval and spread with half the cheese. Turn in the sides and knead. Again press the dough into an oval, and add the balance of the cheese. Knead until the cheese is spread throughout the dough.

CHILL
Overnight

Wrap the dough with plastic wrap or place in a plastic bag and chill overnight. The following morning, leave the dough at room temperature for ½ hour, then roll into a flat piece about ¼″ thick. Fold and roll again to make it flaky .

PREHEAT

Preheat oven to 350°.

SHAPING
15 mins.

Cut the dough with a 1″ cutter; turn each piece over and place bottom up on the baking sheet (this allows maximum rise). Lightly score twice across the top with a sharp knife, brush with the egg wash, and sprinkle with balance of the cheese (2 tablespoons).

BAKING
350°
30 mins.

Place the sheet on the middle shelf of the moderate oven and bake until a golden brown, about 30 minutes.

FINAL STEP

Remove from the baking sheet and place on a metal rack to cool, although they are delicious still warm from the oven. They can be frozen for months.

Jé étvágyat!

Sourdough Starters

THERE are two basic starters used in home baking—wild and yeast-fortified.

Be forewarned: A true starter can be whimsical and maddening in its formative days. Once established, it is a joy to have in the refrigerator and to tell acquaintances about. Some starters are boosted with yeast, but the amount is small and its presence will be lost in the long fermentation period that follows. The yeast, of course, makes it a sure thing and takes away some of the gamble.

All starters and sponges (especially that for salt-rising bread) demand warmth in their formative stages. With the door slightly ajar, the pilot light in one of my gas ovens maintains a perfect 90°. With the door closed, it jumps to 100°, which is also acceptable. I sometimes borrow my wife's yogurt maker, a series of small glass jars nestled in a heated plastic box that holds at a constant 90°. I divide the mixture among the jars and I am certain to get one or more viable starters or sponges.

Other warm places include top of the water heater or refrigerator or in any enclosed area where heat collects. The light in an electric oven can provide heat, too. Turn the oven on for a moment — just until the air inside feels a little warmer than room temperature. Place the starter inside, close the door, and turn on the light — or prop open the door just enough to keep the light on.

There are two easy ways to replenish starters.

One is to replace the cupful taken out of the jar with ¾ cup flour and ½ cup of liquid (water, potato water, or milk). Stir, then allow it to ferment at room temperature for a day or so before returning, covered, to the refrigerator.

The other is to pour all of the starter into a bowl and add 1 cup of flour and 1 cup of liquid. This offers an opportunity to wash and scald the jar in which the starter has been stored. Return the starter to the jar and allow it to ferment at room temperature for a day before returning to the refrigerator.

Ideally, a starter should be used at least once a week. If not, stir down after three or four weeks, spoon out and discard half of it, and replenish the balance. On occasion, I have gone months before retrieving it from the deep recesses of the refrigerator — and, with loving words and warm hands, it dutifully came back with full vigor.

HONEY STARTER

[THREE CUPS]

This is a yeast-boosted starter.

> 1 package dry yeast
> 2½ cups warm water (105°–115°)
> 2 tablespoons honey
> 2½ cups bread or all-purpose flour

Combine these ingredients — yeast, water, honey, and flour — in a quart jar with a cover. Close the jar loosely and let the mixture ferment for 5 days, stirring daily.

Replenish the starter with water and flour in equal portions.

HOPS STARTER

[SIX CUPS]

This starter came from two elderly sisters, Minnie and Ola Turnipseed, who lived on a family farm in northern Indiana and who had baked with this starter most of their 80 years.

3 cups water
1 quart fresh hops or ¼ cup packaged dry hops
½ cup cornmeal, white or yellow
2 cups mashed potato, homemade or instant
3 tablespoons sugar
2 teaspoons salt

In a saucepan, bring water to a boil and steep hops for 20 minutes. Drain and reserve the liquid; discard the hops. If necessary, add water to make 3 full cups of liquid.

Pour 1 cup of the hops liquid in a saucepan and stir in the cornmeal. Bring to a boil over medium heat, stirring constantly. When it thickens slightly, remove from heat.

In a large mixing bowl, combine cornmeal mixture, mashed potato, sugar, salt, and remaining 2 cups of hops liquid. Cover the bowl with a length of cheesecloth and set in a warm place (85°–90°) for 24 to 48 hours or until well fermented and bubbly. Stir every 8 hours or so during this period.

When the starter is frothy and smells pleasantly fermented, pour it into a 2-quart jar or plastic container with a lid. Store in the refrigerator until clear liquid has risen to the top, in about 2 days. Stir down — and it is ready to use.

YOGURT STARTER

[TWO CUPS]

Excellent to give taste and texture to sourdough French breads, this
starter is made with yogurt, milk, and flour — and, later, fortified with
yeast when making the dough.

1 cup skim or low-fat milk
3 tablespoons plain yogurt
1 cup flour

Beforehand: Sterilize a 1-quart glass, ceramic, rigid plastic, or
stainless steel container with hot water. Wipe dry.

In a saucepan, heat milk to 90° to 100°. Remove from heat and
stir in yogurt. Pour into warm container, cover, and let stand in a
warm place.

The starter should be the consistency of yogurt after 8 to 24
hours. If some liquid rises to the top of the milk, stir it back in.
However, if the liquid has turned a light pink, it indicates the milk
has started to break down; discard and start again.

After the mixture has formed a curd, which will flow only slowly
when container is tilted, gradually stir the flour into the starter until
smooth. Cover and let stand in a warm place until the mixture
is full of bubbles and has a good sour smell, 2 to 5 days.

To store, refrigerate. Bring to room temperature before using.

RAW POTATO STARTER

[TWO CUPS]

1 cup warm water (105°–115°)
1¼ cups bread or all-purpose flour
1 teaspoon each salt and sugar
1 medium potato, grated

Mix together the water, flour, salt, and sugar in a 2-cup measure. Add grated potato sufficient to make a full 2 cups.

Pour the mixture into a wide-mouth glass jar or bowl that will hold about 1 quart (to allow for expansion during fermentation).

Place a cheesecloth over the container and allow to rest in a warm place (90°) for 24 hours. Stir and cover with plastic wrap, which will retain the moisture. The mixture will become light and foamy in 2 or 3 days. Stir down each day.

Pour the fermented starter into a glass jar, fitted with a loose lid, and place in the refrigerator. In 3 or 4 days, when a clear liquid collects on top of the mixture, it will have ripened sufficiently for use.

FERMENTED GRAPE STARTER

[FOUR CUPS]

This unusual starter is the creation of Karen Mitchell, whose Model Bakery is in St. Helena, deep in California's Napa Valley. It makes some of the best sourdough bread in the San Francisco Bay area, doing it with a highly successful leavening of fermented grapes and flour.

Not all her breads are made with natural grape yeast, but they are the ones that are the most sought after.

Whenever she needs a new starter, Karen goes to an old vineyard nearby that has not been "nuked" — i.e., sprayed with sulfur — and there picks a bucket of the valley's Gamay grapes.

Here, in her words, is the recipe for the grape starter:

"I crush the grapes in the pail, cover it with a cloth to keep out the fruit flies, and put it aside for a week near the ovens, where it is about 100°. By then, it will be a bubbly sort of wine, with a sugar content of between 1 percent and 2 percent. I strain off the juice, and discard the skins and stems.

"Each day, I lightly feed the juice with small portions of whole-wheat flour. By the end of two weeks, I have a starter the consistency of a thick batter."

Ingredients for the Baker

FLOURS

Flour is the medium for all bread making. While only a few are important to the home baker, the list of flours seems endless: white, whole-wheat, barley, buckwheat, corn, oat, rye, rice, millet, amaranth, soy, chickpea, triticale, and spelt.

Wheat is the principal grain for a simple reason: More than any of the others, it contains an important element, gluten, a plant protein that when mixed with water forms an elastic network that catches the gas generated by the yeast and expands the dough.

Hard wheat, grown in the Great Plains and western prairie states and Canadian provinces, has a high gluten content and is milled into bread flour. Bakers favor it, for it gives dough maximum expansion and also because it can withstand the punishing treatment from heavy machinery.

267

Soft wheat, grown in the Midwest and eastern states, produces a flour lower in gluten, one that is ideal for baking such products as pastries, crackers, cookies, and cakes.

All-purpose is a versatile flour, a blend of hard and soft wheat flours, and takes care of a whole range of home baking needs, from breads and biscuits to piecrusts and doughnuts.

Pastry flour is a soft-wheat flour that can tolerate a considerable amount of shortening without becoming tough. Cake flour has the least gluten and has only enough protein to hold it together until a delicate structure of cells is formed in the oven.

Whole-wheat flour contains the entire germ or fat portion of the wheat kernel. Rye is a grain with little gluten in its makeup; therefore, most of the time, rye flour is mixed with white or whole-wheat to give the dough its necessary framework.

Bromated flour, while heavily promoted on small packages of flour for the home, is primarily for commercial use. The flour is treated with potassium bromate to toughen the dough for the rigors of kneading in big machines, and is of no advantage to the home baker.

The amount given in a recipe is only approximate because flour varies greatly in its ability to absorb moisture, due to differences from harvest to harvest, sack to sack, and the humidity in the room where it is stored. For the recipes in this book, flour is not sifted.

In the latter stages of working dough, add flour sparingly. It is better to *slowly* add the last bit of flour to be certain the mixture is just right rather than discover you have overwhelmed the dough with too much flour. This is especially true of whole-wheat flour, which is slow to absorb the liquid.

Flour freezes and keeps well for a year or more at 0°.

YEAST AND OTHER LEAVENINGS

Yeast is the most important of the leavenings, followed by chemicals such as baking powder and baking soda. Yeast cells, wild or cultivated, feasting on the sugars in the mixture, produce carbon dioxide to raise the dough and make it light.

Manufacturers of yeasts, both in this country and in Europe, have introduced new strains of yeasts over the past few years, designed to speed up the leavening process, i.e., less time for dough to rise before it goes into the oven.

In my kitchen, I have found no clear advantage of one over the others. It is not of shattering importance to me to shave a few minutes off a process that may take an hour or longer. Nor can I detect pronounced differences in the taste of breads made from one or the other. Regardless of the kind of yeast, have all ingredients at room temperature or warmer when you begin. The addition of two or three ice-cold eggs or a stick of butter right from the refrigerator can throw a deep chill into the dough and the ability of the yeast to do its job.

While commercial bakers and some home bakers use large one-pound bricks of fresh yeast, most home bakers will find dry yeast packets and small fresh compressed cakes more convenient. When I travel the country on demonstrations and lecture tours, I always have a few packets of dry yeast in my pocket. Just in case.

Brewer's yeast, by the way, is not a leavening agent and can't be substituted for live yeast. It is, however, an excellent source of biologically complete and digestible protein and is often used in baking.

Baking soda, one of the first chemical leaveners to be used, reacts with acids, such as sour cream or buttermilk, to produce carbon dioxide. The reaction is almost instantaneous, requiring fast assembly of ingredients and immediate baking. However, baking powder has a multiple action that releases a small amount of gas while the ingredients are put together. The main thrust comes from the heat of the oven.

Self-rising flour and cornmeal mix contain baking powder and salt.

FAT

Fat is the baker's generic term for butter, lard, margarine, and oil. It imparts its own unique taste and lubricates the dough so it can stretch and rise without hindrance.

Butter, because of its delicious flavor and rich aroma, is one of the most highly regarded fats for baking. Sweet or unsalted butter is preferred because it indicates a fresher, sweeter product than salted butter, which has a longer shelf life. I have used only unsalted butter in the book. Lard is used in several recipes in this book. Solid vegetable and animal fats are made with oils through which hydrogen has been forced under pressure to produce a creamy solid. Vegetable shortening is a good compromise without a pronounced taste.

MILK

A loaf made with milk has a velvety grain, a browner crust, and a creamy white crumb. The loaf is softer and stays that way longer than bread without milk. It also complements the nutrients of many doughs.

SALT

Salt controls the action of the yeast in dough, strengthens the gluten, and accents the flavor of other ingredients.

SUGAR

Granulated sugar imparts a rich brown color to the crust through caramelization. In moderate amounts, sugar increases the yeast fermentation, while sugar in high concentration typical of sweet breads will inhibit it.

Equipment for the Home Baker

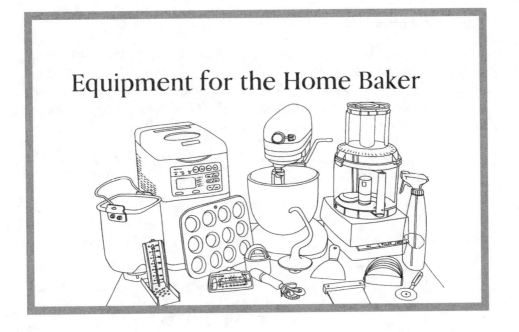

Bread dough is made in two ways—by hand or machine.

BY HAND

Work space is perhaps the most important consideration in making dough by hand, but the space need not be overlarge. An area two feet square is adequate for most bread making—assembling the ingredients, the mixing, the kneading, and the shaping. The height of the countertop or table, whether it be Formica, wood, or steel, is more important than its composition. It should be high enough to allow the palms of the hands, arms extended, to rest on the top surface. Too low, it will tire your back; too high, and you cannot push down with force against the dough.

ELECTRIC MIXER

An electric mixer with a dough hook attachment will take the toil out of bread making. And it does it just as well as by hand. I have used the large-model KitchenAid (K5A) with great success. There are other good mixers with kneading devices; but don't attempt to mix heavy doughs in a machine that is not guaranteed by its manufacturer to handle it. Do not use lightweight or portable or handheld mixers for bread dough because the danger of damage is too great. They work well in batters no thicker than pancake mixes, but that is all.

FOOD PROCESSOR

I was late in accepting the food processor as a viable machine because I believed that only a long period of kneading would make a good batch of bread dough. I was wrong. I don't know the dynamics involved, but I do know that the force of the whirling blade, steel or plastic, is tremendous and can accomplish in a moment or two what otherwise would take long minutes. The recipes in the book have been tested on one of the larger Cuisinart models, the DLC-7 Super Pro. It is a rugged model for the home kitchen and I know a number of chefs and caterers who use it as well.

BREAD MACHINE

The bread machine can be used for mixing and kneading most of the doughs in this book. The shaping of the dough into small breads is done by hand, however.

Whether or not a recipe can be used depends on the size of the machine and the number of cups of flour it can knead. The large one-and-one-half-pound machine will take three cups of flour. The small one-pound machine will knead two cups of flour. Recipes calling for more flour than this must be scaled down. However, the volume of flour and other ingredients in this book is smaller than usual; hence, many recipes may be made by machine without adjustment. Follow the manufacturer's instructions for operating the machine and add ingredients in the order suggested by the bread-machine manual.

BAKING SHEETS, PANS, AND TINS

Get the heaviest and largest baking sheet your oven will accommodate, allowing a one-inch clearance on all sides to facilitate the flow of hot air around it. You may wish to buy baking sheets in pairs so that you can prepare a second batch of biscuits for the oven while the first pan bakes. Never use two sheets at a time, one above the other, because small breads on the bottom sheet will likely burn in the heat reflected from the one above.

Choose sturdy "muffin" pans that are also used for baking other breads, especially rolls. The pans should be well constructed with rounded corners, and cups should be seamless. Most muffin pans of quality are of cast aluminum or heavy-gauge steel and preferably with nonstick coating. Cast-iron pans that have been used by cooks for generations are quite heavy and at times difficult to maneuver in and out of the hot oven but are excellent for baking.

BAKING STONE

A baking stone placed on the lower shelf of the oven is as close as most home bakers can get to baking on the oven floor as bakers have done for centuries. A stone weighs about ten pounds. Unlike a baking sheet that can be moved in and out of the oven to receive the dough, the preheated stone is best left in place in the oven and the bread taken to it. Pans, tins, and baking sheets can be placed on the heavy stone to produce a thicker, crisper bottom crust.

DOUGH KNIFE OR SCRAPER

A dough knife, also called a dough blade, or pastry scraper, is a rectangular piece of metal (about 4″ x 5″) with a wooden handle that quickly becomes an extension of the hand in working with doughs. The French call it a *coupe-pâte*. It is great for lifting and working soft doughs that are sticky during the early part of kneading. A thin, flexible blade is preferred over a heavy, stiff one. A four-inch putty knife is an excellent substitute.

ATOMIZER

The plastic atomizer from a window-cleaner bottle is placed in a glass or bottle of water to spray a fine mist over some breads about to go in the oven, or to spray into the oven to create steam during the bake period.

THE OVEN

A good oven thermometer, the mercury-filled columnar by Taylor, for example, is an excellent investment when you consider the cost of ingredients, to say nothing of your time. In brief, don't ever trust the oven thermostat until you have come to terms with its idiosyncrasies. A too-hot oven may scorch the breads. A too-cool oven will not bake bread. An oven that is just right will produce a masterpiece.

The heat in an oven varies in intensity from side to side, front to back, and top to bottom. Move the pans and turn them at least once during the bake period to compensate for these variations.

All of the baking in this book was done in a Viking gas stove.

Glossary

Atomizer	Small water-filled bottle with spray head to create steam in the oven. I use a glass-cleaner bottle, well rinsed.
Cut In	To mix fat and flour with a wire pastry blender, tips of the fingers, crossed knives, or machine so that fat particles are flour-covered but discrete, not smeared.
Dough Knife or Blade	A metal rectangle about four inches by five inches with a handhold to lift and work dough. It is also called a bench knife. The French call it a *coupe-pâte*. It becomes an extension of the hand.
Dust	Sprinkle lightly or brush with flour, sugar, etc.
Fermentation	The chemical reaction of the ingredient in making dough that causes the forming of a gas, carbon dioxide, which in turn causes the dough to expand.
Fold	To gently incorporate or blend flour and other ingredients into a mixture with a spatula or mixer at low speed so as not to destroy the texture of the mixture.

275

Glaze	To create a glossy finish with a thin coating of sugar, icing, fruit syrups, jellies, and other liquids.
Gluten	The rubbery, elastic substance found in most flours when water is added.
Grease	To rub lightly with butter, margarine, shortening, lard, or salad oil.
Knead	To work into a mass or to develop dough while mixing.
Leavening	A substance that will produce gas to cause aeration within a product, found in bread yeast and chemicals such as baking powder and baking soda.
Light	Dough that has risen and is puffy with gas is spoken of as "light."
Mixing	Blend into one mass.
Parchment Paper	Specially treated paper used to line baking sheets and tins without sticking. Sold in rolls in gourmet cookware shops and departments.
Peel	A flat board used for placing bakery products in the oven and taking them out again.
Pinch	Approximately one-eighth teaspoon, or the amount of the ingredient that can be held between the thumb and forefinger.
Preheat	Turn on and heat oven to desired temperature before putting in breads, usually twenty to twenty-five minutes.
Proof	The stages of fermentation before baking.
Scaling	Weighing materials.
Simmer	To cook just below the boiling point. There are no bubbles, but the surface moves slightly.
Steaming	Injecting water into the oven to create steam while baking.
Stippling, Docking	Piercing dough with tines of a fork before baking or a straight piece of heavy wire to let gas escape during baking.
Stir	To blend with a circular motion, with a spoon, widening circles until all ingredients are well mixed. Used in dissolving.
Wash	To brush the surface, before or after baking, with a mixture usually of whole egg lightly beaten and thinned with milk or cream. If deeper color is desired, use yolks instead of whole eggs.
Zest	Finely grated outer peel of orange, lemon, or lime. (The white beneath is bitter.)

Standard Weights and Measures

Make certain all measurements are level.

Dash	= 8 drops
1 tablespoon	= 3 teaspoons
4 tablespoons	= ¼ cup
5⅓ tablespoons	= ⅓ cup
8 tablespoons	= ½ cup
16 tablespoons	= 1 cup (dry)
1 fluid ounce	= 2 tablespoons
1 cup (liquid)	= ½ pint
2 cups (16 ounces)	= 1 pint
2 pints (4 cups)	= 1 quart
4 quarts	= 1 gallon
8 quarts	= 1 peck (dry)
4 pecks	= 1 bushel
16 ounces (dry measure)	= 1 pound

OTHER MEASUREMENTS

1 lemon   = 2–3 tablespoons juice and 2 teaspoons zest
1 orange   = 6–8 tablespoons juice and 2–3 tablespoons zest
1 cup heavy cream   = 2 cups whipped cream
2 cups water   = 1 pound
5 large whole eggs
6 medium   } = 1 cup, approximately
7 small
8 large egg whites
10–11 medium   } = 1 cup, approximately
11–12 small
12 large egg yolks
13–14 medium   } = 1 cup, approximately
15–16 small

FLUID MEASURE EQUIVALENTS

METRIC	UNITED STATES	BRITISH
1 liter	4½ cups or 1 quart 2 ounces	1¾ pints
1 demiliter (½ liter)	2 cups (generous) or 1 pint (generous)	¾ pint (generous)
1 deciliter (1/10 liter)	½ cup (scant) or ¼ pint (scant)	3–4 ounces

MEASURE EQUIVALENTS

METRIC	UNITED STATES	BRITISH
1.00 gram	.035 ounce	.035 ounce
28.35 grams	1 ounce	1 ounce
100.00 grams	3.5 ounces	3.5 ounces
114.00 grams	4 ounces (approximately)	4 ounces (approximately)
226.78 grams	8 ounces	8 ounces
500.00 grams	1 pound 1.5 ounces	1 pound 1.5 ounces
1.00 kilogram	2.21 pounds	2.21 pounds

COMPARATIVE U.S., BRITISH, AND METRIC WEIGHTS AND MEASURES FOR INGREDIENTS IMPORTANT TO PASTRY MAKERS

INGREDIENT	UNITED STATES	BRITISH	METRIC
Almond paste	1¾ cups	16 ounces	450 grams
Apples, pared/ sliced	1 cup	4 ounces	125 grams
Berries	1¾ cups	6 ounces	190 grams
Butter	1 tablespoon	½ ounce	15 grams
	½ cup	4 ounces	125 grams
	2 cups	1 pound (generous)	450 grams
Cheese	1 pound (generous)	1 pound (generous)	450 grams
Cheese, cottage	1 cup	16 ounces	450 grams
Cheese, cream	6 tablespoons	3 ounces	80 grams
Cheese, grated, hard type	1 cup (scant)	4 ounces (scant)	100 grams
Cornstarch	1 tablespoon	⅓ ounce	10 grams
Flour (unsifted)	¼ cup	1¼ ounces	35 grams
	½ cup	2½ ounces	70 grams
	1 cup	4¾ ounces	142 grams
	3½ cups	1 pound	450 grams
Herbs, fresh, chopped	1 tablespoon	½ ounce	15 grams
Nuts, chopped	1 cup	5½ ounces	155 grams
Raisins (seedless)	1 tablespoon	⅓ ounce	10 grams
	1 cup	5⅓ ounces	160 grams
	3 cups	1 pound	450 grams
Spices, ground	1 teaspoon	1/12 ounce	2.5 grams
	2 tablespoons	½ ounce	15 grams
Sugar, brown	1 tablespoon	⅓ ounce	10 grams
	½ cup	2⅔ ounces	80 grams
	1 cup	5⅓ ounces	160 grams
Sugar, confectioners'	¼ cup	1 ounce (generous)	35 grams
	½ cup	2¼ ounces (scant)	70 grams
	1 cup	4½ ounces (scant)	140 grams
Sugar, granulated	1 teaspoon	⅙ ounce	5 grams
	1 tablespoon	½ ounce	15 grams
	¼ cup	2 ounces	60 grams
	1 cup	8 ounces	226 grams

Permissions

Grateful acknowledgment is made for permission to use the following material:

Bantam Books: Recipe for "Bakestone Herb Cakes" from *The Kitchen Cookbook* by Sylvia Thompson. Copyright © 1995. Used by permission of Bantam Books, a division of Bantam Doubleday Dell Publishing Group, Inc.

HarperCollins Publishers: Recipe for "Earl Grey Tea Rolls" from *The Book of Breads* by Judith Jones and Evan Jones. Copyright © 1982. Used by permission of the publisher.

Chronicle Books: Recipe for "Buckwheat and Hazelnut Muffins" from *The Art of Quick Breads* by Beth Hensperger. Copyright © 1994. Used by permission of Chronicle Books.

Time-Life Books, Time Inc.: Recipe for *"Pergedel Djagung* (Indonesian Spiced Corn Fritters)" from *Pacific and Southeast Asia Cooking,* Foods of the World, Time-Life Books, Time Inc. Copyright © 1970. Used by permission of the publisher.

Recipe for "Petits Pains" and "Beignets de Pommes" reprinted by permission of Simon & Schuster from *Monet's Table: The Cooking Journals of Claude Monet* by Claire Joyes. Copyright © 1989 by Century Hutchinson Limited and Simon & Schuster Inc.

Recipes for "Double Corn Hush Puppies" reprinted by permission of Simon & Schuster from *Around the Southern Table* by Sarah Belk. Copyright © 1991 by Sarah Belk.

Index